HORSE-AND-BUGGY
GENIUS

ROYDEN LOEWEN

HORSE-AND-BUGGY
GENIUS

Listening to Mennonites Contest the Modern World

UMP
University of Manitoba Press

University of Manitoba Press
Winnipeg, Manitoba
Canada R3T 2M5
uofmpress.ca

Printed in Canada
Text printed on chlorine-free, 100% post-consumer recycled paper

20 19 18 17 16   1 2 3 4 5

Cover design: David Drummond
Interior design: Jess Koroscil

Library and Archives Canada Cataloguing in Publication

Loewen, Royden, 1954–, author
Horse-and-buggy genius : listening to Mennonites contest the
modern world / Royden Loewen.

Includes bibliographical references and index.
Issued in print and electronic formats.
ISBN 978-0-88755-798-9 (pbk.)
ISBN 978-0-88755-493-3 (pdf)
ISBN 978-0-88755-491-9 (epub)

1. Mennonites—America—Interviews. 2. Mennonites—Doctrines.
3. Civilization, Modern. I. Title.

BX8121.3.L63 2016   230'.97   C2015-908003-7
                                                               C2015-908004-5

This book has been published with the help of a grant from the Federation for the
Humanities and Social Sciences, through the Awards to Scholarly Publications Program,
using funds provided by the Social Sciences and Humanities Research Council of Canada.

The University of Manitoba Press gratefully acknowledges the financial support
for its publication program provided by the Government of Canada through the Canada
Book Fund, the Canada Council for the Arts, the Manitoba Department
of Culture, Heritage, Tourism, the Manitoba Arts Council,
and the Manitoba Book Publishing Tax Credit.

FSC
www.fsc.org
MIX
Paper from
responsible sources
FSC® C016245

CONTENTS

Preface

This book is based on an oral history project designed by a team of graduate and postgraduate students and me between 2009 and 2012. The subjects of this study are the quiet and reclusive horse-and-buggy Mennonites of Canada and Latin America—the Canadians known broadly as Old Order Mennonites and the Latin Americans as Old Colony Mennonites. Both groups have been the subject of media accounts—newspapers, magazines, radio, and TV—but not often as the focus of the oral historian. Yet both the Canadian and Latin American groups have their stories to tell: perhaps they have lived out their anti-modern lives in starkly different contexts, but they have faced similar challenges in history.

Thus we went to them looking for answers to the basic question of history and culture: what has changed in the life of your people and how have they survived the test of time. At an inaugural September 2008 workshop on this project in St. Jacobs, Ontario, we as a team pondered the specific questions we would ask these Mennonites. We shared notes of our own research experience and mapped ways of undertaking ethical and culturally sensitive research. We were reminded that often the best approach, one standard in oral history methodology, is to ask open-ended questions. Our goal, after all, was not to create a precise history of Old Colony and Old Order Mennonite communities. Rather, it was to record what members of these communities said they remembered about changes that they had made to preserve their communities within the modern world. Certainly the accuracy of memory assists in creating a credible narrative. However, as oral historians like Alessandro Portelli and others have argued, even imprecise recollections point to the greater truth of an event or past era, for memory is a way of making sense of the present. And ultimately the goal of this book is to convey the historically conditioned culture, the genius, of these quiet and communitarian people to the wider world. That genius, we learned, would not become apparent in stilted question-and-answer sessions.

To enable this project we, as the researchers, sought safe spaces for the interviews. And most did occur in the interviewees' own social places: the familiar inner sanctums of their homes, but also on their buggies, in taxis that they hired, in city restaurants that they suggested, or by happenstance in front of the colony general store or on the side of country roads. In the end, the stories the horse-and-buggy people told us in response to our questions were unrehearsed and reflected a world without telephone and Internet where social spontaneity is welcomed. Many interviews were not even planned ahead. Nor were they vetted by local church or community authorities. The result, we hoped, would be stories, uncontrived and told from the heart. Of course, the written transcripts of the interviews, to be deposited in a publicly accessible archive, are filtered documents. They are shaped by the questions we asked, and reflect a long-standing idea that oral history is always a co-production of interviewer and the interviewed, and hence, a social process unto itself.

We were also mindful that the interview transcripts were produced in the social context in which outsiders are distinguished from insiders. The interviewers and research architects for this book were seven committed young scholars, graduate and postgraduate university students (Kerry Fast, Tina Fehr Kehler, Anna Sofia Hedberg, Jakob Huttner, Anne Kok, Andrew Martin, and Karen Warkentin) and me. Trained variously in history, anthropology, sociology, and religious studies, four of these research associates were acculturated Mennonites from Canada, while three were non-Mennonites, one each from Germany, the Netherlands, and Sweden.[1] The language of conversation in the Latin American communities was usually Low German (but also Spanish, High German and English), while in Canada all interviews were in English. Perhaps the interview process itself was not especially strange to the horse-and-buggy people; given the agrarian culture of the Sunday afternoon or weekday evening "visit," telling stories is common in these communities. And, certainly, this cultural divide was bridged in part by the fact that we as interviewers were "present," often as overnight guests, usually at meals, recipients of warm hospitality, or in places outside the home they invited us into. Yet, it was always clear that we were not members of the community; indeed, we had come from afar to ask them about their history and communities.

The stories that these Mennonites told us were those they seemed to want to tell. Following ethical guidelines vetted by the University of Winnipeg, where I teach, we made it clear to the interviewees that we were writing a book that would be read by the wider world. We also reminded them that they did not have to talk to us, that they could stop the interview at any time, that they could contact us after the interview to withdraw their remarks, and that they need not allow their names to be used in the book. The majority, especially the Old Colony Mennonites in Latin America, said that we could use their names, a practice that they employ in writing to Mennonite newspapers. The Old Order Mennonites in Canada, who live closer to many potential readers and have a tradition of using pseudonyms in writing in public forums, were more hesitant; thus, in respect of that tradition, they are referred to in this book mostly by culturally appropriate pseudonyms. And reflecting the sensitivity of horse-and-buggy people to modern technologies, only a third of the interviews were tape-recorded, with the rest recorded by hand during the interview or within the day of the interview as field notes.

The result, I hope, is a transparent work, ethical in nature, innovative in scope, illuminating in a new way.

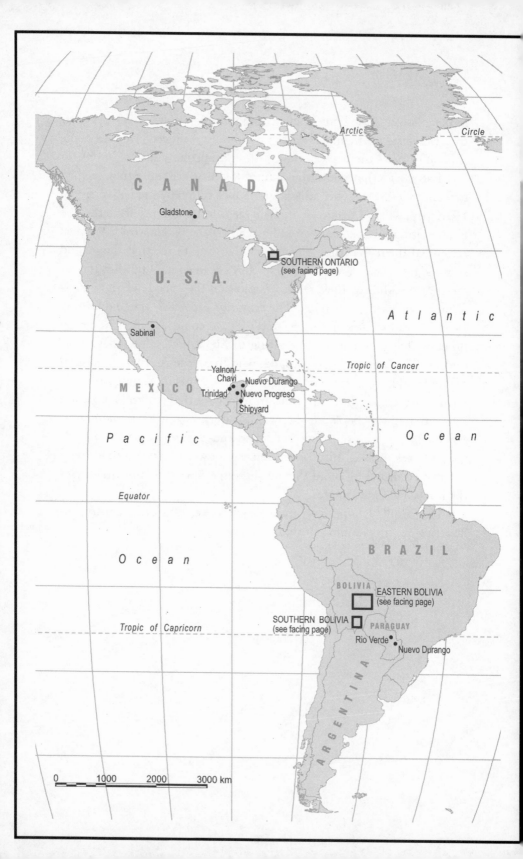

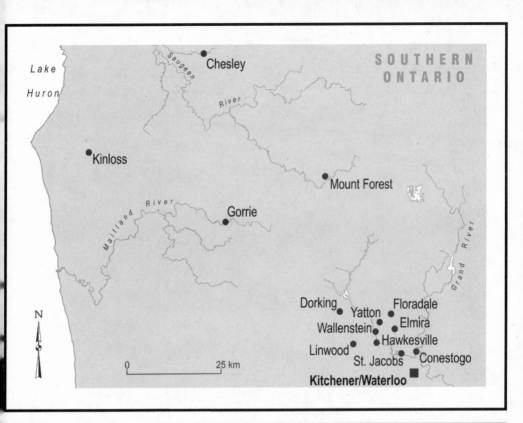

Old Order and Old Colony Mennonite communities discussed in this volume. Map design by Weldon Hiebert.

HORSE-AND-BUGGY
GENIUS

Introduction

An invited guest, he stands conspicuously in the grand Convocation Hall at the University of Winnipeg. You can spot him easily in his dark blue shirt and black suspenders among other conference attendees in tweed jackets and colourful sweaters. When he rises to speak, he jokes that he might be the only "horse-and-buggy" Mennonite ever to have attended an academic conference. Levi Fry, an Old Order Mennonite from Mount Forest, Ontario, has come a long way, travelling the slow way, by train, from Toronto to distant Winnipeg. He has refused to take an airplane or, indeed, to write out his speech on a computer. Reading from his hand-written text, he sets out to confront the idea that his people have been "shallow, ... blindly following tradition," generation after generation.[1]

Why are they, the horse-and-buggy people, labelled legalistic and primitive? Mostly, says Levi, because they seem to be "an intentional misfit in today's super-charged technologically focused world." They reject the car for the horse, the cell phone in favour of face-to-face communication, the slick and glamorous for the earthy and local. To the outside world, he says, they appear to be foolishly out of step with modernity. Their stubborn stance has presented problems. How do you survive in modern society outside the government-funded social safety net, he asks, without "Child Tax Benefits, pensions, employment insurance"? Can you stop the acceptance of new technologies with the simple logic that a "true" community must be built on "a need to help the neighbour or the need to depend on [someone] to help you" and that technologies undermine neighbourliness? Can you convince your youth to follow you in rejecting the car for the simple reason that a car can "travel farther than the distance a horse will go"? The Old Order Mennonite insists that religious faithfulness is linked to a life lived in the local and in simplicity. It is also the best way to live a life. This equation is the "genius," the heart, of their world.

This book relays the stories of people like Levi who have resisted the logic of the modern world and survived. Unlike Levi, the vast majority of horse-and-buggy Mennonites in the Americas do not visit the urban world to talk publicly about their old order ways. For that reason, a research team under my direction and I went to them to ask them about their worlds. In this book, we listen to their answers to a simple set of questions revolving around a single concern: what has changed in your life, and how have you come to terms with it? The result is an oral history that interprets the stories that they tell about their evolving place in the modern world. Inevitably, their accounts emphasize the community over the individual, the local over the nation, simplicity over profit, and peace over violence. They speak of having resisted much of what we "moderns" assume to be true and good: personal achievement, ease, progress, ever-increasing knowledge, certainty, and the idea that society is healthiest when its citizens act in self-interest.

The horse-and-buggy Mennonites implicitly critique modernity in stories about their way of life. Indirectly, they speak to the concerns of philosophers and historians who bemoan some "malaise of modernity," the "inner contradictions" of capitalism, or the short-sighted "ascendency of the individual" over everything that matters.[2] In their own ways, these people talk about resisting the pitfalls of individualism. They are dismissive of a preoccupation with personal rights, and they are critical of an economy driven by personal interest. And they remind us of old "wisdoms," those "remarkable repositories" of preindustrial ways about which anthropologists speak nostalgically.[3]

Ironically, the horse-and-buggy Mennonites' own thinking is often hidden by the very material markers by which they announce their place within modernity. They do in fact drive horse-drawn buggies, the women do wear bonnets or quaint kerchiefs, the men do appear in black overalls or button-up coats, houses are in fact lit by flickering lanterns or battery-powered lights, and everywhere there are obvious symbols of an intentional, alternative way of living. Their picturesque gardens, well-defined fields, physically rigorous children, lanes and earthen roadways, and roomy houses are all easily photographed. But they also signal a particular world view, one infused with religious meaning. Their testimonials reveal complex and dynamic communities, all shaped by contesting the immense as-similative power of the globalized modern world.

Yet this particular story has been overshadowed by the accounts of another group of horse-and-buggy people, the Amish in the United States, a group that broke from the Mennonites more than 300 years ago. Concentrated in identifiable clusters in some of the most densely populated sections of eastern rural North America, not far from the great American metropolises, their story has caught the imagination of modern society. Indeed, the Amish have been the subject of a rich scholarly discourse.[4]

The subjects of this book are not Amish and not American. Rather, they are two sets of horse-and-buggy Mennonites linked to Canada: the first lives in Canada while the second consists of Canadian descendants who live in Latin America. The first includes some 8,000 horse-and-buggy "Old Order" (including "Orthodox") Mennonites who have chosen to remain in Canada despite its modern and integrated economy and culture, charting lives for themselves in southern Ontario, the very heart of modernity, in the shadow of Canada's largest city, Toronto. The second group includes some 100,000 "Old Colony" Mennonites in Latin America, descendants of stubborn western Canadian Mennonites who moved to northern Mexico in the 1920s and then scattered in Central and South America after the 1950s. The two sets of Mennonites have rarely met and have distinctive histories. Old Order Mennonites have stood firm within Canada, whereas the Old Colony Mennonites have run off to the ends of the earth in Central and South America. The Old Orders are of Swiss-American descent who speak English, but prefer their ancestral Pennsylvania Dutch, a South German dialect. The Old Colonists are of Dutch-Russian-Canadian descent, who speak mostly in their ancestral West Prussian Low German, and are much more versant in Spanish than in English.

Despite these significant differences, both the Old Orders and the Old Colonists share a common anti-modern outlook on life: it is most spiritually rich when it is kept simple, lived out in the local, in close-knit and highly self-sufficient communities, on farms, close to nature. In a remarkable coincidence, both the Old Orders in Canada and the Old Colonists in Latin America have concluded that such a simple agrarian life requires horse-and-buggy transportation, limited use of electricity, plain clothing, and oftentimes the steel-wheeled tractor. Both sets of Mennonites have been intent on contesting the modern world.

Aspects of this story have been told by academics with reference to specific sub-sets of these communities. As published graduate theses and dissertations, these works have been a tremendous help to me in conceptualizing this book. Such studies explain how societies of resistance are performed in local contexts, how closed versus open societies function, or how cultures of informality bump against worlds organized by contracts and instruments of standardization. They have also pitted ideas of human agency against restricting social structures, innovation against old habits, and they speculate about dialectical forces between the two. Yet, though I have benefited from the energy directed at understanding Anabaptist groups such as the Amish and Old Order and Old Colony Mennonites by sociologists, anthropologists, geographers, and economists, in this book I do not emphasize social scientific theory to explain the horse-and-buggy people.

Rather, as an oral history, this book reports on answers to questions that we as researchers posed to the Old Order and Old Colony horse-and-buggy people whom we visited.[5] Of course, their answers can be complex because any conversation is always filtered: stories are told, but always in certain ways, with some facts highlighted, others diminished, others still left unsaid. We understand that those answers are spoken by horse-and-buggy Mennonites to scholars living comfortably in the very modern world that they have rejected. Yet the fact that we went to these people in a spirit of curiosity and respect seemed to facilitate the discussions. Of course, in conversing with us, these people had their own unspoken agendas. Perhaps they merely wished to reach out from their rural isolation to a wider world of friendly people. Perhaps they wished to defend their ways, to speak their own stories into a world that has often emphasized their peculiarities, including their shortcomings and relative primitivism, a condition ripe for the spread of fantastic stories of social dysfunction. Certainly, they know that they are a distinct people and that their ways of life are intentional. And even though they are humble, even reticent, they can also recite the biblical injunctions not to hide one's "light under a bushel" and talk about "the hope that is in you."[6] True, outsiders have often come to change the ways of the horse-and-buggy Mennonites, and understandably the Old Colony and Old Order people would rather not talk to people they see as attempting to foist the modern world onto them. Besides which, the horse-and-buggy people do not like to debate with opponents, discuss theological niceties, or even defend their ways. Yet they readily tell their stories to one another and they happily talk to perfect strangers who have come to listen to their narratives.

As in all stories, there are inconsistencies and degrees of narrative messiness. The interviewees often portrayed fuzzy histories, ones that assembled facts in helter-skelter ways. They relayed oral and intergenerational traditions to explain group sacrifices, why they live in the ways they do, so distinctively from the modern world. Oftentimes they seemed to conflate the past and present, indicating the conundrum of all people committed to changelessness.[7]

As such, the very idea of history for them is not what it is for modern citizens. Indeed, most horse-and-buggy people do not feel comfortable with the typical life-story interview approach of oral history. Despite its claim of giving the interviewee the freedom to answer within his or her cultural constraints, it in fact assumes that people love talking about their own progress, unilinear progression in particular, in a teleological fashion. But how can you ask a people about change when they do not celebrate change? It seems that for the horse-and-buggy people history is not what is different from one era to another as much as it is a record of the steps taken to make sure that as little change as possible occurs. For this reason, many of the answers to questions about the past posed to them seemed to slip into descriptions of the present. Because of their commitment to preventing change, they often do not separate past and present tenses. Often they refer to present practice with examples from the past, or they speak in the "present perfect simple tense," talking about "what has been" rather than what "was," an approach used in literature to describe "action that has had an influence on the present" and "action that is still going on."[8] To employ the technical language of theorists, the stories that they tell about the past are by nature both "communicative" and "cultural," both informal and formal, intertwining myths of the "absolute past" with memories of the "recent past," embodied in both life narratives and affective ties to artifacts at once sacred and temporal.[9] In short, story is a fundamental feature of their world.

The interviewees especially liked talking about migration. Occasionally their stories recounted long past migrations, those from Pennsylvania to Canada or New Russia to Canada, or somewhat more recent moves, from Canada to Latin America, or very recent ones within southern Ontario and within Latin America. As the Ontario groups tell their family histories, they speak about having come to Canada and then living within one region for over 200 years. Their histories begin in Switzerland in the sixteenth century, link them to Pennsylvania in the eighteenth century, and then take them to Upper Canada in the years after 1800, to a region they still inhabit today.[10] The Old Colonists in Latin America have a remarkably different story. They speak about grandparents migrating from Manitoba and Saskatchewan in the 1920s to northern Mexico. Then they trace their own migrations ever farther southward, to tropical Belize in the 1950s, fertile Bolivia in the 1960s, East Paraguay in the 1970s, semi-arid Argentina in the 1980s, and Mexico's steamy southern Campeche in the 1990s. For some, these moves became but the first of many, leading to a seemingly endless moving back and forth among these various places, mostly as promises of farmland or greater degrees of distance from modernizing forces presented themselves.[11] Some have even migrated north to Canada or the western United States and then back south.

Migration stories are the easy stories; but more intimate stories of religious duty are told, albeit more often in the second and third hour of the interview. Even though the Old Order and Old Colony stories of migration do not overlap, their stories of faith do. Most members of both groups know their historical lineage, how they as Mennonites had their start 500 years ago in the time of the "martyrs" and the Catholic priest-turned-Protestant preacher Menno Simons who preached simplicity and humility. Some also know the details of how the Anabaptists of the sixteenth century, the antecedents of the Mennonites, confronted the state church—both Catholic and Protestant—with their ideas on adult baptism and nonresistance. Many know details of painful separations from more modern Mennonites:

the Old Orders know that their ancestors endured a series of schisms in the 1890s and again in the 1920s in Ontario; and the Old Colonists speak about the historic emigration from modern Manitoba and Saskatchewan in the 1920s and went through their own separation from modernizing Mennonites in Mexico between the 1960s and 1990s. And they both talk about this history not as an achievement but as a striving: for continuity, simplicity, and obedience.

Indeed, this is their common genius, the heart and substance of the community. It's not a genius as in utopian design or remarkable cleverness and insight; rather, it is an approach to life, reflected in sweeping ideas and symbols, and in the spirit that enlivens relationships with an insistence and intention. *Genius* is not a word that these Mennonites use; it translates poorly into Pennsylvania Dutch or West Prussian Low German, and it potentially violates their implicit humility. Indeed, the horse-and-buggy Mennonites are the first to announce that they are far from a perfect people. Often they agree with people who highlight their shortcomings. They know that they have been severely criticized by the media and by other churches, both national and international, and even by their friends and relatives. They have heard jurists and journalists say that they deal poorly with sexual abuse since they are too quick to forgive, too quick to accept such violence as deserved suffering, stubbornly unwilling to lift peasant taboos about talking about sexuality, and seemingly unaware that confrontation and therapy are the most effective routes to ending the abuse. They have heard psychologists say that horse-and-buggy communities should be more open so that, when young adults choose the sacred vows of baptism, they have considered all the options. They have had run-ins with anthropologists who have cited them as a classic example of a "closed" society, with a strong authoritarian leadership and naive membership, racialized social boundaries, and a dualistic world view. They have been told by economists that their technologies are highly inefficient and lead to unintentional poverty and social problems. They have faced accusations from environmentalists that they cut forests and heedlessly plow the soils of former bushland. The horse-and-buggy people have their share of trouble, and this book does not present them otherwise. They are not the pure

side of a simple binary of good and bad, the contesting and the hege-
monic, the weak and the mighty.

Still, the horse-and-buggy people may like the irony of the word
"genius." They know that in their simple ways they live out a certain
critique of the assumed achievements of twenty-first-century civilization. And admittedly, I do argue in this book that there is a certain genius in how the horse-and-buggy people live in community and *survive*
with so little. I confess that I write this book with this bias. This book is
not a commissioned work; these humble people did not ask me to write
about their accomplishments. When I visited them, unannounced, An-
nie and John Sherk of Huron County, Ontario, did not boast that they
feed eleven children on seventy-three acres of land or beg to show me
how they milk their cow by hand, feed their sheep by wheelbarrow,
or blanket their horses in the cold of winter. I asked them to show me
their farm in January 2015, and they obliged me, inviting me in for
supper to boot. Jacob and Maria Neudorf of Yacuiba, Bolivia, did not
offer to talk about adapting their Mexican-proven farming methods
for a new frontier near the Argentine border and about their dream of
raising chickens for the town's market; I invited myself to their colony
in July 2009 and asked them about their adaptations and dreams, and I
enjoyed a two-day stay. In their very ways of living, the Sherks and the
Neudorfs confront the forces that radically altered the social reality of
most of the earth's rural people during the twentieth century. And in
this respect alone, their stories of survival are worth hearing.

Indeed, these anti-modern people may well cast light on the
nature of our modern society. In comparison to lives in the technologized north, the horse-and-buggy Mennonites leave a tiny
carbon footprint on this earth, they care for their own, they respect
the elderly, they reject factory farming, they are people of the earth.
And they organize their own affairs. Their communities are built on
time-tested institutions driven by values of care and equality. They
live by an egalitarian system of inheritance, local taxation by honour,
rudimentary education geared to simple farm living, a culture of
conflict resolution, and a rough but effective internal welfare system.
Perhaps oddly, they are often rather open and even pluralistic in their
outlooks, expressing deep love for adult children who have rejected

their ways and basic respect for anyone of any faith who struggles to remain true to their own sacred vows.

In this respect, the horse-and-buggy Mennonites are similar to other anti-modern groups around the world who have stood up to modern ways. Certainly, rural groups in every country have resisted the encroachment of modernity.[12] But over the centuries, religious groups in particular have opposed some aspect of modernity or had a radical wing that did so. Christianity has had its desert monks, Judaism its Orthodox Jews, Islam its Wahhabi scholars; Shintoism, Sikhism, Hinduism, and Buddhism all venerate the ancient and mythological. Every modern society also has its peripheral, earthy, off-the-grid "hippies" who emphasize the natural, the communitarian, and the simple, and often embrace a pacifist anarchism. A hundred years ago North American and Western European countries saw groups of anti-modern *fin de siècle* artists and poets reach back to a romantic past in their bid to offer fierce critique of modern, urban, and industrial societies.[13]

In a sense, Old Colony and Old Order Mennonite communities find their place within these broader narratives of protest, for theirs is a particular critique of modern ways. Their protest has been expressed partly through migration but especially through schism. They have endured hard moments in order to separate themselves from more accommodating Mennonites. Both the Old Colony and Old Order communities appeared out of a larger ferment of change linked to religious and political reforms as well as to rapid urbanization and industrialization.

The Ontario Old Order group had its beginning in 1889 in Waterloo County, when, inspired by its counterpart in the United States, it confronted modern trends in the main Mennonite Church and separated from it. The official church history has Bishop Abraham W. Martin (1832–1902) of Woolwich Township, reportedly a "fleshly," affable, and dignified man, stand up to emotional and subjective revivalism. Having refused to baptize youth who were converted in "revival" meetings influenced by Methodism, Martin eventually led a minority of about 600 Mennonites to form the Old Order Mennonite Church. By the 1920s, when the Old Orders rejected the car as a symbol of pride and individualism, they became known as a horse-and-buggy people.

The much more numerous Old Colony Mennonites had their beginning in 1875 in Manitoba. Here, Bishop Johan Wiebe (1837–1905), also mythologized as a warm and conscientious man, organized a disparate group of about 3,000 Mennonite immigrants linked to the original "old colony" of Khortitsa (or Chortitza, as they wrote it in German) established in New Russia in 1789. The most conservative of three immigrant groups in Manitoba, this so-called Reinländer Mennonite Church, or more popularly the *Altkolonier* (the "Old Colonists"), opposed revivalism and Sunday schools as rigorously as the Old Orders did, but also public schools and participation in municipal politics. In 1916, the Old Colony church was one of the most stalwart of Mennonite groups opposed to the introduction of English-language public schools, and in 1922 the church, now located in both Manitoba and Saskatchewan, left Canada for rural autonomy, school freedom, and military exemption in northern Mexico. Its opposition to modern ways was eventually extended after the Second World War to include the rejection of electricity and rubber tires on tractors. The most traditional among the Old Colony community became known as a stalwart horse-and-buggy people.

This story, as these Mennonites tell it, is an amalgam of corporate memory and personal reflection. The first two chapters present stories from two distinct southern Ontario–based Old Order Mennonite communities. The more moderate Old Order folks from Waterloo County speak of the historical foundations of an anti-modern life within the shadow of booming Kitchener-Waterloo; the more traditional "Orthodox" Old Orders from Bruce County, 100 kilometres west, near the town of Gorrie, talk about how they have reinvented old traditions.

The next set of chapters introduces the worlds of the Old Colony people in Latin America—Mexico, Paraguay, Bolivia, and Belize (a tiny English-speaking country intricately linked to the Latino south). In Chapter 3, these people tell stories of migration, of arriving at their current localities in the Global South, and recall their sacred vows of simplicity and the process by which the religious community was transplanted. In Chapter 4, Old Colonist men and women tell stories of adapting old institutions and farm practices to new physical and social constraints in Latin American contexts. In Chapter 5, the Old Colonists talk about their lives unfolding in family time, a set of intergenerational bridges lending stability to their worlds, and moving inexorably from birth to youth to middle age to old age to death. In Chapter 6, they tell their stories of crossing social boundaries marked by religion, social class, and race, all the while using these links to build a moral economy. Finally, in Chapter 7, they speak of how they have reconnected with ancestral Canada or found places in the United States, sites at once attractive and frightening.

The very idea of a community resisting modernity is worthy of close study. We might not appreciate the horse-and-buggy stubbornness and rural simplicity. Yet as other works on the merits of anti-modern or even ancient societies—as diverse as those told by Wade Davis or Ronald Wright, Thomas Merton or Kathleen Norris, Clifford Geertz or Fredrik Barth—these stories not only add a critical dimension to national histories and global discourses, but "trouble" the implicit assumptions of modern life. The narratives in this book contain ago-old maxims, lore of yesteryear, folk medicines, ancient wisdom, and slower and smaller ways of farming from which we can learn. These stories speak to a communitarian culture, rooted in the past, critical of the homogenizing global impulses of the twentieth century. Hearing accounts of how the horse-and-buggy people believe that they have survived the forces of modernization in two remarkably different cultural contexts—Canada and Latin America—reveals not only an account of a particular cultural resilience, but an implicit critique of our own advanced societies. Indeed, despite their maddening primitiveness and untenable dualisms, their overall story just might illuminate something foundational about our own. By the end of this book, we might have been reminded of the degree to which the ideas of the ascendancy of the individual in a consumption-oriented society have won the day in our world over a moral economy and communitarian wholeness. Perhaps we may have learned something about our own culture from the histories of a people whom we thought too anti-modern to have relevance in today's world.

PART ONE

OLD ORDER MENNONITES IN CANADA

CHAPTER ONE

Changelessness in
Canada's Heartland

"Some of the neighbour men came to do the plowing..."

We slowly drive past the simple, wood-framed Linwood Old Order Mennonite church in southern Ontario, in March 2008, as a long line of horse-drawn buggies turns into the churchyard. They stop in turn in front of the church, and poised women in neat garb of yesteryear and smartly dressed children alight. Then, in sequence, each buggy pulls away to the hitching posts, where men and boys dressed in dark suits tether the horses and make for the "men's" entrance on the church's far side. We are outsiders, hoping to enter this world of plainness and tradition. We stop one of the Old Order families in their buggy on the roadway: "We are from Manitoba, may we attend your service?" we say. The friendly husband responds, "You are most welcome, just park your car on the roadway across from the church." Then he adds, "By the way, if you are from Manitoba, do you live close to Brandon? I've got an agent out there selling the ventilating system I build on my farm." It seems strange, a manufacturer of a piece of modern farm technology, with a national market, on his way to an Old Order church!

Other moments of incongruence follow. As my travel companion, Tim Snider, a veterinarian, and I walk into the church yard and approach the men's entrance, we find a circle of farmers curious about our worlds. A friendly man about my age, Noah Weber, engages me on the challenges of rural life in a modern world—volatile global pig prices and government-issued chicken quotas; the Old Order pig farmers are struggling, but state-regulated poultry farmers are doing okay; I wonder how economic disparity caused by outside markets and politics affects Old Order congregational unity. Noah smiles and invites us into the church building. Plain white walls announce the inside space and a pattern of wood-slat benches provide a unifying matrix, demarcated by four gendered sub-spaces, one each for men, women, girls, and boys. A plain wooden podium centred by a pulpit speaks of authority. Once everyone is assembled, a lengthy service ensues: German hymns sung a cappella in long cadences, an hour-long sermon, extemporaneous, in Pennsylvania Dutch. Then comes a surprise ending when a younger minister steps onto the podium and takes the pulpit. He announces in English that the regional ministerial conference has met and that before the next communion service the baptized young men who played hockey shall confess to the leadership. He adds that the church *Ordnung* has a new regulation: tractors on public roadways must not exceed ten miles per hour, presumably the speed of a good team of horses.

Ironically, a visit to a service that we thought would be a throwback to a previous century has brought us face to face with a social reality within the Old Order community: you can't easily escape from the modern world. The Old Order Mennonites of southern Ontario number about 8,000, the largest concentration of horse-and-buggy Anabaptists in Canada. Their history as a separate Mennonite denomination dating to the 1889 schism puts them at odds with more acculturated, modern Mennonites. The Old Orders still reject modern-day church services that highlight the individual and emotional displays of joyfulness; instead they emphasize humility and close-knit community. They decline the "worldly" car and electronic media, the ease of electric devices, and town living. And they put a lid on farm commercialization and progress, for one, by tamping down the speed on Old Order-driven tractors. Their theology of simplicity and absolute non-violence requires adults to live lives of self-denial, meaning that the grown men leave sports and raucous living to the youthful boys. They also reject most associations with the state, including medicare, old age pensions, and social assistance, but they live in a world of markets, nakedly subject to global forces and state policies. They're committed to rural life, and even as affordable farmland disappears, many turn farmyards into manufacturing sites, thus energizing their households' economies. The Sunday morning visit to Linwood introduced us to plainness and simplicity, but set in a complex and dynamic world.

Scholars who have studied these Old Order Mennonites stress their unique and successful attempt to breathe life into old ways within the Canadian industrial heartland. Certainly, they fit nicely the classical models of sociology that separate formal, urban life from farm and village ways of face-to-face interaction and a more holistic and affective world. Historians who write about the Old Orders emphasize their beginning in the 1890s and long contestation of modernity; they document their growing list of restrictions and the bewildering array of small splinter groups—the David Martin Old Orders, the Orthodox Old Orders, the Kinloss Old Orders, the Westbourne Orthodox in Manitoba—as each sub-group sets its own path of anti-modernity. But these studies have not often reported on the words of the Old Order Mennonites themselves. Based on oral history, the next two chapters report on what these Ontario Old Order members themselves say about their history.

That history begins by seeing a past residing uneasily in the present, dynamic and volatile. The conversations between thirty some Old Order Mennonites[1] and Andy Martin, a doctoral student at the University of Toronto and the grandson of an Old Order minister, suggest that, where outsiders see changelessness, Old Orders might well see constant negotiation and perpetual contestation. Their stories are about alterations that they have made in response to outside forces, constant changes in order to keep life simple, slow, and local. Their lives are lived out in the shadow of Canada's largest city and in some of the most densely populated rural districts of Ontario. Theirs is an anti-modernity honed within the very heart of modern Canada.

Musings and Mindsets

When Old Order Mennonites reflect on the past, their differences from and conflicts with modernity stand out. Their symbols of horse-and-buggy transportation, neat peasant garb, enclosed farmsteads, and night-time lanterns are all intentioned. But they demarcate more than cultural difference; they are symbols of religious faith lived out in everyday life. Faith, at the centre of their world, has been best expressed in lifestyle, not in words.

Long-time Old Order schoolteacher Paul Bowman of Linwood says that religious words have not often been spoken in their communities, for it is the way of life lived in community that counts. Thus, it is not a particular religious "doctrine" or even "personal relationship" but "the life of Christ [that] is the centre óf the Old Order life." Ministers, ordinary farmers chosen by lot, do not typically teach theology in Sunday morning services, for Christian doctrine learned at baptism is assumed. Old Order interviewees say that belief is the easy part of faith; practice is what is difficult. Reuben Wideman, a retired farmer from Mount Forest and the father of fourteen children, says that it's "like we heard on Sunday" at the church service, "salvation is free, discipleship is costly." What matters is how seriously you take discipleship, the call to live simply in this world. As Reuben puts it, it matters "to what extent ... you take [discipleship], that's where a lot of the differences come in." Sermons thus focus not on correct belief but on willingness to live the plain life.

This struggle for simplicity is at the crux of their history. And the Old Orders ponder this challenge daily. Elderly Anson Weber of St. Jacobs is known by his neighbours as a thinker, even a sort of rural philosopher. He still lives in the house of his birth and says that the idea of "simple" itself is not simple: "We can always use it for wrong or right.... If everything were black and white, this world would be different, but there are more grey areas than black and white. Like, can you distinguish the difference between improvement and covetousness? ... There are some areas that we hardly know exactly.... Selfishness is actually one of the greater hindrances of our life." It's not easy to keep to the old ways in a modern world, but keeping to the old ways and staying humble, making sure that self-denial is life-giving, that is the real struggle.

The Old Orders know that they have been criticized for legalism, even for self-righteousness and pride. Anson says that he has come to appreciate the fact that "Christ came to this world without observation," an infant in a barn, and then he became a simple prophet, rarely "openly visible." Yet a religious mystery attracted the simple and the humble. He says that 2,000 years ago "the Pharisees, they saw it and rejected it," but "the poor people picked it up." The call for the Old Orders has been similar, a humble acceptance of the inexorable cycle of life. We know that our bodies "came from the earth to begin with," recognize that "food comes from the earth," and realize that, "when we have passed our time, the earth again takes care of our body." The real meaning of life, and this requirement of submission, says Anson, remained unsettled in his mind until only ten years ago. The life of simplicity is a lifelong calling, a vocation.

Religion for the Old Orders has thus been less about doctrinal certainty and inner peace than about submission and humility. Veteran schoolteacher Cyrus Martin of Yatton says that his people hold to basic Christianity. In a way, he even sounds similar to an urban evangelical when he says that we "preach Christ crucified" and that "salvation is what happens when I accept Jesus Christ." But, Cyrus insists, to claim salvation, to say as evangelicals do that "I was at a meeting last night, and I was saved, that is totally foreign ... to what we teach." Religion is ultimately about obedience and hope. The "whole experience is salvation," he says; "that's why we have always said we 'hope' to meet each other in heaven, not 'I know' that I will be; you know what I mean?" This meaning can become complex since religion cannot be separated from the everyday. To make his point, Cyrus talks about a "home orientedness we have in our hearts." It's demonstrated in the way that Old Orders have had funerals and weddings within the home and not the church. These central moments in the cycle of life cannot be made sacred by a church building.

Old Orders have always seen life as a stark choice: the long-term goal of getting to heaven versus the short-term lure of capitalism and consumption. David Reist, a middle-aged farmer from Chesley to the north, for example, talks philosophically about human confusion between the words *needs* and *wants*. He recites the gospel song lyrics "this world is not my home, I'm just a-passing through," to explain the underlying reason why he rejects modernity. All materiality is a fleeting reality. He says that "I feel we should just want the things we need, not the wealth and fame—they have no value for our salvation." Certainly, there is no virtue in poverty, but wealth is much more problematic. It can easily pull him into the consumer market in the city. He sounds moralistic when he says that "if we make money it should be used to help others," but he describes specific ways in which money has been shared within the community, given to deacons to hand out to the needy or "loaned out to help others." Even within the Old Order community, it's been tempting for those with money simply to invest it in order to obtain more land or larger farms. The irony is that "some of the smaller farm operators seem to be more generous because they aren't upgrading buildings and equipment and have more money to loan out." David says that it's formulaic: scales of economy bind you to the world; he has seen how large farm equipment has sometimes derailed the Old Order person from a life of contentment.

This level of theologizing is as much as Old Order members ever undertake. Surprisingly, they often say that they haven't "taught" their children this behaviour but merely "modelled" it. Retired schoolteacher Jesse Martin of Hawkesville recalls the 1960s, when the Old Orders quit the public school system and he taught in their new private school. The parents who made up the school board told him not to teach religion. In fact, they were "clear they wanted to have the Lord's Prayer and scripture reading, but [the teacher] was not supposed to comment on the scripture reading." Certainly, the parents cared what their children learned. They opposed book "titles that included the words *magic* and *make believe* and *sex education*." But the school has not been a place for indoctrination. Former teacher Paul Bowman adds that ordained men were not invited to be on the private school boards: church and school were supposed to serve different functions. Yes, church funds paid for the schools, but the money flowed without strings attached: "School board secretaries [simply] let the deacons know how much money [was] needed for the school year, and then the deacons let the various churches know how much money was required." The parents, not the preachers, run the schools.

The Old Orders might treasure actions over words, but they have not generally been moralistic. True, over the past decade or so, Old Orders have adopted the more personalized ethical code of competing evangelical groups, a new order sometimes elevating good personal habits above healthy, community-enhancing social interaction. But many Old Orders see this move toward personal accountability more as a political step to ensure that they are respected and understood in the shifting faith landscape of modern Canada than as a deep religious conviction. Paul Bowman says that "today alcohol and tobacco are [increasingly] banned in the Old Order community," a result of the "influence of fundamentalism" encouraged by the more evangelical Conservative Mennonite and Markham Mennonite groups. He is frank in outlining the equation: these more modern groups consider themselves "better" than us, "so we kind of [went] in that direction." Many Old Orders have even begun to embrace evangelical vocabulary. But many are also openly opposed to this development, seen as a step toward modernization and individualism. Surprisingly, the Old Orders see the individualism of the more verbal, moralistic, evangelistic, car-driving Mennonites as more rigid than their horse-and-buggy ways: for evangelical Mennonites, it's "like one little cigarette, and they miss their chance for baptism that summer." For the Old Orders, religious action is not so much the personal act as the community-oriented action.

Usually, when the Old Orders muse about life, they tell stories. Their accounts are not of large church events or times of great accomplishment or miracles in history. They are of assisting one another in everyday life or of staying close to nature on the farm. Long-time schoolteacher Elvina Sauder of Elmira recalls that when her nephew's wife had a stillborn baby they had only a small graveside funeral for family and close friends. But the community showed its support later when "some of the neighbour men came to do the plowing for [the] nephew even though he wasn't expecting it." And when the Old Orders venture from stories, most stay with ideas rooted in the everyday. They like to talk about farm life as a guarantor of communitarian wholeness and humility. Farmer David Reist says that "we like the lifestyle of the farm" and worry "when people work out [for wages] and have evenings free; leisure time at night is not good." The farm is the place where family members assemble without distraction. Thus, it is important to keep the family farm from falling prey to the logic of agrarian capitalism.

Yet Anson Weber worries that this logic has crept onto the Old Order farms. He recalls that in his youth he "knew that the 'book'" said they were "to work with sweat on the brow, and I tried to stay with that." But the way in which his grandson approaches work is different. Anson describes his grandson's farm: the "work is done so much faster—'fed with the loader and gone for the day.' ... He cleans out the stable once every two weeks with the loader, and then when it's time for the fields, in a day or two, everything is taken out, and there is the liquid manure which takes another day and sometimes into the night." Perhaps this new technology-embracing ethos has had its good side. The horses, for example, are no longer overworked, and as they say tractors don't suffer, "they just wear out, that's all." But Anson is adamant: horses are healthier when worked steadily, and people who work with them are in a better frame of mind. Besides, patience learned while dealing with horses is the same trait needed to get along with people. And ironically, though tractor power has put horses to rest, it has also resulted in people working too hard: "We never [used to] work ... after nine o'clock. If ever I worked after nine o'clock—sometimes ... filling bags of potatoes at night till 10:30—it robbed me of energy the next day." Anson tells a personal story as he muses about the important things in life.

The Old Order community's handful of rural philosophers, ironically, excel at arguing verbally the limits of a verbal faith, indeed for the need for a religion based on action. But of course Old Orders won't argue that the horse-and-buggy system is superior. Placing themselves ahead of other folks is not their way. Rather, they choose to tell stories that emphasize harmony, patience, and humility.

The Preachers and the Practice

If faithful action has superseded correct belief, how can the former be achieved without talking about the latter? The simple answer is that Old Order Mennonite society is organic and face to face, not a formal and highly structured society. In fact, their communities have been much less fully organized than one might think. They insist that their leaders are chosen for character rather than skill, for humility rather than charisma. And they readily admit that this process produces messy, heartfelt social exchanges, not neat and orderly ones.

Even when Old Orders talk about voting for minister candidates in the past, they describe having looked for the candidate's reputation and humility, not for speaking talent or theological brilliance. It is about action, not about vocabulary. Farmer David Reist explains that patriarchal leadership has historically consisted of local men trained only in elementary school and chosen for life. Their work—preaching, baptizing, performing marriage ceremonies, administering communion—has been hard and without pay. But the uniquely Old Order task of revising and enforcing the *Ordnung* in changing times has been especially demanding. To do so requires patience and authority, the latter stemming from example rather than hierarchy. To establish that authority, says David, it is "recommended that ordained men should stay back from the line a little further." Thus, they should resist fashion with special rigour and wear more conservative dress and even hairstyles, the kinds that match older people's styles. The preacher's vocation is thus arduous in a variety of ways. In fact, when a person is elected to office, there is little reported joy; rather, it's a time of personal crisis for the one chosen. David says that "nobody desires an office of bishop," and ironically it's those feeling unworthy of it who have often been chosen: "The Lord can use us better if we [feel we] don't ... qualify."

Moses Frey of Mount Forest was only twenty-eight when he was ordained to the ministry in 1975. He recalls that "I felt unworthy. And of course it took quite an adjustment for Sunday. You usually sat in church and listened to what others had to say, and now you had to be one of those that got something together to teach others." He told himself that he shouldn't worry because the people must have had faith in him. And it helped him to have a strong sense of the spiritual. He says that at his first service as minister "it wasn't the first time I thought about God or the Bible or something, like my life just took another turn, right?" His vocation had been a long time in the making. In time, he learned to relax in front of an audience, realizing that "you've got a reason to be there, and you've been ordained, and you've got to quit thinking that everybody else can do better.... There's really no more required than to give what you have, right? It's not competition, it's contribution." But learning that confidence for the young preacher took time.

Veteran church leader Christian Shantz describes his vocation in the context of his church's leadership history. He says that he was "ordained to the office of bishop in ... 1986" after having been "ordained a minister in 1970 at twenty-five years old." His election as bishop came at a particular moment in Old Order history, after members decided that they needed to find a companion bishop for Edward Bauman. Knowledge of the lineage of the other bishops is important: when

Bauman died "in 2002, Onias Frey was ordained bishop to replace Edward. [Then] Peter Brubacher was ordained bishop in 2010, making it six bishops, three for Waterloo County, two for Mount Forest, and one for Kinloss." The lineage of senior-most bishops matters.

The authority as bishop resides in this narration of vocation rather than in any clerical symbol or title. True, ministers wear somewhat more conservative dress than do ordinary Old Order members, and they can read and write in Pennsylvania Dutch. They are also more likely to perform the "holy kiss," the intragender lip-on-lip kiss described by Willard Wideman of St. Jacobs as an act of affection usually reserved "for something special—meeting the ministry, at a funeral or viewing, or meeting a friend who has not been seen for a long time." But it seems that persons of authority don't revel in these symbols and symbolic actions. In describing his work as a bishop, Christian talks of hard work, sometimes meaning that he "has Sunday clothes on every day for two weeks." An Old Order minister works and demurs; he does not strut and pronounce. In fact, Old Order leaders will sometimes emphasize a minister's or bishop's relative lack of power: these leaders are chosen by members and possess no seminary training.

Yet they have always led the *Umfrage*, the closed meeting of clergy and groups of laity. It is a place where a bishop can consolidate clerical power, but it's also a place where it can be challenged. For one, at the *Umfrage*, change is negotiated between the ministers and the people. Literally, *Umfrage* means to "give counsel." These special counsel days are held in the women's cloakroom at the church just before the biannual communion services, and they have been the dynamic sites of debate, admonition, and even confrontation and contestation. Here especially middle-aged and older persons are welcomed to offer their views of the state of the community, to challenge, and to be challenged. Willard Wideman says that once "a couple has a fifteen year old" they are considered to be "a good age to start going to give counsel." The *Umfrage* has no set agenda. The members simply go into the cloakroom to talk to the ministers "by group, a younger men's group, an older men's group, a younger women's group, and an older women's group," and no one knows how any of these submeetings will turn out. The *Umfrage* has been a dynamic place for community discipline. Folks raise concerns about the community but also confess matters and state "whether they are at peace with God and the community." Clearly, giving counsel must also entail receiving it.

Issues at the *Umfrage* come from the right or the left, refining just how the community is shaped over time. Store owner Allen Metzger says that it was at an *Umfrage* some twenty years ago that members challenged the appearance of bicycles and even the use of taxis to take people to town. Even in later years, some members raised the issue of "using the bicycles too much," first because social boundaries could be crossed with such ease and second, if the boys started to bike, would the "girls ... start to bike to church" as well, and "what effect" would arise from "young girls out biking late at night alone?" But Allen himself has used the *Umfrage* as a place to contest certain conservative trends in the church. He has never believed that traditional "structure and order should dictate exactly how every individual has to do this or that." Some time ago, for example, he and others protested the dismissal of a young minister who believed that the church should shed its historic isolationism for a fuller engagment in community outreach. Allen and others were deeply disappointed when the young minister felt driven from the Old Order community and compelled to join the nearby Charity Church, an evangelical body. It was a bitter moment for Allen.

Ministers have taken local *Umfrage* issues to district meetings, gatherings of ordained men from a constellation of congregations, presided over by the district bishop, who assumes a neutral voice. As Willard Wideman says, "some people have in mind that the bishop is the head of the church, and whatever he's got to say, that's it, I don't have it that way in mind." But no matter just who wields power, the combination of *Umfrage* and district meetings shapes the world of the Old Orders. In rejecting both girl cyclists and Old Order mission workers, both advocated by Allen, the leadership reinforced the closed nature of the community: borders are not to be transgressed.

Matters of sexual abuse is one issue that some Old Order member say the *Umfrage* has not always addressed well. Like all "closed" communities—residential schools, sports locker rooms, the highest of government offices, the closed doors of a suburban home—the closed community of the horse-and-buggy community has its history of sexual abuse. Old Order Mennonites believe that within their church structure, they have strong proscriptions against sexual assault of any kind, including excommunication. However, from time to time serious cases have arisen that the community has not been able to deal with in a healing or expeditious manner.

Nehemiah Wenger,[2] a farmer from an outlying community some distance from Waterloo County, says that sexual abuse among Old Order communities has not been addressed well in the past. He refers to the highly publicized Adam Biesenger[3] case in which an Old Order man in his eighties was sentenced to two years of prison after pleading guilty to seventeen counts of sexual assault involving twelve boys and five girls, all under the age of sixteen, between 1967 and 1986. Nehemiah was one of the victims, and he is frank in his analysis that the long history of abuse in this case related to pitfalls of easy forgiveness offered to perpetrators by the church. He says, "You can forgive in a bad way, when you forgive sexual abuse." He speaks of the elderly man as "a pillar of the church" and "a wealthy Old Order man," who had been able to commit the crimes over a long time because he had honed the skill of "a professional liar," one who would confess, endure a short excommunication, and then be reinstated by bishops who felt he required forgiveness. The Old Order leadership, said Nehemiah, seemed to be "unaware of how much damage a pedophile can do." At the trial, said Nehemiah, he did something rather surprising for an Old Order member: "I found myself congratulating the investigating officer and the social worker for being more 'Christian,' caring more for Old Order children ... than did our own leaders." Later, said Nehemiah, when he shared his thoughts with his leaders, he felt ostracized for speaking out.

Nehemiah thinks there are limits to a fundamental principle of the Old Order world, the traditional Mennonite theology of the "two kingdoms." He agrees with the teaching, stemming from sixteenth-century Anabaptism and calling the true disciples of Christ to be non-resistant to violence and live in communitarian unity, in contrast to the wider world, which ultimately relies on police power for order, and sees individual liberty as an ultimate measure of social well-being. Nehemiah recalls how at the trial both the family and church of the accused argued that he had already paid his dues. They said he had suffered shame and indignation in the public eye, in stories carried by urban newspapers in Guelph, Kitchener-Waterloo, and elsewhere, with stark headlines that read "Mennonite Farmer Admits Molesting Young People."[4] Indeed, the old man had been excommunicated for a short period of time and had been permitted to attend only certain church services and forced to eat at a separate table. It made sense that the Old Order leaders wished that he be spared prison time. In fact at the trial Biesenger had been humble, repentant, and contrite, declaring that he would never again assault a child, and indeed the bishops had worked with him to make sure he wouldn't reoffend. At the trial the victims had spoken of having forgiven their assaulter and not wishing him any harm, some even going so far as now insisting that the assaults had had no lasting effect on them. Nehemiah recalls that the judge, Justice Norman Douglas, had seen it otherwise. He emphasized how the accused had hurt his victims, perhaps to the extent that they would have life-long trouble in establishing trusting, intimate relationships. The judge had said that perhaps the Mennonite elders' job was to forgive, but his was not to "judge a man's soul, but to enforce Canada's law." Nehemiah says that at the trial "I cried for this man; but I should also have cried for the sins he committed against me." He remains ambivalent: the Old Order church leaders rightfully advocate an alternative form of justice, but to his mind it is one with limitations.

Gender and Generation

At the centre of an Old Order narrative of continuity is the family. In this community of more than 200 years, most members have a strong sense of lineage and even kin-based or household-grounded lore. The ability to link farmsteads to specific families is common. Schoolteacher Elvina Sauder knows well that her parents are "the fifth generation living on this farm," that it is a farm "passed down through the male side to [her] father," and that indeed the "current house is the third house that was built on this farm." Retired farmer Silas Martin says that his parents bought the historic family farm in 1934, but he also knows the lore that it was "the coldest winter on record," when in one month "the temperature never came above zero degrees Fahrenheit" and when "a lot of apple trees froze out in southern Ontario." The elderly Anson Weber says that both he and his father Henry were born in the house in which Anson now lives, and he knows the year without having to do research: "Grandfather David moved to this farm in 1898."

But this sense of historical rootedness only hints at the efforts required for the farm household to survive culturally and economically over the generations. It does not reflect the changes required to ensure this reproduction. Yet this struggle is apparent at almost every stage of the life cycle of the family.

Historically, Old Orders expected their religious culture to be passed on at the family level, not at the church level. Grandmother Emma Wideman says that Old Orders rejected Sunday school more than 100 years ago for the simple reason that "we strongly feel the parents are responsible ... to teach their children about God and his word at home." And it happens without a lot of elaboration, in "everyday living," perhaps as parents use a beautiful rainbow or sunset to make a point about creation or human fragility. However, some changes have been introduced, especially as modern society has beckoned more forcefully. Indeed, some Old Order families have borrowed a page from more evangelical groups and begun having daily devotions, Bible readings, and readings from other devotional materials at breakfast.

In order to pass on the skills of farm self-sufficiency, Old Order children have left school at fourteen and begun working either at home or at other homes. Working for other families has allowed them to learn their ways, a sort of local cultural cross-fertilization. Elvina Sauder recalls that, when she finished her studies at fourteen, she worked at home, and when she reached sixteen she began working for Old Order neighbours. But she says that household technology—electric ovens, fridges, freezers—has changed the time of apprenticeship. For example, teenaged girls have found it increasingly difficult to find work as live-in maids. Because of the prevalence of modern conveniences, maids now work by the week or the month. For example, "when a woman gives birth, she may have hired help for [only] six to eight weeks," a time in which she "would work ahead by doing extra baking and cooking that could be put in the freezer to be used later after she is gone."

Boys have been more affected by laws dating from the 1960s directing children to attend school until age sixteen. To make sure that the state "turned a blind eye" on their practices, Elvina says, after Old Orders started their own private schools in the 1960s, they revised their educational policy manuals to say that "children must not enter the workforce until sixteen years of age." Some years ago, Three Bridges School, a unique public school geared to Old Order and Old Colony Mennonite children, began circumventing the issue by creating a special school program in which the school issued "a letter" allowing boys to "work for a local company as part of their school experience," even though they had left school upon completing grade eight.

The time of youth has thus become more complicated and certainly was once less of a concern than in recent years. High birth rates and surprising retention rates keep the problem of youth in sight. In Old Order parlance, store owner Allen Metzger has a very indirect way of measuring this phenomenon: "I am only thirty-seven years old, but … at our local church, on a Sunday morning, … I find that I am among the old…. I'm not on the front bench, but I'm on the older men's benches now." Just how to keep the youth within the fold has been a concern historically. The Amish and Old Order youth culture of *Rumspringa*, a time of rowdy drinking and dancing among youth, is well documented. But Paul Bowman thinks that an encroaching world has made alcohol abuse "more prevalent." Unfortunately, little can be done, though in the worst cases "the parents would be approached and made aware," and occasionally "deacons may become involved as the intermediary between church and home."

Parents have become more assertive over time. Take, for example, the Sunday-night youth "singings" that draw together most youth. Up to 100 youth gather in some farmyard and "mill about," sing, dance, and play volleyball, all "at the same time." It has been a primary place of courtship. Schoolteacher Cyrus Martin says that he "got to know [his] spouse at singings" after first meeting her at the place where "she 'worked out'": that is, working for another household as a maid. He would find ways of offering her a ride to the singings on Sunday nights. But parents have become concerned about the unsupervised nature of these large gatherings, the "big singings," and have introduced "small singings," shorter meetings of an hour super-vised by parents. There youth engage in orderly innovation within the framework of faith as they sing in four-part harmony from English songbooks that guide them with shaped notes. Now, says Cyrus, "the youth who drink do it in private or away from the crowd because they don't want to be caught."

Greater parental control has also been seen in what girls wear at the singings. Schoolteacher Jonas Bearinger offers this observation: "The age of when girls start wearing coverings has changed in the last twenty years.... Today most of the young women here start wearing their coverings all the time once they are baptized.... But I remember twenty years ago women quite often would start wearing the covering for every day all the time [only] when they were married.... I don't know what brought that about." Some of the influence might have come from the more evangelical car-driving Markham Mennonite group, among whom girls wear coverings at a younger age. But Jonas insists that no formal decision about the change was ever made: "As more and more people did it that way, it became the accepted thing." Old Orders have begun to accept some of the ideas of adolescence, the sense that teenagers are malleable and should not be allowed to sow their wild oats until the age of baptism.

Yet little has changed regarding the age and culture of baptism, says grandmother Emma Wideman; this rite of passage still occurs between the ages of eighteen and nineteen. Baptism is still a time of intentional and voluntary joining of the community. And generally youth haven't had to be manipulated to join it. Manufacturer Na-thaniel Martin says that actions always speak "louder than words," and if "parents demonstrate satisfaction and contentment with the church the youth will also be more likely to be content." Old Orders don't seem to worry about youth following in their parents' footsteps. Willard Wideman says that only occasionally, "if a youth's actions don't show that they are ready to join the church, they are asked to withdraw from the baptism class," often an embarrassing time for ev-eryone. But again there are new signs of change, especially of greater parental guidance. Besides "straightforward preaching," Willard says, Old Orders have come to rely on Amish reading materials such as *Family Life, Young Companions,* and *Blackboard Bulletin* to instruct youth in moral living. Such materials might stem from other traditional groups, but they advocate that parents intervene more decisively in the lives of their children.

In recent times, the church leadership has also become more assertive, especially in the way that boys are prepared for baptism. Baptism, says Christian Shantz, was once more laissez-faire. He says that as always youth are to "let their ministers know before New Year's [Day] if they want to be in the [baptismal] instruction class that year." But in a new move, Old Order bishops have begun dividing the names of young men among themselves and meeting with them individually in meetings of an hour or two. The bishops want to know why the boys wish to join the church and just how serious they are about this step. It was a necessary change, says Christian, for the "fruits seemed to not correspond to the seriousness of the situation." Why boys and not girls? "They are more into mischief than the girls," and "the girls are not as independent" as the boys. In recent times, too, "silly living is coming into the country," especially with electronic gadgets, which boys can use to "put the world in their pockets."

As in times past, weddings occur a few years after baptisms. Old patterns persist even as new ideas are introduced. The bride's family asks a few married couples to be the *Foregehr*, those who go ahead to manage the wedding according to tradition and the family's plans. The family then prepares all the food and hosts the wedding at its home. The event begins with men serving "plates of cookies and shot glasses of wine," commemorating the time that Jesus "turned water into wine at a wedding," says bike shop owner Mannasseh Weber. After a short ceremony in which the bride and groom are both dressed in dark attire and say their vows, tables are set up for the midday "dinner," served to 100 or more invited guests, often in two settings, the first for the closest friends and relatives.

But despite the hold of tradition, times have changed somewhat, says business owner Lovina Wideman. In the past, the event was an "all-day wedding," beginning by 9:30 a.m. and continuing till the late afternoon, when adults would return home. Only the "waitresses," half a dozen single girls, and the "chore boys," who would have looked after the horses, as well as the bridal party of six or seven young couples remained behind. Then, in the evening, the community youth would reappear, visiting and playing group games, all "very competitive and exciting, ... played with lots of enthusiasm." Occasionally, square dancing would take them into the night. Reflecting the influence of evangelicals, says Lovina, some families have replaced the wine with grape juice; reflecting a faster-paced life, some weddings have become merely "afternoon" events. And increasingly, the entire youth cohort stays for supper, and then after a "small singing" and some organized games they leave for home by 10:00 p.m. instead of midnight or even 1:00 a.m. as in the past.

Making a somewhat radical departure from the past, some youth have chosen not to marry at all. In recent years, singleness has risen sharply among Old Orders, especially for women. Schoolteacher Elvina Sauder says that single women have simply "gained independence" in recent times. Until recent decades, this outlook was virtually unknown. In the past, when a young single woman left her family, it was to "move around to various families, like a hired maid." Elvina thinks that the Old Order's private school system begun in the 1960s was a turning point. She recalls vividly "a day in February 1968 [when] a couple [of] Old Order men who were on the board of the North Waterloo [Old Order] school came calling" to ask her father if she "wanted a job as schoolteacher, and he said 'no' because he knew" that she was satisfied with her work at home. They were dissatisfied with his answer, so her father sent them to her place of work, but she too declined the offer. Only when they persisted did she finally agree, having "no good reason to say 'no.'"

Many other single women have found independence in business. Lovina Wideman grew up Old Order and recalls fully expecting to get married. But instead she eventually became a partner in a thriving food supply business, Kitchen Kuttings, with her sister, Elmeda, and a friend. Lovina recalls being socialized to become a homemaker. She says that she reached the dating "age of independence" of fifteen, asking boys for rides to the "big singings." After turning sixteen, she worked as a maid for Old Order families, and at about twenty-two she even lived with two Old Order bachelors, helping them to keep house. She says that it was "quite common for a single Old Order woman" to provide this service, even though "some people ... frowned upon" the practice. All signs pointed to a normal life, with an eventual marriage. But then at about twenty-five Lovina and her younger sister moved to North Waterloo and began working part time at jobs in town. She recalls feeling anxious "because a lot of our friends were getting married and having their own home[s]," yet "this just felt like something for ourselves, that we would want to do." After a few years of cleaning, clerking, and nursing home work, Lovina was coaxed into purchasing the Elmira Cheese Shop with her sister and a friend, the sister of the bishop. In little time, the business—with its 75 percent Mennonite clientele—was "bursting at the seams."

The young women began organizing their own social interactions, gathering on Sundays with other women over twenty-five, and soon after she and her sister asked their father to help them buy a horse-and-buggy unit. Lovina marvels: "I tell my nieces things have changed so much, because on a Sunday they go their own way [as girls]. They decide with their [girl]friends what they are going to do, and they hitch up the buggy, and they go.... In [our] youth, when you were fifteen to sixteen, you rely on the boys, and if there are no boys in your household you have to rely on the neigbourhood boys to come and pick you up. And that has all changed." Despite their new freedoms, Lovina and her sister eventually did leave the Old Order, mostly because their growing business demanded the use of a car and computer. The decision was difficult, and fortunately they were shunned only partially (not allowed to eat at the same table as their family members at their father's funeral) and only for a short time, until they actually joined a more liberal Mennonite church.

The majority of young people marry within the understanding of an officially patriarchal community. But the system has had its critics. Allen Metzger, single, says that one reason he has never been elected minister is because it is understood that "a minister needs to have a wife to lean on for support because the life of ministry is not easy, and he needs a soul companion." Allen's concern is that women are expected to serve men, and some women are concerned that upon marriage they will lose their independence. Seleda Horst, a single woman no longer with the Old Order, says that even today the "average housewife struggles to speak English.... She can speak English well enough to sell her produce and ... [go] to the doctor.... [But] her faith, ... she will ... think about it in German, like she hears the preachers do in church." Marriage has isolated women from the wider world. Seleda is especially critical that the "men are the head of the family and expected to understand these deep mysteries and to lead the church; the woman's place is to raise her children in love and submission to her husband and the Lord." She recalls her own mother, well spoken and able to converse about faith matters, as an exception.

Patriarchalism, say Old Orders, has been tempered too by the mutuality of the agrarian household. Paul Bowman says that farms have never been about the men and their successes. The basic understanding is clear: "When a young couple gets married and moves out on a farm, ... they have the support of the whole brotherhood." Then, too, the Old Order's centuries-old system of egalitarian inheritance means that the couple can receive gifts of land from either the maternal or the paternal side, with husbands often moving to land inherited by their wives. Middle-aged Ishmael Burkhardt recalls that his "parents moved onto the farm in 1965 a few years after they were married," a farm owned by his "maternal grandparents, the Mathias Martins." The same culture of inheritance has encouraged both widows and widowers to remain on their farms. Ishmael recalls that Grandfather Mathias obtained his farm only sometime after his father died in 1932: that is, after having "first worked for his [widowed] mom on the farm." Most often the matrilocal lineage is stated without explanation. Tilman Brubacher says matter-of-factly that in 1959, when he was in grade one, his parents moved "west of Floradale" to take "over from ... mother's parents' farm ... on the 4th of Peel," that is the fourth roadway concession in Peel Township.

Their stories indicate that these long-standing legal and economic structures have given Old Order women greater agency than their patriarchal ordinances might suggest. More recently, women have also benefited from certain technological advances, lightening their workloads and presenting greater degrees of mobility and leisure. Emma Wideman lists the innovations approved by the church during the past fifty years: "fridges, freezers, rototillers, electric stoves," and anything else using electricity. Even the family's annual butchering of a hog or steer, which itself replaced the old beef and pork rings and drew from twenty to forty families together, has been discontinued. Some Old Orders now "own government-inspected butcher shops." Despite these changes, however, the woman's role is clear: keep the house, nurture a large family, and work alongside the man on the farm as time allows. Family size has decreased slowly over time, but given the high degree of self-sufficiency—clothes sewn, gardens kept, the elderly tended to— hard work and cleanliness remain central virtues.

Old people have almost always lived their final years out in the "doddyhouse," a self-contained wing of the house, constructed after the original house was built, where the couple retire to when the youngest child marries. Often retirement actually means a step-by-step process. Men might first take a job off the farm, thus allowing the younger generation a chance to farm, and later they might take up less demanding roles. Bishop Christian Shantz says that he has been helping his sons on their farms since his fifties, and since he enjoys mechanics and they don't, he has a role to play. He jokes, quoting a Pennsylvania Dutch maxim, "when you work for free and eat at your own table, there is always more than enough work to do." Sometimes the pathway from active farming also takes the farmer from farming itself. Retired farmer Silas Martin of Conestoga says that in 1987, when his daughter married, he and his wife "moved into the doddyhouse," and he "got a job at [the] Home Hardware warehouse ... set[ting] up the warehouse where the annual Spring and Fall Home Show[s] are held."

Usually, old age has been a time when respected elderly members have helped to launch the next generation, both materially and culturally. Both men and women speak about remaining closer to the hearth, not tending to the fields or cooking large meals but forever busy with crafts. Women make rugs out of old dresses, produce quilts, and patch worn clothing; men turn woodworking shops into places of creativity. Both men and women cherish genealogy and know the place of each member in the family lineage. David Reist can recite his with just a bit of trouble: "Father [was] Melchior [Reist]; grandfather Anthony [Reist]; great-grandfather Jeremiah [Reist, who] always wore a beard, and he had a 'different' personality," and it was "Jeremiah and his wife [who] joined the Mennonite church, but ... [I'm not] sure where they came from." They can also tell stories of old. Silas Martin recalls a specific story told by his father, about the time when "their ancestors came from Pennsylvania in the early nineteenth century" and his grandfather worked for "'Cooper' John S. (Shirk)

Brubacher, ... [who] built a stone house with large stones," and he moved them by training "a young ox to walk a scaffolding, and as this ox grew he could use it to drag heavy rocks up the wall of the house; this house is still standing today." For the Old Order, artifacts may be inanimate, but they are objects with stories.

The final stretch of life is one fully entwined in the traditional ways of the Old Order. But it has required a dynamic engagement with younger members. Elderly Anson Weber says that he has not worried about attending church as he ages; in any event, his daughter and her husband "would take [us] along." Support for the elderly is simply assumed, no matter the social cost. Elvina Sauder says that she moved home after teaching near Waterloo for fourteen years "to support her mother, who was in her sixties," and found work at the "school at the end of the lane." When family resources are inadequate, the community pitches in. Siloam Brubacher, handicapped and in her seventies, is assisted by her husband, who has altered their buggy to be able to carry a wheelchair. She also relies on weekly visits from ten neighbourhood women. Ishmael Burkhardt says that even as "a single person [I don't] fear old age as I guess I just trust that I am a member of the church, and somebody in the church will fill that need."

If dealing with old age has not changed much in the past two generations, neither has the final ceremony, the funeral. Elvina Sauder says that it still resembles "a Sunday service in that it opens and closes with a song, but following the sermon there are no testimonies as there are on a Sunday." Some Old Orders practise an old European ritual, stopping the clock at the moment of death and keeping it still for the funeral period. More importantly, death is a time when the community comes together. She says that upon a death close neighbours and friends assemble at the home of the bereaved, and the family forms a committee from among them to organize the funeral: the women "plan and prepare the food for the funeral and clean the house, while the men ... do the chores and the [necessary] farm work."

Some changes have filtered into the Old Order community over time, but they have actually enabled that community to seek changelessness as a general principle. The wider society has been threatened with new disruptive technologies and new ways of thinking in more individualistic ways. To meet this challenge, parents have become more vigilant and ministers more proactive in dealing with youth. Old ways are being taught more intentionally, just as a greater degree of piety and moralism, borrowed from the evangelicals, bolsters those old communitarian ways.

Invention and Innovation

Old Order stories of change over time are accounts of accommodation. You can't survive as a horse-and-buggy culture without engaging the wider economy, and in this account, with the economy of Waterloo County. Just as Old Orders are changing some of their practices to ward off competition from both evangelical Mennonites and the wider secular world, so too they are opening up to a wider world, driven by a changing farm economy and new technologies. It's a selective adaptation to an economy made ironically, in order to avoid being consumed by it.

At the root of much change has been simple economic imperative. Over the past generation, an increasing number of Old Orders have chosen to derive at least a certain percentage of their income from non-farming means, some through farmyard manufacturing, others through wage labour. Jesse Wideman, a retired small farmer, says that in recent years worldly wise "cash croppers who farm thousands of acres and who are able to afford to pay top dollar for land," and who are enabled by high commodity prices, have entered the county and chased up farmland prices, in Waterloo as well as in outlying districts such as Linwood and Mount Forest. Manufacturer Nathaniel Martin offers a detailed narration of this rise: "Dad bought his first farm for $8,000 around 1948"; then in 1966 he "bought a 100-acre farm for $21,000, which was quite run down"; in 1978, he bought 100 acres of "good well-drained land only (no buildings) near Millbank" for Nathaniel's sister for $85,000. "By comparison, in 2011, a local 100-acre parcel of land with a large new $200,000 shed on it sold for $1.25 million," an amount so large that it required financing through local banks.

Old Orders have responded by farming more strategically. Christian Shantz notes that Old Order farmers have begun contracting with large agricultural corporations and selling livestock on the futures index. He says that "succeeding financially in farming inevitably [has] led to getting involved in some of these things." But there are checks and balances in the system. The Old Order's most far-reaching new marketing response, formation of the Old Order–owned Elmira Produce Auction Company (EPAC), for example, has decidedly communitarian roots.

Nathaniel Martin recalls EPAC's beginning in 2003 when mad cow disease hit farms, thus collapsing beef prices. Old Orders then drew on their knowledge of the highly popular farm produce auctions among American Amish and Old Orders. "Someone set up a public meeting," and then another with American Old Order speakers, and some 300 people showed up. With tacit support from church elders, a corporation was soon formed, a five-director board was elected, shares—both "membership shares" and "preferred shares"—were sold to Old Order members, a manager was hired, a set of very talkative non–Old Order auctioneers was lined up, and soon some 350 growers, 75 percent of whom were Old Order, were selling produce at EPAC. Nathaniel says that the "goal is not to make money on the investment" but "to create a cooperative that promotes local producers and gives them a fair return on their investment." He also says that "any producer (including non–Old Order producers) is allowed to sell at the auction whether they hold shares or not, but the produce must come from a seventy-five-mile radius to protect and promote local produce," with an exception made for unique Niagara region produce.

Farmers have also learned to deal with institutions and even state regulations in innovative ways. When Anson Weber purchased a farm for his son in 1980, and the local bank quoted a rate of 16 percent, he looked "to other places for financing" and found money within the community at 6 percent. But more recently, Old Order farmers buying million-dollar farms have begun borrowing from the federal government–owned Farm Credit Corporation, even as they reject the government social safety net. Then, too, they have readily latched on to Canada's government-supported supply management system for poultry production. Christian Shantz says that his "dad built a broiler barn in 1955–56 and started raising broilers" and supported the quota system introduced in the mid-1960s to stop a "market ... flooded with birds," helping "to raise the price and profitability." The justification for Old Orders signing on to supply management was simple: it wasn't a government subsidy. According to one Old Order man, "those who took the risk to get into the business have been successful, and those that did not ... were now grumbling because of the success they missed out on." Even in Old Order communities, financial success sometimes seems to justify a particular action.

Old Orders have also learned to adapt to rapidly increasing local government regulations affecting land use. Often they need to combine their practical independence with local knowledge and even with feigned deference to bureaucratic egos. Middle-aged Ishmael Burkhardt recalls stories from 1962 when Old Order farmers got together and rebuilt the low-level bridge near St. Jacobs after years of fording the "river there with [our] buggies." After the Woolwich Township Council declined their requests for a bridge, Old Orders simply asked for permission to construct their own bridge and maintain it themselves. Ishmael recalls that they named "Dan Kramer and Alvin Martin to a special committee" and hired "cementer Eph [Martin]" to do the work. Silas Martin recalls another incident from about 1998 when Old Orders took on the Grand River Conservation Authority (GRCA), which had been "very dogmatic about changing any areas in the floodplain." Old Orders convinced the authority to relocate a bridge over the Conestoga River by telling them a story. Ishmael recalls the special hearing in which he rose to his feet and asked the young, educated commissioners if they recalled how Hurricane Hazel had rerouted the river in 1954 from its original bed, thus discrediting the idea of an original "floodplain." Of course, they didn't, and the lore of Old Orders won the day; they got the bridge extension. This general attitude to local authorities—a fusion of healthy self-respect and deference—has shaped other points of contact, including the Workman Safety Insurance Board's mandates for farm safety; Old Orders comply with the regulations but have also organized one committee to explain their culture to the board and another to teach Old Orders about safety.

Farmers have also considered new degrees of mechanization. The idea of selective mechanization is not new. Some rather innovative changes go back to the Second World War and its aftermath. Silas Martin recalls that in 1942 his parents acquired a milking machine powered "by a gasoline engine running a vacuum motor." Just five

years later Emmanuel Reist developed a welder powered by a tractor's power-take-off shaft and then used the welder to invent a line
of snow blowers and grain swathers. Other changes have been more
recent. Anson Weber says that when he started farming at midlife,
in 1981, he copied his parents, using "horses for seeding, cultivating,
spreading manure, and bringing in the crop," but when his daughter
and son-in-law took over "it wasn't long before the one horse was too
old, and then he used a tractor." But a tractor was never just a tractor:
elders worried that it could be used to get to town more quickly than
with a horse, and thus its potential was accepted only by degrees. For
a time, only steel-wheeled tractors were allowed, and then they were
accepted with rubber wheels but reserved for fieldwork. By the 1990s,
even ministers and bishops had replaced the steel wheels with rubber
tires on their tractors.

New farm economics have also increased non-farm vocations. Often young farmers have begun combining farming with other forms of
business. Christian Shantz has helped to establish two sons on farms
of their own, but "recently his son on the home farm installed a ...
Planer, ... finishing the rough-cut lumber for the other son," who
retails it. Nathaniel Martin exploited the world's Y2K scare in 2000
by building wood stoves, leading to "a huge boom" of Martin brand
stoves sold across Canada, using dealers who, ironically, promoted
his stoves on the Internet. Other farmers have drawn on homegrown
inventiveness, linked to farm necessity, to produce machines required
by any number of farming subsectors. Silas Martin's son-in-law, for
example, has invented and begun manufacturing the "cattle squeeze,"
an invention that "lifts the cow up so the hooves can be trimmed."
Farmyard inventions geared to agricultural advancement have
breathed life into Old Order rurality; it's industry, usually within the
household, intertwined with rural life.

Cyrus Martin says that a new generation of Old Orders is moving off the farm altogether. Mannasseh Weber, the bike shop owner,
says that, upon his marriage, his dad thought that land prices were
too high, and instead of helping the young couple to purchase a farm
he helped them to buy a house and small acreage at Wallenstein. In
1997, Mannasseh began working for Cardinal Cabinets, owned by a
car-driving Markham Mennonite family nearby, and with a steady

income now he has stopped his search for a farm. Allen Metzger, the store owner, tells a similar story. Without the prospect of farming, he taught school for six years, then feeling that he "needed more open space," he started growing a garden for a hobby in fresh air, selling his produce "at a roadside stand." But then, just as the garden hobby increased, the Ministry of Transportation told him to leave the roadway. So he purchased property and built a store. At first, he focused on providing bulk foods for Old Orders, but today he also relies on summertime tourist business from folks en route from Toronto and area to lakeside cottages. Clearly, Old Order ways have learned to feed on the most suburban of habits.

Despite the sacrosanct horse-and-buggy culture, other changes in the Old Order community have included transportation, with the ironic effect of strengthening church life. The covered buggy, for example, was once considered prideful, but its growing adoption has allowed young parents with small children and the elderly to attend church during the winter and cool spring months. Ishmael Burkhardt says that covered buggies can easily become elaborate, costing four times as much as a good "used two-seater carriage," worth between $1,000 and $2,000, and thus when they were allowed restrictions applied, with windows, for example, "no bigger than six inches by twelve inches." Increasingly, only younger people, wanting to be out in the outdoors and under open skies, drive open buggies. Also, some time ago, Old Orders began renting vans or taxis to cover distances within Old Order country. Retired schoolteacher Jesse Martin regrets the passing of a tradition of staying overnight when taking the buggy beyond district lines: in bygone times, they "would frequently go away for two days and stay overnight with families or friends." In what might appear to be a strange new practice, ministers and bishops have begun using hired buses to follow a selected "ministers' route" to take clergy to their special semiannual conferences.

Other technologies, especially those related to communication, have caused serious conflicts. Allen Metzger says that 1989 was another important year for the Waterloo County people, when, after decades of allowing the telephone only for farm business, and restricting its location to a booth on the farmyard, it was allowed into the home. The action "caused quite some serious ripples in the church. Some people said [that] it had been 100 years since the split from the [more moderate Old Mennonites] and that it was time for another." New battle lines have recently appeared. Nathaniel Martin says that he "got a phone in the house in 1989 when the church gave the permission for it," but he has deep concerns about the electronic world, the Internet, smartphones, and iPods. The real problems are that a device that "used to require a suitcase can now be put in a shirt pocket" and that a "fifteen-year-old [Old Order boy] has the same brain as Joe Blow, he is not a born-again Christian," meaning that he can access the Internet for dubious reasons just like anyone else. The church thus decided to forbid even word processors; as schoolteacher Allen Metzger says, "we got rid of anything with a mouse, or a touch pad, or a spreadsheet capacity."

Often the road to accepting an innovation has been bumpy. When Christian Shantz's father got his farm in the 1950s, he disconnected the electricity, but when Christian himself took over the farm he reconnected it. Then, in 1970, when he became a minister, he again disconnected it. When his son took over the farm, it was connected a third time. When electricity did come to the county, it was controversial. Tilman Brubacher recalls that, when "electricity was installed on the Fourth of Peel," his grandfather was one of the Old Orders "lobbying for electricity to be installed in their district, but there were others who were opposed." But Tilman understands the progressive stance of his grandfather, for he was among those who "owned large farms and bought tractors and other modern equipment."

Bank loans, but also old forms of credit, have enabled this new technologized and capitalized world. Individuals have always loaned money to struggling families, and the church has set up committees to help the poor. Willard Wideman says that, "when families run into financial difficulties, a committee of three other families is formed to help the struggling family," either with advice or with a loan. The elderly harnessmaker, Anson Weber, affirms that Old Orders in financial trouble can expect help from him, especially young families, and he has helped others out even when he himself has felt strapped. He recalls how someone once asked him how he had become involved in giving out loans to younger families, because surely he had not yet paid off the farm debts. His answer was a little brazen: "I said 'no, we just loaned money'"—funds that he had borrowed from other people. He adds, humbly, "but it's not what I have done but only what I have tried to do." Anson might be more generous than the average Old Order, but his approach to local need is not unusual.

It is not only financial needs, he says, that Old Orders have been addressing. Recently, they have also considered mental health issues instead of simply tolerating or spiritualizing them. Anson recalls that about 2004 his bishop was asked by Harmony Haven Home in Michigan if any Waterloo Mennonite couples might serve as house parents, as "people helpers" for Old Orders with emotional problems, sometimes manifested as spiritual in nature. Store owner Allen Metzger says that he favours this incursion into mental health work: "I think Christians in a brotherhood need to help each other, or else there is no brotherhood. If your barn burns down, we'll flock in there and help you build your barn, but if you get depressed we can't ignore it, we've got to be there to help you as well." Not everyone agrees, though, and the church has declined to support a counselling centre.

None of these various changes has come easily. Old Orders ponder the consequence of every change. Willard Wideman "feels the Creator allowed more production on farms because [the Creator] knows there are more people in the world to feed." But Willard also knows the risks of technology and has spoken to "people in Third World countries where the rich get richer and the poor get poorer." He recalls how thirty years ago tractors were allowed into the barn. He says that the entire community was apprehensive: "We all knew at that point, if that happens, we will see changes out there. Like farmers, instead of having fifty to seventy-five head of cattle, they had 100 head. Well, today we got guys with 300 head on one farm." In order to keep a check on farm growth, the *Ordnung* now limits tractors to 100 horsepower and mandates only small, pull-type combines. The list of dos and don'ts can be bewildering: tractor loaders are allowed, but "stable cleaners" are not; silo unloaders are, but large round balers are not; "call waiting" is, but "call display or answering machines" are not. The problem, as Allen Metzger sees it, is that modern ways don't improve life but simply make it more hectic. He recalls that in "grandpa's day they would mail a letter to the feed mill saying they need feed. How would that sit today?... So, for efficiency sake, for decency sake, we have to sort of evolve with society around us, providing we don't get carried away by it; we kind of have to adapt to it."

Conclusion

The stories by horse-and-buggy Mennonites in Waterloo County, Ontario, and its immediate environs have never been merely ones of maintaining old ways. They have been accounts of a search for cultural and economic simplicity in the name of a religious ideal. Old Orders believe that words are less important than actions, that trust and hope are better than boastful certainty, and that rural simplicity is better than urban knowledge. But they also insist that these actions relate to conventional Christian doctrine; they just happen to believe that living out their faith is more important than talking about it.

They also know that nothing can remain the same forever. They do engage in selective adaptation, sometimes tweaking old ways to ensure their continued use, sometimes resetting old lines of restriction, as need and demand allow. Certain kinds of change are simply accepted with no debate at all: new products are invented to keep rural households viable; variations in the family life cycle ensue to accommodate youth in a changing rural economy; new codes of ethics stave off competitive outside religious forces. These historical changes are acceptable, especially when they might be indiscernible to the outside eye. But changes can also lead to strident internal debates. Sharp exchanges can take place in the surprisingly egalitarian households officially cast as patriarchal, or within the age-old institution of the *Umfrage*, or among members of the newer ministerial conferences. Leaders might have power, but a great deal of emotional pondering, admonition, defence, and questioning characterizes the apparently staid community.

Where outsiders might see a long narrative unfolding in unilinear fashion, Old Orders themselves tell somewhat more ambiguous stories. They consist of well-honed farmyard genealogies and family histories mixed with the challenging personal experiences of being Old Order in their own lifetimes. Every Old Order member has a story of the arrival of new technologies and then the uneasy wondering whether the innovations strengthen old ways or threaten them.

Old Orders express uncertainty about border crossings, moving beyond old farmsteads with intention, judiciously into nearby towns, or strategically into lower-priced counties north and west. They worry about the next generation, especially about their youth in a world of electronics and wage labour, and hope that experiments with new ways to keep them in the fold will work. They debate which new markets to engage, which technologies to consider, which state initiatives to confront, which lures of leisure to contest. The distant urban retailer in western Canada, the speedy tractors on Waterloo highways, the baptized young men on ice rinks, the supply-managed farm programs, all are reminders that old ways are never just simply passed on from one generation to another. Anti-modernity is in constant negotiation with modernity.

CHAPTER TWO

A New Orthodoxy in Backwoods Ontario

"This was a crazy kind of thing to 'move out of the Promised Land.'"

Early one sunny Manitoba morning in July 2014, I made my way to the bus depot near the Richardson International Airport in Winnipeg. There I met with a delegation of Old Order bishops and deacons who had just completed a thirty-two-hour bus trip from southern Ontario. They had come to Manitoba—accompanied by their wives—to seek to build bridges and engage in truth, reconciliation, and accountability talks with a break-away Orthodox Old Order Mennonite group that had settled in Manitoba in 2008. The Ontario leaders had come to reconnect with an Old Order community too far from "home." I met them because I had been retained by a law firm in Winnipeg to write a background paper on Old Order history and society for the judicial team looking into charges of physical and psychological abuse in the Manitoba community that had fallen sway to a lay charismatic community member, now facing criminal charges. To accomplish my task, I asked to meet with the leaders and sat with them for an hour over coffee in the meeting room of a hotel next to the bus depot.

According to Old Order tradition, the women, wearing their dark dresses and white bonnets, sat on one side of the large table, while the men, in black coats and buttoned-up shirts, sat on the other. The delegation included leaders from the main branch of Old Order Mennonites, mostly located in Waterloo County, Ontario, and described in Chapter 1. But two of the bishops in the room, Paul Martin and John Sherk (acutal names, used by permission) represented Mennonites who had moved away from the home base in Waterloo County, albeit within southern Ontario. They lived in new settlements across the Ontario peninsula, not far from the shores of Lake Huron, near the towns of Gorrie and Kinloss, in Huron and Bruce counties. Like the Manitoba group whom they had come to visit, they too had used a physical move to distance themselves from the more ideologically moderate horse-and-buggy Mennonites from Waterloo. Their relocation to southwestern Ontario had helped them to turn the clock back, hoping to breathe new life into old traditions.

To complicate matters even more, the two more traditional bishops represented communities that had drawn the line against time at two different places. True, the two men described their faith in similar ways. Paul, the Old Order bishop from Kinloss, said that all "discipline needs to be in love," that Mennonites are a "non-resistant" people who aim to be "quiet and peaceful, ... keeping in mind our martyr history" and charting a life of "following the teachings of Christ." John, the Orthodox bishop from Gorrie, similarly spoke about "lead[ing] a God-fearing life out of love," "salvation ... by grace ... in Jesus Chirst," and "being judged by the fruits of your works." Still, the former is less strict than the latter. The community at Kinloss, though it has resisted cell phones, electricity, and rubber-tired tractors, is still in fellowship with the original Waterloo group. But the community at Gorrie has long ago broken fellowship with the Waterloo moderates and formed its own branch of the horse-and-buggy community, which they refer to as Orthodox Old Order Mennonites. The technological restrictions of the Orthodox group are similar to those of the Kinloss group, but the former group of Mennonites are stricter in other ways: their men are bearded, and their women have plainer headcoverings; they also practise shunning errant members.

This chapter focuses on the stricter of the two groups that have moved away from Waterloo County: that is, the Orthodox Old Orders in the vicinity of Gorrie in Huron County. From my readings, I know that when the Gorrie bishop speaks about the "fruits of your work" he means a reinvigorated and stricter interpretation of Anabaptist simplicity. Although the main horse-and-buggy community in Waterloo County has made a series of small changes to accommodate modern ways, the Gorrie Mennonites in Huron County have gone in the opposite direction. They have sought a stricter separation from secular ways well away from the urban areas of Kitchener-Waterloo and the shadows of the Greater Toronto Area. They have embraced the idea of a limited diaspora to secure old ways. Although the majority of Canada's 8,000 horse-and-buggy Mennonites live within fifty kilometres of Kitchener-Waterloo, an increasing number have found farm settlements in more remote districts, such as the Orthodox Old Order community near Gorrie.[1]

Diaspora and Devotion

The Gorrie group were willing to leave Waterloo, the historic site where the first Mennonite immigrants to Canada arrived in significant numbers from Pennsylvania after 1800. They also left their ecclesial birthplace, the site where Old Orders were born from the schism in 1889. But stories from the Waterloo moderates indicate that a departure from this geographic heartland has long been considered risky. As Waterloo County resident Ishmael Burkhardt puts it, even when his grandparents moved to Hawkesville in 1918, just nine kilometres west of the heart of Old Order country at St. Jacobs, they were told that "this was a crazy kind of thing to 'move out of the Promised Land.'"

Indeed, as late as the 1960s, when urbanization in the Kitchener-Waterloo region was threatening Old Order ways of life, movement from this venerated geographic centre in Waterloo County was seen as controversial. For example, in the early 1960s, when Old Order families moved twenty kilometres northwest of St. Jacobs, to Linwood and Dorking, they were met with suspicion. The Waterloo County bishop recalls that, when his father purchased the family farm along Highway 86 at Dorking, he was considered "radical ..., pushing the boundaries of the community." His only defence was that his good-sized farm of 150 acres cost only $16,000, compared with farms near St. Jacobs going for $40,000. Even more controversial was the move by Old Order Mennonites sixty-five kilometres north to Mount Forest in the late 1960s. It didn't matter that they were being pushed north by the construction of a four-lane highway that displaced four-generation Old Order farms.

Historically, migration from Waterloo has spelled trouble. Retired homemaker Emma Wideman recalls Mount Forest's main problem in the first years: "It was simply too far to come regularly to an existing church service." A horse and buggy doesn't easily cover sixty-five kilometres. And then came the rumours that Mount Forest settlers were too conservative and had moved in reaction to modernizing reforms in the south. Emma recalls stories that her grandfather "apparently asked the bishop, Edward Bauman, if some of the old traditions could be brought back again." This question "caused some to think they were dissatisfied and were going to found a new church." But retired farmer Nelson Knorr disagrees and says that there were suspicions that the Mount Forest folks were actually attempting to get away from old ways. When the move occurred, "there was community pressure not to have electricity, but, as more people moved out of the Waterloo area into new areas where the farms had been previously owned by non-Mennonites, the Old Orders started to leave in the electricity, and others began to install electricity." At Mount Forest, old borders began to crumble. No matter whether the shift was progressive or traditional, the very geographic relocation was enough to rouse suspicion.

Farmer David Reist recalls even more distressing rumours when in the 1990s Old Order families moved yet another sixty kilometres north of Mount Forest to the Chesley area. The rumours, he says, were inflamed by "distant memories from the longer Mennonite history about how families moved away from the Mennonite community and ended up in other [more liberal] churches" that would tolerate new technologies. The migrants did stay within the old church, but cheaper lands with larger acreages at Chesley led to temptations to use hitherto forbidden technologies and large farm equipment, for example self-propelled combines. Not surprisingly, the Waterloo County leadership hesitated supporting the Chesley initiative. David says that in "1999 there would have been about fifteen to twenty families in the Chesley area" when at an *Umfrage* "one of the older Old Order members in the Chesley community asked the question 'when do we know that it is time for our own ministry?'" As David remembers it, the bishop and ministers said no to this request, suggesting that the settlers should first erect a building, thus demonstrating their seriousness about building a fully fledged community at faraway Chesley.

Despite these troubles, schoolteacher Allen Metzger says, the flow westward and northward from Waterloo County was inevitable and perhaps unstoppable. He sums up the recent history: "Well, if you stop and think, when I was a teenager, we had Mount Forest, that was the only other community [other than Waterloo]. Now we've got Kinloss.... We've got Chesley—it's growing fast—we've got Lindsey out east, then Massey up north, it's small, but it's growing." More than simply listing a geographic dispersion, Allen is outlining a significant cultural divergence.

The name Kinloss, for example, denotes not only a place clear across the Ontario Peninsula, 100 kilometres from Waterloo, but also stands as an example of a geographic move that led to an attempt to turn back the clock on reforms. It marked a move to try to reclaim yesteryear's purity. The bishop from Kinloss explains how new rules were meant to keep farms simple and small: only horses for hauling things, only tractors with steel wheels, only electricity derived from diesel generators. New rules also kept the household simple and close to nature: only "indoor hand water pumps or gravity-feed" water pipes, only wood stoves, and food preservation only by storing items in cool basements or through canning.

For a number of Kinloss Mennonites, transplanted from Waterloo, the new restrictions seem to be life giving. First established in 1994, the Kinloss community had a solid footing with eight families within twelve months, and even after a painful split just three years later the group numbered eighty families by 2010. While still in fellowship with the Waterloo group, members within this confident young community speak openly of aiming to restore true Anabaptist ideals of simplicity and community.

Still, the newfound traditionalism of the Kinloss group is overshadowed by the even more conservative Orthodox Old Order settlement at nearby Gorrie. There followers of Elam S. Martin (his real name), who began his own branch of Old Order Mennonites in the 1950s, have grown in number. The group began in 1956 back in Waterloo when about a third of the ultra-orthodox David Martin Mennonites organized a new church with several smaller groups, including a few Low German–speaking Old Colony Mennonites from Mexico. In 1979, members of this consolidated Elam Martin group moved to the Gorrie district, where they chose the name Orthodox Old Order Mennonite. Minister Isaiah Bauman says that the word *Orthodox* was chosen after the more moderate Waterloo bishop objected to the Elam Martin group using the name Old Order, reserving the historic term for the parent church. When the Gorrie congregation discussed a new name, recalls Isaiah, "Anson Hoover's father, Menno Hoover, who was a bit of a scholar (he had attended college and had a motorcycle at one time), suggested that if they [were] about going back to the old original ways then that [was] being 'Orthodox.'" Thus, the official name Orthodox Mennonites was born, which Isaiah and others admit does "sound ... too exclusive."

But the Orthodox members don't think of the word as denoting staidness. They talk openly, for example, about schisms, outmigrations, and strangers joining their ranks. Orthodox minister Ananias Martin says that in the 1980s his "father moved away from Ontario, warning about how there were evil influences, and it was not a healthy place to live," and he found refuge in isolated places, first in Pennsylvania and then in Tennessee. At the same time, in the 1980s, a dozen Mexico and Paraguay Low German–speaking Old Colony Mennonite families who had been assisted by Old Orders also left Ontario. Some returned to Mexico, where, according to farmer Daniel Sherk, they could buy inexpensive Mexican land with Canadian dollars. Others chose to move farther south, to Belize, Central America, where they joined up with the ultra-orthodox Barton Creek Mennonite community, which disallowed any engine power whatsoever. These were painful breaks since over time a small number of these Low German–speaking Old Colony people had become fully Orthodox, even intermarrying. Philip Wiebe, one of the Old Colonists who stayed and married an Orthodox woman, says that it was worth the price of learning the "very difficult" Pennsylvania Dutch.

The 1990s and first decade of the twenty-first century marked similarly bumpy times for Orthodox Mennonites. In about 1997, eight of the sixteen families with ties to Mount Forest separated from the Kinloss congregation and joined the Orthodox group, citing Kinloss for carelessness, even as they themselves were called malcontent, demanding, and less than transparent. But then in 2008 this group in turn split from the Gorrie Orthodox group and headed for far-off Manitoba when sharp differences over leadership and child discipline arose amid charges of physical and sexual abuse. As one community member put it, the Manitoba group consisted of families who had originally gone "to the Kinloss area with demanding attitudes toward the church, and there was not a spirit of wanting to work with the church."

Despite these upheavals, however, the Orthodox horse-and-buggy community at Gorrie grew to well over 100 families by 2009, with a daughter colony in the Algoma district, 900 kilometres northwest. The community had its own school, set of local institutions, *Ordnung*, and leadership. Most importantly, it had its own identity and oral history on which to establish the notion of recapturing a past set of ideals.

Praxis and Preservation

The Gorrie Orthodox Old Order members are aware that their community signals a significant variation from the more moderate Waterloo Old Orders. They know that the latter community has allowed selected new technologies in the past few decades and that they, the Orthodox group, have gone in the opposite direction. The members speak openly about becoming more committed to simplicity, to a cohesive local community, to a more full separation from the wider world. They also speak of how difficult it has been to seek older pathways of life.

They recall the bitter negotiations within the community over striking changes in visual appearance. Men's untrimmed beards, for example, stemming from the influence of similarly traditionalist Old Orders in Kentucky, were highly controversial when the practice started in the 1980s. Minister Isaiah Bauman says that, "when that beard movement started, the church split, and I ended up on the other side of [it] with [beard-wearing] Anson Hoover, ... [who] took about two-thirds of the people out of the church.... The issue was 'so many changes,' but the beard sort of brought it to a head, for sure." When the matter settled, the Orthodox members had agreed on untrimmed beards for men.

It was a similar pattern of specific visual appearance for women. Over time, Orthodox women have embraced more conspicuous headcoverings made of solid white rather than see-through white fabric, and they wear them regularly. Isaiah Bauman says, "I do remember [the time when] the headcovering is one thing that they used to just wear in church"; indeed, upon arriving at home, "the headcovering went off with the bonnet!" Young women, too, were more lax about headcoverings in the past. In fact, they didn't wear them till they got married: "Usually, on the wedding day, ... [they took] 1 Corinthians 11, the part on the headcovering, ... [but merely] as part of the wedding service, [agreeing] now it's time to wear the headcovering." The Orthodox group changed this practice and insisted on the headcovering at a much earlier time. Isaiah recalls that their first leader, Elam Martin, believed that girls should begin wearing it at puberty, "but eventually it was agreed that when a girl was done school she would wear a covering."

The Orthodox members have also addressed more personal moral issues. On the one hand, they have maintained some old practices deemed immoral by evangelical standards. For instance, farmer Daniel Sherk reports, they continue the old tradition of serving a bit of wine when guests arrive at "all-day" weddings. Some wine has always been tolerated, he says, most often "for medicine, and when [we're] threshing and there's a lot of dust in the air, and ... [we] kind of feel like [we] should have something to clear up [our] throat[s]." On the other hand, the Orthodox Mennonites have also introduced new moral codes, such as the prohibition against tobacco use. Indeed, the initial leader, bishop Elam Martin, forbade the use of tobacco in 1956, long tolerated by Old Orders, says Daniel. Smoking was deemed a sign of assimilating with the world.

The most far-reaching prohibitions within the Orthodox community, however, relate to technology. Many older Orthodox members recall the liberalizing times of earlier decades. They remember that the David Martin group they left in the 1950s had begun using power tools and welders, while those from the Old Order itself recall rubber-tired tractors, electricity, and telephones, as well as snow blowers enabling year-round car and truck traffic. Over time, the Orthodox group has prohibited such technologies; indeed, the list meant to shore up social boundaries and keep life simple includes no electricity, no cell phones, no rubber tires, no power tools.

This level of anti-modernity has not come easily, but it has gradually been embraced by Orthodox members. Isaiah Bauman says that, when "I came up here and everything was done by hand, ... the shock was almost too big." In fact, he "sort of moved away from carpentry work because I was so used to the [circular] saws and the chain saws." He recalls a particularly difficult day when he had business in the nearby town of Wingham: "I was up here ... walking down the sidewalk, and the town works people had cut down a maple tree, and ... the fresh sawdust and the fumes of the smoke from the chainsaw, together, it got into me, and I just cried. I mean ... that's my life.... I was so ready for something like that again for a change." Yet his longing for power tools was always fleeting; he says that giving them up was worth it. In fact, the Gorrie people have embraced the romance of a world without power. Isaiah says that today "I see ... [we] can put up buildings in a day.... I mean they'll put up a barn and everything closed up and the barn doors hung same as the power-saw people," and they do it using only high-quality crosscut saws. "In fact, we have taken races with a chainsaw, and ... with a good, new, sharp ... bowsaw they can cut very fast." For these Orthodox Old Orders, old ways of craft and skill trump new technologies.

Even Lucille Dawson, an Orthodox member of non-Mennonite background whose father worked for the Canadian Broadcasting Corporation, says that the cost of becoming more simple has been worth it. "Coming to the Orthodox community was a very difficult transition," she says; "you give up a lot." But the big benefit is living within a close-knit community in which members care for one another. She gives as an example her grudging acceptance of Orthodox patriarchalism even though she fancies herself "a bit of a woman's advocate" and has even "written to the leaders of the Orthodox community to tell them how ... women should be seen as equal." But, she says, "if there is genuine love in a marriage, the woman will experience equality, and ... there is real strength in their community." Clearly, Orthodox strictness enables local expressions of love.

Rules of Life

The Orthodox members might have their *Ordnung*, but it does not comprise a set of unchangeable rules. For example, they have had to make some allowances just to survive economically. Like Old Orders, they too hire taxis and vans to transport them to town or back to Waterloo for visits. They also hire non-Orthodox Mennonites with bulldozers to build driveways and rubber-tired tractors to do the fall plowing. Daniel Sherk says that "we are getting to the point where we have to compete with a lot of other people, with our farming, and you can't really spend much time doing things like it's not economical. So we do end up hiring people to do work for us, but we try to limit it to the things that we can't do with our horses."

Making these sorts of decisions always involves a fine line: although farms are not to become too big, they must also be viable. Ananias Martin says that the "average farm in the community is about 100 acres with about 80 cultivatable," an operation that he can handle with his "six heavy horses and two medium horses, that can also be used as a wagon team." He says that this is the size of farm that can feed a family and serve as the foundation of a close-knit community. At that size of farm, he says, the Orthodox group can focus on selling commodities at their own "cooperative market, where [we] sell retail and wholesale, ... open six days a week on the main highway ... sell[ing] produce and some baked goods from May to October." This cooperative market goes hand in hand with the small farm operation.

Surprisingly, for the outside observer, the Orthodox have never written down their rules. Indeed, they don't see themselves as legalistic and insist that they are not a rigid people. Daniel Sherk says that, unlike the Old Orders, the Orthodox don't have a written *Ordnung*, "like everything written down on paper, what is allowed and what isn't allowed, and then after their preparation service [for communion] they read off those rules.... We don't do it like that." Their emphasis is on unity, consensus, and uniformity. So citing a neighbour for violating a rule is done carefully:

> If people do something that another person is offended at, ...
> they can go talk with him ... and see if they can understand
> each other.... And [perhaps] that person ... [will] just leave it

for the sake of the other person. And if he feels that he can't leave it, then he'll probably get more opinions together, and ... [if] most of the people would think that it would be a better way of doing it then we might get a gradual changeover into that direction. If people see harm in it, or something that would lead to something that we don't want, then it will probably be discouraged, and they'll drop it.

However, there are ways to pressure members to conform, including the ministers' biannual meeting or the newly established annual December meeting at which ethical matters are discussed.

And members can be disciplined, even excommunicated and shunned. In fact, the Orthodox members have learned strict discipline from their Amish neighbours. Unlike their Old Order antecedents, the members of the Orthodox group are willing to excommunicate and then ban the wrongdoer. Lucille Dawson supports the process. The ban is meant to "put fear and trembling in the hearts of people that we don't accept sin, 'banable' sin," different from "besetting sins" such as anger. She agrees with this level of accountability. Although she and her husband were never excommunicated, she does recall the time that they "had to confess, have a church confession, once for our [domestic] fighting; it was so bad that I had to move away." But, Lucille says, it felt good to be within a disciplining community: "It was really commendable for what the church did. It gave us security and stability to be surrounded by the Orthodox.... For five and a half weeks, we had committee meetings every Saturday morning here [in our home]." Over numerous weeks, members even took turns spending meal times with the couple.

The Orthodox Mennonites insist that such actions are meant not to enforce rules, or for the sake of rules, but to guide the congregation to a fuller restoration of a plain past. Indeed, since their beginning in the 1950s, the guiding principle has been the restoration of Anabaptist purity, or as Daniel Sherk puts it, "trying to reclaim ... lost practices." He uses as examples the beard for men and the headcovering for women. He "thinks that the original Anabaptists would have had beards and not had neckties and had plainer headcoverings and that gradually these things just changed." The Orthodox members, to his mind, have merely sought to arrest this drift away from original practices.

Importantly, it's not that the leaders dictate the terms of the restoration; rather it evolves slowly, arising from debate and consensus building among the members. Daniel recalls the debate over whether Orthodox men should wear beards or not, and his account includes no hint of schism or anger. As he recalls it, the process of reclaiming the beard in the early 1970s followed a long consensus-building process. He emphasizes the halting process, the give and take, the quiet debate:

> It was brought up for discussion, and we found that we
> wouldn't have any scriptural reason not to have [it], but
> there were different people that had their reasons why they
> didn't want it. That was an issue that took quite a few years
> before that really came about.... And then the church finally
> came to the conclusion that, as far as the church would be
> concerned, like, it wouldn't be an issue if someone wanted to
> wear the beard. Then people felt, well, if it's okay to do it and
> there's nothing to stop them, then they started, maybe about
> half a dozen people or so started with it, but then there was
> still a few that had problems with it to the extent that they
> stopped it and shaved again for a while, but that really didn't
> bring any peace either, so eventually ... it just ... it took time.

It's hard to imagine that a symbol as important as the beard would be adopted in such piecemeal fashion, but it is telling that the Orthodox members do not see themselves as legalistic.

They also insist that their prohibition of technology is not a form of legalism but a tool to encourage humility, submission, and community bonds. They worry most about the slippery slope that one technology will lead to a whole host of new ones. They insist, for example, that hydroelectricity is not evil; it's the lifestyle associated with it that can hamper community life and social relations. Daniel Sherk says that, "if we open the doors to electricity and we run our motors with electricity, then we would end up with a host of things that you could run with electricity too.... [Once] you can plug in a washing machine, then you could plug in a toaster, a blender. There

would be no end to things that you could plug in there." He means
the radio, television, and computer, which would radically alter the
simple agrarian world that the Orthodox members believe provides
the best basis for a spiritually rich life.

In keeping with the idea of consensus building and principled
living, Orthodox Mennonites also say that they have not sought to
enforce human-made rules as much as to embrace nature and natural
ways. And they do so from many different angles. They view the body
from that perspective; about the beard, Daniel says, they "just leave it
up to God, ... just let it grow when it grows.... God makes hair grow
on the face, and so ... just allow that to happen." And he would say
that the same applies to fertility and thus opposes birth control, to
tiredness and thus opposes electric lights that tempt you to work after
the sun sets and keeps you from sleeping at night. Lucille Dawson
says that the logic of agraria holds a similar simplicity that counters
theological abstraction. She also says that it's a rootedness that doesn't
require a lot of complex thinking and that her people don't debate
theological niceties, such as what are the truest biblical translations:
"It is interesting that when you get this far back from the regular society there's not really that much to think about the standards and that,
where with the car, ... there were a lot of issues to hassle out, but here
people don't spend a lot of time thinking about it."

Certainly, they see themselves within a natural world. Ananias
Martin says that in the past when he couldn't sleep he went outside,
even at 2:00 a.m., and "looked at the stars, ... sitting and looking at
the stars." Doing so made him consider "his connection to God" and
indeed how "humankind can reject God with all the evidence of God
in nature." This simple connection to the natural world is also the
Orthodox group's approach to technology. Reverend Isaiah Bauman
says that "our lives are not that backwards, we just don't bother with
all that technology. It's not that ... I couldn't run it [technology] as
well as you can, it's just that I have chosen not to." These people see
technological innovation as taking them away from nature. Technology, Lucille Dawson says, can also separate you from your neighbour.
She adds that the ways of the Orthodox are meant to make sure that
they "don't put themselves higher than the common man" and likes
how this approach to life means that people "are accountable to each

other." Lucille might see herself as an advocate for women's status within the community, but she clearly sees social and class-based inequality as more problematic than the relative status among genders.

Orthodox Mennonites know that by quietly denying the world they also have something to offer it. Isaiah Bauman recalls meeting a cousin who left for Toronto a long time ago. His cousin asked him if in the Orthodox community "the young people [were] staying in the church." Isaiah was able to tell "him that 99 percent" were, that "only a very few have left out of a few hundred that have stayed." His cousin's response was "I wish my parents would have stayed with the Mennonites. You're living here, you've got your grandchildren all around you, and you can go and visit your grandchildren, they can come home." The cousin spoke of family upheaval, of messy divorces, of single motherhood, of second marriages, of agnosticism. Isaiah answered that "I don't really feel like we are missing out on a lot" and recalls his cousin's response: "You are missing out on nothing." Where the outside world looking in sees rules and restrictions, the Orthodox members looking out see confusion and social alienation.

Idealism and Invention

Mostly, the Orthodox group insist that their newfound simplicity is linked to a spiritual discipline. Isaiah Bauman says that he has heard that back in the 1950s their leader, Elam Martin, "was a reformer." Indeed, "he felt that the churches [had] left the old Anabaptist [ways], like the old Anabaptist foundation, and he wanted to go back ... there." Isaiah also recalls how the early leaders scoured early Anabaptist writings for a model for life: "I remember when I was growing up Sunday afternoons we were sitting in the rooms, in the living rooms, whatever, and the older men were reading out of the *Martyrs Mirror* and things like that and all the old happenings to get this back into our blood, I guess, and it sort of worked." They were looking for the spiritual quality of early Anabaptists willing to suffer privation for their faith.

Isaiah says that Elam Martin tried to take the best from a number of traditions. He even pursued a personal pietism, the kind emphasized by car-driving Markham Mennonites and even the Missionary Church, groups in which he had immediate family members. Despite his backward glances, Elam certainly "was an open-minded man, [and I] never heard him criticizing other churches." As a "good speaker," adds Isaiah, Elam sought to reach young people: "He was already quite concerned that the young folks know what they are doing when they are baptized. Like it's not just a matter about making application and being baptized, there's more to it than that." He also emphasized prayer, not only nighttime prayer but also morning prayer. And he encouraged table grace before and after the meal, having learned the practice from the Old Colony Mennonites in Mexico, who "were sort of shocked that we [their Canadian hosts] just walk away from the table" after a meal. The Orthodox approach to life is to do everything with an intention meant to guard against greed and complacency.

The Orthodox members say that they emphasize spiritual vitality. Isaiah Bauman, for one, is especially concerned with the spiritual health of Orthodox young people. He asserts that "for us it is very hard to separate" the simple life from the spiritual, for "our lives are part of our [spirituality]." Personal faith and costly discipleship go hand in hand. Orthodox Mennonites are more than horse-and-buggy people with an "Anabaptist" label. Sure, they have a historical identity, but Isaiah insists that just being simple is not what the sixteenth-century Anabaptists wanted: "We are always in great danger ... [since] we do shun technology that we don't get onto the impression that that is our religion." He tells of times when visitors have applauded them for contesting middle-class values. He recounts "a visitor from Germany, ... and he was ... just sure ... that for us the most important thing in life is to live plainly.... That is the be all and end all of everything. But that's dead yet, just shunning technology alone isn't [enough], there is no life in that.... We want our life in something more, ... we want a living faith in Jesus."

Yet the Orthodox group insist that by "living faith" they don't mean a personal piety or evangelical joy. Isaiah has evangelical neighbours in mind when he says that, "if you go to the Sermon on the Mount, which is sort of [a] fairly basic foundation of the Christian life, ... I for myself cannot see how a person can really live in a faith in Jesus and not be non-resistant." Faith for Isaiah demands actions, and ones that counter ideas of patriotism and military service.

Daniel Sherk is more explicit in his criticism of evangelicalism. He says that, though "we do emphasize that ... our salvation is through the shed blood of Christ, ... we do believe that our walk of life will reflect on the end, our destination." Eternal life is not secured by uttering religious phrases or claiming a conversion. In fact, says Daniel, "we put a lot of emphasis on the new birth, or a new creation," just not on an emotional "experience" as a moment of crisis when "we have to crucify the old man and be born to a new life in Christ." For Orthodox members, religious sincerity is measured by how fully one comes out from the world. Daniel uses the term *"Abgesondern* people" to denote this idea of a "separate" people: "We are in this world, but we are not of this world. And we feel that our walk of life should be something that is not a part of the world. And that's what the *Abgesondernheit* is." This strict dualism is fundamental to their understanding of themselves.

This identity has also shaped their view of child discipline. Reverend Isaiah Bauman, also a schoolteacher, says that Orthodox members spank their children, even in school, but only if all other disciplinary avenues have been pursued first. He adds that it has been years since he as a teacher has spanked a child. He thinks that as an older man he naturally has greater authority than the young women who teach alongside him. But as the senior teacher, Isaiah thinks it important to reserve any physical discipline for prepubescent children. He recalls a time when he "did punish a grade eight girl" and found out later that "she respected [him] even less." He insists that, given parents' historical involvement in education, the home is the place where discipline should be meted out if necessary. And even there corporal punishment should be used sparingly. Isaiah believes in reading to children to help shape their lives—"there's quite a few Bible story books that are acceptable for us"—and in "praying before children go to bed." Children are trained in the Orthodox faith, but discipline should be constructive and not received in fear.

Yet Daniel Sherk explains a particular philosophy of child discipline, one that trains the child to become a full member of the community and lead a successful life within the congregation: "I believe that a child when it is growing up has to learn submission. It's not really born with any submission. Parents have to teach their children

... what submission is." Not until a child becomes an adult can he or she make decisions that matter; before that time, it is a matter of obedience. Only after a period of youth, "when he wants to start thinking about joining the church, ... he ... starts seeing the need that he is lost in himself, that he has to have a new birth before he can be part of the Christian community." At that point, the young person starts "asking himself questions. Why do we do things like that? What is the best way of doing it? And where is the most danger?" It is during youth that parents let go for a time; the years of discipline end with puberty and the time of *Rumspringa,* literally "jumping around," a time of youthful unruliness that their parents tolerate, at least to a degree.

At the end of the period of youth, at baptism, eyes are supposed to become open to the meaning of life, and the eighteen articles of the 1632 Dordrecht Confession of faith are presented to young men and women. Daniel says that the articles are studied intensely, "three each for six Sundays," and then the youth go through a prebaptism *Umfrage* "to see if ... we feel that they are a regenerated person and have crucified themselves and are living a life for Christ." Even then the congregation recognizes that, though baptism is a solemn event, it is "just a start, it's not something that is completed.... It's like a child that's learning to walk, like he might be a little bit wobbly at the first while, but as you progress in it you mature in it." Young members are given a period of grace as older members reach out with moral support.

This generosity of spirit comes within a contradictory package. Orthodox Mennonites live in a world of social boundaries. They know that keeps them from entering the modern world with its lure of consumer goods and individual ascendency. But they also know that it keeps them from meeting other Mennonites. They recall their old kin in the David Martin group, whom they left in 1954 and who still shun the Orthodox group to this day. Isaiah Bauman says that "two weeks ago I got word that they buried my sister this morning, the first I heard about it. That was rough. We ... had plans to visit them again this summer, and ... if nobody else was around they took us into the house. They were nice if it was just one to one." He is critical of groups that won't meet with outsiders to discuss their beliefs and practices. His problem with the David Martin group is that they "see their church as something too sacred to talk about, ... refus[ing even] to talk to outsiders about their church." Ironically, the Orthodox themselves shun other Mennonite churches. They do not attend Old Order services at nearby Kinloss or in Waterloo, for example. Nor do they allow "children from families who have radio or TV" to attend their schools.

At the same time, the Orthodox members believe that they do not judge other groups. Daniel Sherk says, "the way that we do things and the way, for example, that you do things might be quite different. By us doing our things the way we do, it's not that we're saying that the way you do things [is] going to be wrong.... But we have to choose what is the least harmful to us. And that is the same for you or for me." It's not that the Orthodox people feel more threatened by the outside world but that they feel a religious calling to separate themselves from the "harmful" ways of modernity.

Conclusion

An account of the anti-modern pathway is a story of folks imagining what the world might look like if values of the past shaped present-day society and then contesting what they see as the inexorable march of modernity. In the Gorrie district near Lake Huron in southern Ontario's Huron County, a group of Mennonites, originally from densely populated Waterloo County, near the sprawling city of Kitchener-Waterloo, have done just that. A dynamic group, splitting, reamalgamating, and splitting again, the Orthodox Old Order Mennonites have developed into the fastest growing church in the area. They embrace simplicity and humility with considerable rigour. The long beards of the men and the full cloth headcoverings of the women, as well as the horses in the fields and the homes without electricity, distinguish them from the more moderate Old Order Mennonites.

In the process of living the simple life, they have been accused by outside observers of legalism and exclusiveness. Their communities are patriarchal and insist on obedience from children. They seem to embrace ascetic values even though they know that such actions are economically counterproductive. They reject most technologies on which farm communities elsewhere have come to rely. Yet they describe a community that is not only viable but also believes in itself. At the foundation of this confidence is their belief that they have reclaimed sixteenth-century values and are successfully passing them on to their children.

This Orthodox community has moved beyond old rural community boundaries to new locations in order to acquire new farmlands. Simultaneously, it has also embraced ways that its members imagine previous generations lived. And in doing so, this horse-and-buggy community sees itself not only as arresting the flow of history, but also as a dynamic force within it, offering an alternative to society as imagined by members of the wider world, the middle class in particular.

PART TWO

OLD COLONY MENNONITES
IN LATIN AMERICA

CHAPTER THREE

Vows of Simplicity in the South

"And he got ready to leave right away."

We sit by candlelight in a home in Colonia Del Sur, Bolivia, just ten kilometres from the Argentine border on a cool winter night in July 2009, speaking in Low German. A taxi has just dropped me off, and Abram and Helena Guenther, in their sixties, have offered a warm welcome to a perfect stranger. Their daughters have reheated the soup, and Abram and Helena sit at the table taking turns describing, in soft voices, the founding of the colony just a dozen years earlier. The last leg of their trip from northern Mexico was the twelve-hour road trip south from Santa Cruz in large trucks. Pitched plastic tarp was their crude first shelter in the bushland, an array of rough boards on dirt their first floor. Wind tugged hard at the moorings on the first night, and in the morning they began the slow process of unpacking furniture and goods shipped from Mexico.

The next day I hear another account of the founding of Del Sur from Jacob Neudorf, the stout, unflappable former colony mayor (*Vorsteher*), sitting in the ticket room of the colony cooperative truck and wagon scale. The story of legal wrangling and financial risk is long and complex. It was a legal morass since Jacob, the chief land scout, found out too late that the land sale was invalid since it violated Bolivian law that no foreigners could purchase land within fifty kilometres of an international border. It was a horrible burden that he carried secretly until the Mennonites' lawyer suggested another way—be pragmatic, he counselled, and register the colony in the names of Bolivian-born Mennonite kin of the Riva Palacios Colony founded in 1967, 300 kilometres north. And, just like that, the owners were no longer considered foreign.

Later that day schoolteacher Benjamin Guenther and I embark on a two-hour journey by horse and buggy to neighbouring Colonia Florida. We have a lot of time to talk. Benjamin says that Del Sur and Florida are friendly enough but not in full fellowship. They attend one another's auction sales, the Ältesters will even shake hands, but they do not attend one another's churches. Back in 1967, the Florida group were "obedient" and fled modernization in Mexico with its symbolic triad—rubber-tired tractors, trucks, and electricity—and dutifully followed the head minister, bishop, or Ältester, Bernard F. Peters, and re-established the sacred *Ordnung* in Bolivia. The Del Sur people, however, had stayed in Mexico, thinking that new settlements in isolated semi-arid northern Mexico, close to the American border, could stop the advance of the world, that is, of consumer culture, and unchecked capitalism. The Florida people had been faithful, the Del Sur had not. A long generation later modernization caught up with them, and the Del Sur people pulled up stakes and likewise went south. Too bad that it was thirty years too late; Florida feels the need to shun Del Sur at least to an extent.

Three accounts tell the Del Sur story: the first night in open air; the days in lawyers' offices; the migration south to protect an anti-modern faith. They are all components of the Old Colony narrative of migration. And they indelibly separate the Old Colonists in Latin America from the Old Orders in North America. As indicated in this book's introduction, Old Colonists and Old Orders certainly have much in common—their insistence on plain dress, their travel by horse and buggy, their concerns about electricity, their histories with steel-wheeled tractors, their veneration of the one-thousand-page seventeenth-century *Martyrs Mirror* and the Dordrecht Confession, the latter speaking about "a visible church" and "chosen generation." But in other aspects, they differ significantly, and in no way more completely than on their idea of migration and diaspora. While Old Order groups have become deeply rooted in Canada, Old Colony groups have emigrated from Canada to the Global South. They have become a people of the "walking staff," committed to diaspora. They are a people not of place but of mobility. Old Colonists have been in constant negotiation with various national governments to secure their alternative worlds. They have faced and adapted to unfamiliar local markets and new climates. They have had to contend with competing evangelical churches that followed them south. And thus their histories are filled with memories of pulling up stakes and moving, of uprooting and transplanting. They speak of lines drawn in the sand to resist modernity, sometimes with success, other times with failure.

And they tell a variety of stories. Stop by their colonies and ask them about the migration south from Mexico, whether in the 1960s or 1990s, and they will recount the first days in tents in the bush and bothersome government officials. But it takes another day, a private audience, a patient visit for another layer to appear, a story of contestation and conflict. The answers arising from a typical oral history question—"Can you tell me what has changed in your life?"—begin with the migrations and early days of settlement, but then proceed to the idea that creeping modernity led to the migration. The first set describes a move, the second the nature of a diaspora.

This chapter, like the four that follow, reports on about 200 interviews conducted by Kerry Fast, Tina Fehr Kehler, Anne Kok, Jacob Huttner, Karen Warkentin (graduate or postgraduate students) and me with Old Colony Mennonites in their communities in Central and South America. The horse-and-buggy Old Colonists left their original colonies in Chihuahua and Durango, Mexico, between 1958 and 2009 (the year when most of the interviews took place). In the simplest of terms, in the 1950s they founded new colonies in British Honduras, in the 1960s in eastern Bolivia, in the 1970s in East Paraguay, in the 1980s in central Argentina, in the 1990s in Campeche in southern Mexico, and in the years between they moved every which way, though typically ever farther southward, mostly to the Bolivian Oriente and Mexico's Campeche state.

Their migration stories reflect a two-tiered narrative, a "communicative" memory of the everyday on the one hand and a more profound "cultural" memory on the other. The first set of stories of pioneering lies at the surface, for the Old Colony people are folks of the material, the everyday, and they like to talk about pioneer times. But just below the surface is another one encouraged by church teachings, explaining what they do as horse-and-buggy people, contesting the modern world with sacred symbols. It is the story of an expressed religious principle: migration will strengthen the underlying religious faith of their communities, a version of a biblical "test by fire."

Departure and Diaspora

The Old Colony migration stories are accounts of social distance from the original Mennonite colonies, founded in Mexico between 1922 and 1924; these original colonies in Northern Mexico have all modernized, as signified by the use of rubber-tired tractors, trucks and cars, and electricity. It is among the second- and third-generation colonies—established a long distance from the parent colonies—that you can still find the stalwart horse-and-buggy communities, which make up about one-third of the descendants of the original Old Colony Mennonites in Mexico. The more modern two-thirds consist of those Old Colonists who have remained in the South and those who have returned to the land of their parents, Canada, mostly in southern Ontario.

The various sub-communities that my research team and I visited were founded between 1958 and 2009. Shipyard Colony (1958) in northern Belize is the oldest. It was established by settlers from northern Mexico looking for land under the British crown and distance from the social security policies of Mexico's government. Riva Palacios, Swift, Santa Rita, and Sommerfeld, the latter not Old Colony, (1967–68) are located in Bolivia, just south of Santa Cruz, and were founded by settlers who rejected modernization in northern Mexico. Bolivia's Valle Esperanza (1975) was founded by settlers from northern Mexico looking for land as were East Paraguay's Rio Verde (1968) and Nuevo Durango (1978). Chavi (1982), Yalnon (1983), and Progreso (1987), located in the southern Mexican state of Campeche, were also established by Old Colonists from northern Mexico in search of more land. A decade or so later Trinidad (1998) and Nuevo Durango (2000) were also established in Campeche as protests to modernity in the north. Likewise, Sabinal (1993)—the only horse-and-buggy colony remaining in Mexico's northern state of Chihuahua—was founded by Old Colony Mennonites who protested modernity in the central state of Zacatecas. Oriente (1993), Valle Nuevo (1993), Manitoba (1995), and California (2007) were founded by second- and third-generation

Bolivian Old Colony Mennonites who crossed the Rio Grande in search of new land in the country's vast Oriente. Nuevo Durango (the third thus named, 1994), Neuland (2002), and Bajio Verde (2007) all have roots in East Paraguay, whereas Del Sur (1997), later renamed El Breal, stems from northern Mexico, and Florida (1997) is an offspring of Riva Palacios. These colonies, located in eastern and southern Bolivia, were also founded because modernization was creeping into their mother colonies.

These are only a third of the horse-and-buggy communities in Latin America, and this list only hints at their constant scramble for new sources of land, whether to ensure farms for new generations or to protect old ways or some combination of both. Hidden here is Old Colonists' theology of migration, which links farmland and religious simplicity that has shaped the Old Colony story in Latin America for almost 100 years.

Ask about stories passed down from parents of olden days, and you hear these two rather different accounts: there are the seemingly banal, often conflated, and imprecise, but also the epochal, those heralding an era-shaping event of grave theological consequence. But even what appears to be banal can be of greater significance than you might think. The banal is evident in numerous stories of the old homeland of Canada in the 1920s, especially those relating to cold and inclement weather. Abram Wall of Nuevo Durango in East Paraguay recalls his father speaking about the sound of river ice breaking up in spring in Canada, while middle-aged Katherina Dyck of Progreso in southern Mexico says that her "mother-in-law talked about having to get warmly dressed to go slaughter pigs in a 'double box' wagon."

But even these simple stories recounting Canada have religious significance, for many memories touch on thorny issues of technology. Katherina, for example, remembers a story of "a steam engine being pulled [in place] by work horses" and, more pointedly, how when her "*Mamme* saw her first car [she] thought the world was at an end." The first technology was fully accepted by the Old Colony church at the time, whereas the second was non-negotiable. The memories of Katherina's neighbour, middle-aged Martin Martens, simply relate to "work with horses. My dad talked about how they used horses in Canada in the tobacco fields." He is mistaken about the existence of tobacco fields in 1920s-era Manitoba, but his conflation of tobacco fields of southern Ontario, of which he has heard, with horse-drawn implements of early Manitoba does romanticize a time uncluttered by technological innovations. The recollections passed down to Margaretha Hildebrandt of East Paraguay are also of sweet days before the tractor in Canada, though recollections made more real with reference to the accompanying physical discomfort for young women working in the fields; her grandmother "had to plow the fields with horses; after a day on the plow, her feet hurt so much she almost couldn't walk anymore." These are fragments of memories from a time before temptation to modernize transformed most Mennonites in Canada.

Old Colonists know that there is nothing implicitly sacred about the past or its artifacts. Old things have no value in and of themselves. On Sabinal Colony in northern Mexico, Justina Hiebert,[1] soon to be a great-grandmother, comments on a neighbour's broken fence and then explains that the fence along the street actually serves no purpose because nowadays the common pasture has been replaced by plowed fields; it is merely *Moud,* "the fashion," "from a time when cows were taken to the village pasture along the street.... Now cows are looked after by each individual farmer." As an outsider, you might think that certain practices are significant until you hear the stories below the surface. Her husband, Johan, has heard that in the parent colony of La Honda, a car-driving colony 1,000 kilometres to the south in Zacatecas state, the "horse and wagon are still used to carry a body to the grave." He finds it strange that a colony that allowed itself to be seduced by truck-driving businessmen still maintains this anti-modern practice. As Johan sees it, there is nothing significant in a signpost of past times for its own sake.

What matters is a particular practice in the lineage of faithfulness. Elderly Peter Wiebe of Yalnon says that he reads "a variety of books, whatever interests me, I buy it and read it." However, he is especially drawn to the "one about the martyrs, where they killed them." The reference to the venerated *Martyrs Mirror* depicting sixteenth-century Anabaptist ancestors is not unusual. But most Old Colonists see faithfulness in more recent struggles. Many can repeat stories of how the government of Canada attempted to force their grandparents to

attend English-language public schools after 1919 when courts up-
held the validity of both Manitoba's and Saskatchewan's new School
Attendance Acts. Indeed, asking them why their grandparents left
Canada in the 1920s can elicit imprecise answers; Anna Banman
of Bolivia believes that it was "because they didn't have freedom,"
whereas Katherina Wolfe believes that it was because of "schools
and military service" (or *Militärdienst*, as she puts in German). Both
are somewhat mistaken, but they hit upon the truth as they see it:
the migration was about protecting the pacifist German against an
encroaching militaristic English.

But take a bit more time, and a detailed story of Canada as the
great betrayer surfaces with more detail. Widow Katherina Woelke
of Progreso recalls a story of property confiscation and imprisonment
in Morden, Manitoba, in 1919. Her grandfather was a preacher who
said that his children would not go to school, nor would he voluntarily
pay the fine they imposed for breaking the law. So the authorities
came to get his oats as payment for the fine, but still he didn't send his
children to school. Then they took his best horse, but still he wouldn't
send them to school. Finally, they came to arrest him as he worked in
the field. After he washed up at home, they put him in jail. A night in
jail led to a heady decision on leaving Canada. As Katherina puts it,
"And [still] he didn't want to send the kids to English school. Saturday
they got him, and Sunday they let him out. A man, I can't remember
his name, bailed him out, and he didn't have one meal in prison. And
he got ready to leave right away [for Mexico]. That my mother told
me." It is a story of mythological proportion, rendered with affect and
passion, clearly outlining why Katherina lives in the south and her
distant cousins in the north.

Arriving in New Lands

Arriving in new lands in the south is told in stories of the surface.
They might well recount times of difficulty, but they are not about
resistance and conflict. Farmer Peter Knelsen of Manitoba Colony,
Bolivia, has heard a single story of arriving in Mexico in 1922: "They
… communicated … through body language," and "the Mexicans
helped them unload their baggage from the train." Perhaps he is

implicitly saying that there is no need to speak a national language if members of the host society are thrilled to have them become their neighbours. But mostly Peter's story is about warm and friendly intercultural exchange.

Later moves can be told in similarly temporal terms. In the story of the 1958 move from Mexico to British Honduras, now Belize, for instance, there is no sense of betrayal or hostile government. Elderly residents of Shipyard recall the standard story of the trip from northern Mexico by chartered bus lasting three days and two nights. Oldtimers such as Franz Penner talk about the difficulties posed by the Belizean jungle: the fifteen-foot-high vines and the wild pigs. Johan Knelsen recalls crossing into British Honduras at age fourteen on 18 April 1958, at Santa Elena. But he especially remembers arriving at Blue Creek, not far from Shipyard, where they had no place to sleep except "outside on a tarp, ... too tired to notice the mosquitoes," until they were able to rent a "house with a straw roof." The reasons for the move to British Honduras can be quite personal, with barely a reference to religion. By happenstance, several male accounts highlight the role of women in their moves. David Friesen says that he moved because his wife wished to be close to her extended family; Heinrich Wiebe moved from Canada in 1966 as a boy because "almost all of my mother's relatives" had moved; Franz Penner moved because the doctor suggested that a tropical climate might cure his wife's lung cancer.

Yet at least some religious concern lies beneath the surface of this storytelling. Johan Knelsen might talk of mosquitoes, but he also emphasizes the continuity of religious community. In "the first few years in Shipyard," he says, "there was no Ältester. The Ältester from Mexico came to baptize the youth, that was in 1959." He also describes "the first church" doubling as "the first school building, in Campo 1," and how in "1961–62 the first church building was built, in Campo 2," still in use. He notes also that "all the Bibles and songbooks and [religious] material was brought ... from Mexico." Oldtimer Johan Dyck relates that the first settlers at Shipyard arrived from Chihuahua in 1958, and the first from Durango came in 1959, and then a cohort of Canadians arrived directly in 1960 because provincial governments had closed their schools in their isolated northern communities during the late 1950s. The question of schools lingers from one generation to another.

This two-tiered storytelling—of the pioneer times and the more sacred elements of the migration—also shapes the accounts of the relocation of hundreds of Old Colony families in 1967 to Bolivia, where they established Riva Palacios, Swift, and Santa Rita Colonies, each named after the colony left behind in Mexico. At the surface, it is a story of gutsy migration. Numerous Bolivia Mennonites readily recall the primitive conditions in settling the land beyond Santa Cruz, with its thick bush, frightening monkeys, screaming "bush cats," wild pigs, and sudden floods. Other oft-recited stories recount the difficult separation and journey. Four married sisters from a Friesen family in Bolivia—Treen Fehr, Marie Hamm, Ann Buhler, and Sara Buhler—reminisce together, highlighting the auction sales in Mexico and emotional partings. Justina Reimer of Manitoba Colony recalls at least two ships, one carrying Ältester Bernard Peters, who came in 1968, and the difficult trip, including the ocean voyage: a bus to Mexico City, a train to the Pacific coast, a multi-day voyage in horrific storms, and the bus caravan through the mountains to La Paz. Johan Sawatsky, now of Neuland, was only three months old in 1967 when his family boarded their ship. He retells the stories that he heard about illness and fear of death, culminating in the death of a little girl and how they "tied her up in a sack with rocks and threw her overboard," a fate that he thinks "is worse than a grave." To make matters worse, another child died as they crossed the mountains to La Paz.

Even those who travelled, ironically, by airplane to escape modernity readily tell stories of a difficult relocation. Cornelius Berg, the father of fourteen children, describes the pain of separation, how in Mexico City his fifteen-year-old daughter balked terribly at leaving Mexican soil and her boyfriend, while their neighbour's teenaged son actually ran away and was forced back by the Mexican military personnel. Cornelius remembers especially the creaky, propeller-driven plane carrying the immigrants from Lima to La Paz and his panic during the flight through the mountains, quite convinced that the plane would crash. Men "slid together on the seat in fear" as the "plane tilted one way and then the other" during takeoff through the mountains. Once they arrived in Departamento de Santa Cruz, travel continued to be a challenge. The Friesen sisters recall how they made their way from Santa Cruz to their new home, Riva Palacios, in a district still known as the *Brechas*, "the clearings," by "flatbed [truck] together with all ... [our] belongings, ... standing or sitting wherever [we] could find room." The immigrants to nearby Santa Rita, Swift Current, and Sommerfeld Colonies, begun at the same time, share similar accounts of treacherous travel.

It's a narrative full of sadness, but in a subsequent interview, after the sun sets, a story of even greater anguish is told. It is an account of the reasons why the Mennonites left Mexico in the first place. Peter Knelsen says that the migration was a protest against modern ways in northern Mexico after church leaders, directed by Ältester Bernard Peters, urged the wholesale and tremendously costly migration. Peter reports that an urgent migration fever developed after "people were starting to use tractors as they came from the factory": that is, new tractors equipped with rubber tires. Peter says that the *Jemeent*, the church, realized that it "couldn't stay 'true'" if the youth used the new fast tractors to frequent the city, so it passed a new *Ordnung*: if a machine "has an engine, it can't have rubber tires." And to discourage nighttime fieldwork or driving, neither could it have electric lights. When a group of Old Colonists used the modern tractors anyway, they were banned, and conflict escalated to the point that the most outraged "started beating up the others." Cornelius Berg, having told his airplane story, now recalls Mexico again and offers that the most difficult part of the whole migration was the conflict that set it off; he remembers a moment when the Ältester went to distant Torreón for medical treatment. He had instructed a younger minister on how to keep the peace in his absence, but while he was away the rebel group, those shunned for buying trucks, came to a church service and refused to leave. In keeping with the historical practice of shunning, the presiding minister was forced to end the service and vacate the building. The terrible rupture between modernizers and traditionalists began well before the historic relocation.

The migrations involving East Paraguay are told in a similar bifurcated manner. Ask about the 1969 migration to East Paraguay, and it is all about release from the dust of the semi-arid mountain valleys of Chihuahua and Durango. Johan Neufeld remembers precisely the moment of landing with a group of fourteen families at the Asunción airport at 2 p.m. on 23 April 1969. Any emotion in his recital of the migration consists of an old regret. Johan recalls his father's "great longing for Canada," ruing the day in 1922 when he left Canada and joined the migration to Mexico, "*das verdammte Land.*" Heinrich Loewen of Rio Verde also remembers a bit of nostalgia, his parents speaking of the fertile "black soil back in Canada" and a similar regret that his family had ever tried farming the pebbly grey soil of northern Mexico. He mentions Mexico's "storms from the southeast [with winds] incessantly blowing for three or four days at a time." Then he contrasts both to the massive, warm, well-watered jungle of East Paraguay.

But there is a religiously based hope that accompanies Johan's and Heinrich's materialist interpretations. Oldtimer Cornelius Bergen at Rio Verde emphasizes the hope felt by the poor who received an automatic 10 hectares per family from the 23,000 hectares purchased by Manitoba Colony, the parent colony in Mexico, and the chance to buy another 50 hectares at a later date. Pressed on just why they moved, both Johan Neufeld and his friend Abram Peters say that it was for land for the next generation. With only 30 hectares on Johan's farm in Mexico, and only 50 on Abram's, "there was no land to give to the children." The beginning at nearby Nuevo Durango a decade later in 1978 is a similar story. Abram Wall has "shortage of land" at the top of his list for reasons to move. Margaretha Schmidt tells the story from a slightly different perspective. She recalls the sheer joy of working the new, difficult, abundant land; being "more of a boy than a girl," she "especially enjoyed rooting out the stumps of the trees with a pick and ... pull[ing] up weeds in the field." Farmland was the only guarantee of continued Old Colony ways.

Similar words mark the initial migrations to Campeche in southern Mexico, where Yalnon, Chavi, and Progreso were established in the 1980s. They were third-generation colonies in Mexico, founded by colonists from the original 1924 colony in Durango state and its 1960s offshoots La Batea and La Honda in nearby Zacatecas state. The settlers begin their stories by saying that they moved south because of land and often link their move to a moment in a family's life cycle. As a young man, Heinrich Bueckert and his wife, Aganetha,

moved to Campeche shortly after their wedding: "We had our engagement party, the *Falafnis*, in August 1983, and three months later
we moved to Yalnon, on November 24 we came here with my parents
and their eleven children, two of whom were married.... We came
because of land." It was as if the young couple's union was closely tied
to his parents' pulling up stakes, thus laying the groundwork for the
next generation of households. *Vorsteher* Abram Dyck of Chavi tells the
same story, albeit from the perspective of the middle-aged parent. He
and his family came from La Batea, where they had only "eighteen
hectares ... [of] oats" and "nine cows and some young cattle [that]
gave a hundred litres a day," so "we moved because we needed more
land for our children." The small parcel at La Batea certainly wasn't
enough to distribute among the children, but with the move each of
their nine children could receive five hectares of land—"enough for
now," says Abram, but only because their "children are young."

Land shortages, however, are but one part of the southern Mexico
story; church and religious concerns also infuse it. Wilhelm Penner
of Progreso is clear about the role of the church in the move south:
"Our children needed land, and [when] Campeche became available
... I didn't want to [go], but the preachers said that the parents had
'to go to show the children'" the value of farm life in the jungle. Johan
Woelke, Progreso's *Vorsteher* at the time, remembers the Ältester en-
couraging the move when a delegation of nineteen farmers returned
from the south and presented their findings at a *Broudaschaft* ("church
business meeting"): "The Ältester said we should find out how many
hectares people wanted. The most people could have was 100 hectares, and the least was 25 hectares, ... [of the] 17,000 hectares....
[Even though] the Ältester sounded like he did not want to come here,
he let the nineteen speak about what they had found."

Moving to Campeche turned out to be a good move economically.
Johan says that "my daughter [just] sold her land for $53,400 for ten
hectares next door to my place." But it was also understood that the
move was a church-sanctioned relocation, even a religious act of settling children on land of their own. In fact, careful steps were taken
to ensure that the poor and younger families had the opportunity to
acquire land. Veterinarian David Friesen describes the complex process of the land purchase at Progreso:

There was a meeting, I was at it, where they talked about this land. Some wanted [to purchase it] and some not, and so [it was decided] if enough wanted to then they would. Then many did. The poor could not afford it, and the rich wanted lots of land, and after a while they came to an agreement, 25 hectares, for the poorest, ... [with a] quarter [down and] to be repaid each year to help the poorer. The middle ones got 50 hectares and had to pay for half up front and later the other half.... The rich got 100 or 150 or 200 [hectares] or more. They had to repay more quickly. At first, everyone only got 25 hectares.

He concludes his account by outlining the specific process by which the poor farmers were helped out: "For many years, the *Jemeent* took ten cents for every litre of milk that was brought to the cheese factory, and it was saved up to buy land in Campeche." It was a carefully laid plan, one that promised to address a social tension within the colony created by landless families whose only other option was migration north to Canada or the United States.

A much more overt religious motivation infuses the narrative of the migration to southern Mexico's most recent colonies, Trinidad and Nuevo Durango, each founded in the late 1990s. The women at Trinidad have their two-tiered account. Helena Wieler says that in 1998 she, just recently married, and her extended family moved from semi-arid Virginias in northern Mexico to Trinidad because "irrigating was too hard" in the north, and "here [there] was rainfall." But her mother, Anna Thiessen, interjects that the move occurred after "it started with the vehicles" and that she and her husband refused the temptation. She asserts self-assuredly that "my husband has never sat behind [a] wheel." Her family stayed true to the old ways, largely because of the migration south. Another woman, grandmother Anna Harms, tells a similar story: she says at first that they moved for "fresh land" but then adds that the move occurred because in Virginias Colony, the roads "started to get chewed up, trucks were being driven, and we didn't want that." In short, she and her family moved south "because of our beliefs."

Another bifurcated account describes the later founding of Nuevo Durango in southern Mexico. Farmer Jacob Peters begins his description of the move thus: on 5 February 2000, "we left Durango [in northern Mexico] and came here [in the south]. On 7 February, a whole busload came, forty plus or forty-four people together with children. I hired the bus." Having established the base of the story, he adds a religious note. In Durango, "they wanted to live more in the world, and we did not want to." And the world, he says, is what drove his grandparents from Canada in the first place: "The scriptures say we are to live in the world but not [be] of the world, and those who are of the world, God is against." His neighbour, *Vorsteher* Jacob Wall, is at once less religious and more specific. He outlines the issue of the rubber-tired tractor: "Rubber tires are not bad in themselves, but it always goes further, then they want to get cars, and nothing is good enough, and then [they] go to high school and are in the world. It just all goes further." The new colony allowed them to stop the slide down the technological slippery slope. Anna Wiebe agrees that the reason for the move from Durango was "because everything was going to vehicles, and we wanted to keep things as we had had them": that is, "horse-and-buggy [since] it doesn't go so fast." But more importantly for her, "our beliefs ... taught us that vehicles are for worldly people and [that] horse-and-buggies are for us." Similarly, "electricity is for the worldly people, and we are not worldly people." These material markers accomplish three things: they keep life simple, reinforce a social boundary, and provide a religious identity.

During the decade that the parent Durango colony was contorting over trucks and electricity, leading to the formation of Nuevo Durango in southern Mexico, similar turmoil raged in East Paraguay. The result was that Paraguay's own 1978-spawned Nuevo Durango colony bade farewell to 500 families who moved to Bolivia in 1994. Half of them settled 300 kilometres south of Santa Cruz and formed yet a third Nuevo Durango. At the same time, Rio Verde Colony residents also began to leave East Paraguay for Bolivia, and with the other half of the earlier settlers they founded Neuland in 1994, and eventually El Tinto in 1997, El Palmar in 2003, and Nuevo La Honda in 2004. These colonies were all located east of Santa Cruz and across Bolivia's massive Rio Grande. The central contentious issues in East

Paraguay were the arrival of hydroelectricity, inexpensive and easily accessible because of the nearby Itaipu dam, and the gradual acceptance of vehicles on the colonies.

The religious underpinnings of the move from East Paraguay to Bolivia are echoed by middle-aged Leona Reimer of Neuland, who says she and her family "moved from Rio Verde because things were changing there. They were starting to use cars and phones, things that were part of the world. Rio Verde has become like Mexico. So the people who didn't want to be part of the change left for Bolivia. Electricity was brought in ... in 1990, ... [and we] became accustomed to using it, ... [with] a water heater tank too. It was cheap to use the state electricity. In Bolivia, [we] use fire to heat the water and solar panels and batteries for electricity." Leona adds that the main objections came from others in the community: "[I don't] think it would hurt to use electricity for small household things, but others in the colony won't allow ... electricity because they say it's part of the world." Leona moved to keep the peace. But she also knows that the move placed her in the flow of a history of faithfulness. In fact, it's a life contrasted to that of her grandparents in Mexico in the 1920s but then she catches herself: "we haven't had it as difficult as they did." Still, she is part of that broader narrative: "The *Dietsche*," we Germans, "are like ants—always wandering to new places," and "as long as there's room for them in the world" they will continue wandering to protect the faith.

Grandmother Katherina Wolfe, also from Neuland, has a similarly constructed narrative. She is open about the reason for the move, that is, it occurred after some colonists "started to use cars," knowing that "with this change ... other changes will come." She too places the move in a broader historical context of religious suffering. She says that the move from Rio Verde "wasn't so difficult because if one [really] wants to move then it's not difficult." Making the move possible for her family was that "it was like [we] were persecuted, like in Russia." Katherina operates within a collective memory.

The largest migration during these decades occurred when second-generation Old Colonists in Bolivia moved east across the Rio Grande into the heart of the Oriente, a move driven by hope for new land. Many of the names themselves speak of anticipation: Valle

Esperanza (1975), Oriente (1993), Valle Nuevo (1993), Buena Vista (1999), El Este (1996), and a dozen other colonies. As in previous cases, this search for land was not without religious meaning. Although each colony is an offshoot of an Old Colony community with roots in the 1967 migration to Bolivia, each folds its story into the larger one of religious faithfulness, a step blessed by the parent church. Thus, while the young mother Frieda Guenther[2] links Colonia Oriente to the parent colony of Santa Rita, another young mother, Margaretha Bergen, highlights the role of the *Jemeent* in choosing the land and organizing the move. Similarly, Marie Reimer and her husband, newly married, recall being anxious to get to California, the newest of these colonies, in time for the 22 July 2008 deadline to obtain their free fifty hectares of land from the *Jemeent*. New colonies never merely spell out "more land" but always include a wider congregational network.

Yet a more explicit linkage of land and religion is indicated by the older members of the colony. Elderly Johan Wall of Manitoba Colony relates its recent founding to establishment of the parent colony Riva Palacios, when his family "moved from Mexico to Bolivia in April [one year] ... under *Oom* Bernard Peters," the very term *Oom*, a prefix of respect for a religious leader, especially an Ältester, inscribing this historic move with religious faithfulness. Elderly Anna Banman might speak about the sequence of migration, with her family moving to Valle Esperanza because "the children moved ahead" of them, but she also contextualizes it with reference to the initial 1967 move from Mexico. It was a time when the "*Ordnung* broke down" as rebel members "set it aside." Even on the Bolivian frontier east of the mighty Rio Grande, where land is in abundance, the story of spiritual compromise in Mexico holds.

Vows of Obedience

If religion and conflict eventually infuse the narratives of relocation, talk about community and religion inevitably returns to themes of migration. It is as if by migrating Old Colonists know they are on the right path, narrow and difficult. Their stories are accounts of conflict, of resistance, of uncertainty. But always the migration offers religious hope.

Religion has been at the foundation of the culture of the Old Colony. David Friesen of Campeche says that he once confronted a Mexican atheist: "I asked if he had ever been to school; 'No,' he hadn't. Had he ever read the Bible? 'No,' he hadn't. I asked him why he kept laws. He said, 'To stay out of trouble,' otherwise he would have problems and be put in jail. I said, 'Who made the laws?' 'The government,' [he said]. I said, 'And God set up the government with laws.'" It may be a strange answer coming from Old Colonists who have their own histories of civil disobedience, but it reveals a particular cosmology nevertheless. God's role in history is not questioned, as "giver of life and death," protector, and judge. Wilhelma[3] Penner, recalling the cyclone in Campeche in 2002, says that it was "amazing that no one died and no one lost a building.... God's hand was in it." But the divine does allow tragedy. Katherina Dyck recalls stories of the horrific murder of her mother's beloved stepfather, Abram Braun, when she was only fourteen, "taken away as God the Heavenly Father had ordained it."

But behind most of their migrations are a set of divine demands. At baptism, according to farmer Johan Woelke of Progreso, "the young people meet with the ministers [and] say they will hold to God and the church, and what is meant is the church, the *Ordnung*." But, if they don't, God is also always ready to forgive. Aron Guenther of Nuevo Durango, Paraguay, says that, in preparation for communion, "the Sunday before the members are called to sharpen themselves, ... to renew their hearts, encouraged to make things right with God, to receive communion." Although God demands obedience from the baptized, surprising mercy is granted the unbaptized. Katherina Dyck worries about poverty, but she is also saddened as her teenaged children "are looking for more room, ... getting weak in their belief, that's just very unfortunate." Even as she laments being "tested from above," she insists that while "I never thought my children would drive trucks ... they are also God's children." She will not denounce her own children for leaving the old ways.

What is unforgivable is the breaking of the "vow" at baptism to avoid the lure of the world's offering of the "easy" and the "handy." Franz Wall of Yalnon says that "[we] have no phones or cell phones or radios or TVs, that would be too handy." But what really matters is that by acquiring the "handy," people are breaking a "promise." As Franz says, "we have those rules in our *Jemeent*, and we vowed to keep them, and we do not want things that are handy." Keeping the "old ways" from one generation to the next is crucial, and it begins with the vows of baptism.

This conversation about vows returns to the meaning of migration. Susanna Wall, a grandmother from Nuevo Durango in southern Mexico, says that they left modernizing La Batea in the north because they made vows at baptism. Many of her siblings stayed behind and modernized, not wanting to make the sacrifice for anti-modernity, "to have such a hard living." She is especially upset with her sister in Canada, not so much because she works as a married woman "cleaning houses" and speaks "English fluently" but because she has joined "a 'second-baptized' church," an evangelical church willing to rebaptize people of Old Colony background. Susanna cannot think of a worse offence: it is "a sin, … just not right, going from one church to the next; one should stay in the church in which one has taken one's vows." Anna Thiessen of Trinidad makes a similar judgment about Old Colonists who break their vows: at a recent funeral, her husband sadly observed his friends of old, "those who [had] knelt together [at the time of baptism] … [and] vowed to remain true to the church until the end, now they were all … gone [from the church], they had thrown it all away, like that." This religious tension infuses the story of migration.

Debating the Work of Ooms

Ministers, the *Ooms*, are the ones charged with keeping the colonists committed to their vows of baptism. Their job has been to enforce the *Ordnung* and resist modern ways, but they speak of it as a difficult task. As farmers, they have had no special training, and aside from an occasional premonition they have been elected without prior warning, in part because members are asked not to talk to anyone about a favourite candidate. They are simply ordinary farmers, always a relative or neighbour, usually elected as young men between the ages of twenty-eight and thirty-two. Yet, as Deacon Jacob Wall of Nuevo Durango, Mexico, says, they are expected to be "a light to others and write the sermon to read to the people, to those who are straying, to show them the scripture and hold them to the right path."

The way in which a preacher has promoted this right path varies little from colony to colony. At Sabinal in northern Mexico, Reverend Franz and Elisabeth Harder speak of the historical pattern of preaching on a circuit, with one minister preaching two weeks in a row, first in one church on the colony and then in a second one, and then taking a four-week break. Franz apparently uses his "grandfather's [sermon] book," but he "also writes [his] own sermons," though the other "*Ooms* also use the books of two deceased *Ooms* and an Ältester to preach from." Franz "finds writing sermons very difficult" and would welcome the help of Elisabeth, but unfortunately she "didn't learn to write German" as she grew up in Canada. He finds the extemporaneous "Low German parts," placed at critical junctures in the sermon and explicitly addressing moral issues on the colony, "the most difficult." These words in the vernacular matter the most, for with them the preacher applies the scripture of the day to specific events on the colony.

The most pressing day for all preachers, says Reverend David Redekopp of Yalnon, has always been *Donnadach*, literally "Thursday." Specifically, it is "the first Thursday of the month [when] we have a gathering of preachers, the Ältesters and deacons, and have the people who are straying come to the meeting or discuss who will go where [to visit and admonish them]. If something [special] comes up, then the Ältester gets preachers together to deal with it." On larger colonies, *Donnadach* might be held weekly, but at a minimum it occurs just before the semiannual communion service, at which members who wish to partake of the bread and wine must have made their peace with God, their neighbours, and the *Jemeent*. Reverend Aron Guenther of southern Mexico says that it comes at a time when the ministers gather "to see that there is not someone doing wrong and to speak to wayward ones, and if they do not stop from their wrongdoing then ask him to come to *Donnadach* and request him to turn from sin." It can mean that members need to be *oppjemolt*, "redrawn," or renewed spiritually.

One of the most common issues discussed at *Donnadach* has been emigration from Latin America. Aganetha Hiebert[4] of Sabinal recalls how she and her husband faced *Donnadach* after their sojourn in the United States. Given the fact that they did not live there for long, they didn't also have to appear at *Nokjoakj*, literally "after church," a meeting of members after the Sunday morning worship service to hear confessions and vote on a reinstatement of membership or to confirm an excommunication: "Others have [had] to do so and for two Sundays in a row; it depends on what kinds of things they have done, ... truck driving and having TVs and radios. One has to believe in God." But other members who have returned from times away and recall the shame of appearing at *Donnadach* or confessing at *Nokjoakj* now speak of it as having been worth the joy of reintegration. Jacob Klassen[5] of Nuevo Durango in Bolivia mentions the emotional well-being of colony life. He introduces himself in perfect English as "Jack Klassen" and says that he came back from a dozen years in Ontario because "I wasn't my own boss," felt cheated by dishonest Canadian Mennonites, and "suffered depression." The "return" was easy enough, even though he and his wife had to recommit to Old Colony ways at *Donnadach* and he had to confess for "two very nervous minutes" at *Nokjoakj*. He has no personal objection to cars, but now "no car" is the rule, and he wishes to live within the *Ordnung*. He even refrains from powering his house with solar panels, still considered somewhat too handy by many in his colony; he certainly "doesn't want to be the first" to use them.

Women in particular have been rather critical of church leaders who can't control members, leading to out-of-control emigrations. True, middle-aged Maria Froese and her daughter Sara of Trinidad respect their ministers. Their job is to "take it upon themselves to ... remind [us] when one does something wrong"; Maria and Sara emphasize the *Nokjoakj* when "the [ministers] really tell people how it must be and everything." One "can't always meet the expectations," though, according to Maria, and "if we simply don't listen in church then they come on a weekday and come onto the yard and ... help us remember '*this* we must not do, and *this* we must not do, and *this* is wrong.'" Her ready examples of "wrong" behaviour relate to clothes, those considered too worldly and fashionable. For men, "the waistband pants" are wrong, "the kind of pants that lighten with washing.... They don't stay as dark.... Those kind of pants are not supposed to be used here." For women, it is more often about hairstyle. Maria says that women "are not supposed to cut their hair, [and] they are not supposed to have bangs ... [or] braid their hair" a certain way. It is understood that these ministers have successfully carried out their duty to maintain the simple ways.

Other women, however, complain about weak Ältesters. Anita Peters[6] of Bolivia is not yet baptized and is upset by inconsistencies. Her father, but not her mother, was excommunicated because their daughter started dating when she was fifteen, then moved to the Bolivian town of Pailón to be baptized into an evangelical church. Anita does not understand why the Ältester held her father responsible, but seemed to fear her mother and never reprimanded her. Anita points to another example: a "man in [our] colony has been excommunicated many times, nearly fifteen times, ... because he sees women when he goes into Santa Cruz; he's about seventy years old." The moment that he confesses, the Ältester allows him back into the fold. Other women highlight "weak" Ältesters on other grounds. Middle-aged Katherina Wolfe from Neuland talks about the changes in her home colony of Rio Verde, especially the coming of electricity and trucks. Her diagnosis is sharp: "It started to change because the Ältester wasn't strong enough to keep the *Ordnung*. It's important to keep the *Ordnung* because [we] were taught it this way, that [we] should have a distinctive appearance from the world.... The world needs to see that [we]'re different." Migrations could have been avoided had strong leadership been in place.

Justina Froese,[7] the mother of twelve children on Swift Colony, applauds her Ältester for having managed the founding of new colonies east of the Rio Grande but is critical of one whom they have chosen at the new colonies. She questions the new Ältester at a newly established colony where her sons live because she thinks that they were scapegoated when a boy was seen loading beer onto a truck that the leaders believed to belong to her sons. She thinks that the Ältester has been inconsistent and weak: "He is too much of a people pleaser." Her sons have told her that at a recent meeting to elect a new junior minister on their colony, "someone made the comment that first they needed to elect a [real] Ältester." Her own Ältester on Swift Colony is different, indeed a wise man. For example, the husband of one of her "granddaughters wanted to farm on [one of the frontier colonies] but live on Riva Palacios," the parent colony. Doing so would mean long periods of separation from his wife and children. He went to the Ältester for advice, asking him what he thought of the plan: "The Ältester ... advised against his idea, telling him dividing his family like that was not a good idea." Justina was impressed with his counsel; it ensured order within a regional diaspora.

As in other horse-and-buggy communities, cases of sexual abuse have been the most difficult for the church leaders to deal with. The situation has been more difficult in the south in a context of a lack of state-directed Family Services and inconsistent policing. Officially the position of the leaders is clear: incest and rape are sins that result in excommunication until repentance by the perpetrator and forgiveness from the congregation. Yet a horrific case of more than 100 rapes of women in their sleep at Manitoba Colony in eastern Bolivia in 2009 showed the limitations of traditional approaches to such cases.

The story had not broken publicly when research for this book was undertaken on the colony in 2009, but in February 2012 Ältester Johan Neudorf of the colony spoke at length about it. *Time* magazine had earlier quoted him as saying that the rapes were "something we just don't understand.... There are good people in this world and bad."[8] Johan was more pointed in our conversation. He named the accused perpetrators by name, noted how each one had "confessed," at first readily, identifying the colony veternarian who had provided the Belladonna-infused sedative spray, the specific houses that the assaulters had targeted, and their rape strategies. He said he wished that they as elders had acted sooner.

Johan also named the two married women who came down his driveway one day in a horse and buggy to confront him, telling him that they had woken to dirt and blood on their beds in the morning and demanded that he do something about it. He recalled replying "but what can I do? We don't know who is doing it." He said the colony officials acted immediately upon observing an actual break-in, accosting the men; and, given the horrific nature of the crime, they took an unprecedented step, made their problems public, and handed the men over to the Bolivian police. Reports from the men that they had been tortured by neighbours to force confessions, he said, must be untrue. His only explanation for the terrible crime was that "we read about 'evil' unbounded in the end times." Healing, he said, comes from God, and then added that the colony held no lasting enmity against the men imprisoned for the crimes in Palmasola prison in Santa Cruz. "If only they confess to their sins, they will be forgiven and welcomed back."[9]

It's a fallback to an old Anabaptist idea of two kingdoms, that in the "Kingdom of Christ" one does not retaliate but forgive, does not defend but turn the other cheek. But even Johan admits that occasionally old ideals have not addressed the worst of local crimes.

The Temptation of the Truck

The diasporic community in the south reassures itself with stories from former communities in northern Mexico. Members recite biblical accounts that call for humility and love but then juxtapose them with stories from the north. Anna Harms of Colonia Trinidad in southern Mexico talks like a minister: "Our laws of the *Jemeent*" remind her of "the story of the rich man and Lazarus; the rich man burned in hell, and Lazarus was sitting in the lap of the Lord. We try not to be too rich.... We still watch that [we] do not go too far." To maintain the humility of a "Lazarus" and seek protection from unchecked capitalism can require a physical separation. Indeed, such a move might be necessary to ensure the final migration to a blissful eternity.

Old Colonists confess to times of complacency in everyday life, and they are not above telling frightening stories about the devil and hell to keep one another in check. Local undertaker Helena[10] Rempel of Swift Colony in Bolivia recalls one woman who committed suicide by hanging herself and was "found in a kneeling position with her knees just inches off the floor," as if the devil had kept her from falling all the way to the floor, which would have saved her from death and ultimate perdition. Old Colonists also know that "eternity" can mean losing the favour of God and going to the place of the devil, eternal hell. Young Isaac Wall of East Paraguay has been introduced to the idea of no hell by two young, blonde, female, German-speaking Jehovah's Witnesses, and he sees it "as a great mistake ... not to believe in hell, because when I wouldn't believe in hell I could do anything." His hope for his own two children and those yet to be born is that they "will go on living in a colony with decent ways and rules, no 'naked' girls, girls showing their belly or wearing short skirts, and no partying."

Yet, they have heard of these very moral failings on colonies where modernity has become the norm. Many Old Colonists link the car and truck to crime and disbelief. Abram Redekopp of Shipyard recalls the "Friesen family from Camp 20 who were in the mafia" and involved with drugs. "They were 'big,' at least they thought they were because they had so much money, and thought they were important and very rich, and wouldn't take any passengers while driving through villages. They drove pickups, so they were excommunicated." Johan Klassen from Nuevo Durango in East Paraguay is even blunter about the car: "The car makes people lazy and stupid; they go and buy everything at once with their cars, small things they don't need or could easily have bought another day.... Like this they spend a lot of money needlessly. Furthermore, cars produce envy [and] invite assaults.... [Look] at the Sommerfelders, who often drive around with guns in their trucks." Bring in the car and immorality and pride of every sort will follow.

Both Abram and Johan are referring to people whom they know on neighbouring colonies within their respective countries. The most disturbing stories arise from colonies that they as horse-and-buggy people have left. Anna Thiessen of Trinidad, in southern Mexico, lays out the problem: "Drinking and driving, if they now have a bit of a bottle and they drink a bit and they have a bit of music," then driving becomes a horror. She relates the story of a horrific accident in Cuauhtémoc in northern Mexico: "With one hand on the steering wheel, and then here they listen. Five boys have been struck dead there.... Those little cell phones, ... they have them in their pocket, and it rings, and ... they [are] tearing around, and they can't have both, and then they scream there is a vehicle in front of them, and then they are hit and are killed." Sudden death among Old Colonists often sends a divine message, and in the case of the five boys that message was unequivocal.

The simple conclusion from such stories is that Old Colony humility and non-violence require a society without vehicles. Helena Wieler of Trinidad, Mexico, states, in a matter-of-fact manner, "I often say ... one would want to live where there are no trucks." Such a place in her mind is related to religious faithfulness. Anna, her elderly mother, is more specific and links a world without vehicles to a particular mindset. She speaks assuredly and with a sense of familial pride: "My husband has kept this 'way'; here we sit, and not one child has learned [the ways of the car and truck], and he has made it that way, everything is produced with patience, and [all of life] is still and content." A history of commitment to the *Ordnung* has resulted in a community that celebrates the slow and peaceful.

Similar stories highlight the peace that has come from farming in small ways with tractors on steel wheels. Such machines are venerated even though the steel wheels make no sense from an economic perspective—they lumber along at slow speeds, are very bumpy, and require local blacksmiths to construct expensive and precisely produced parts unavailable from factories. The ministers, though, have seen steel-wheeled tractors as an expression of self-denial that keeps the farms small and the youth from the cities. Johan Wall of Colonia Florida in southern Bolivia says that it is a mistake to think that the steel wheel will get anyone to heaven. He recalls that his father, who once drove rubber-tired tractors in Mexico, was told that he might not go to heaven on account of his tractor. Johan is adamant that the "steel wheel will not take me to heaven," but he still defends it as a guarantee against slipping into the world: "If we allow rubber tires, the next thing I will want an air-conditioned cab, then a car, and then city life." And city life spells noise and mayhem. Abram Redekopp of Shipyard defends steel wheels with a bit of romance. As he sees it, steel-wheeled tractors "keep the speed down" and allow him as he "drives on a bumpy road ... [to] just think ... about the less fortunate, instead of complaining."

Wilhelm Wall of Nuevo Durango in East Paraguay is more philosophical about abiding with technologies that slow people down. He introduces the term *Privilegium,* that venerated charter of privileges that Mennonites in the diaspora have negotiated with various national governments. Those privileges have usually guaranteed the Mennonites their military exemption and church-run schools, but Wilhelm sees them as also being connected to a society without cars. The *Privilegium,* he says, is a contract: in exchange for their privileges, national governments expect Mennonites to live as the "quiet in the land." He adds that "as Old Colonists we live apart from the world because we have been granted the *Privilegium*. We have been 'invited' to Paraguay to live as farmers and [are expected] not to mix with the country's politics as some Mennonites have already begun." Mennonites are expected to be self-sufficient, and indeed their social cohesion "gives strength to each of us in our everyday lives." The main problem, though, is that the system crashes if Mennonites come out from behind the social boundaries produced by the *Privilegium* and embrace the world. Wilhelm is unequivocal: "If we switch to cars, everyone could go here or there, and we would lose a lot of that cohesion." A car or truck is never just a piece of technology; it is a symbol of a way of life for a people in diaspora.

A Spirituality of Simplicity

Old Colonists talk about religion by telling a specific historical narrative. It's a story about migration in search of land and simplicity, about being faithful and obedient to the *Ordnung*, and about seeking places of peace and community unity. And it's a story of spirituality even though Old Colonists do not readily talk about God or angels or the devil or heaven. Yet after the first hours of the interview process, sometimes only on the second day of "visiting," they do become reflective. They also become introspective, sometimes critical of their old ways, a sentiment encased in a variety of emotion, ranging from slight derision, to humour, to worry, to hope.

They ponder their ways, even the most sacred of them, their church holidays, for example, and historicize them. They know that their ways have changed over time, conditioned by their migrations, even shaped by interactions with other cultures. Reverend Aron Guenther of southern Mexico recites the many holy days that Old Colonists have come to observe: "School ... is closed on December 24th and 25th for Christmas, and on the 31st and 1st for New Year, and on the 5th and 6th [of January] for *Dreikönige* ['epiphany']." Having listed the holidays, he adds without prompt that the actual reason Old Colonists have kept these holidays is "because of the Catholic Church" in history, since "it's not in the Bible, so why?... We do not know when Christ was born. I do not know; there is no 'biblical ground,' [no] biblical injunction, that we need it." He knows that history is fluid and thinks that Old Colonists need to remember this; their calling is not about a practice for the sake of it but about a particular spirit that the practice signifies.

It's the same with their distinct clothing, which has no meaning in itself, but which has been a point of contention among Old Colonists. Johan Thiessen of Progreso suspects that clothing styles have changed "from the time in Russia; we can see that in pictures." But at the same time, it's "not that we can remember that it has changed." His father and grandfather wore the same fashions as he does, but his great-grandfather in Canada or Russia would have been dressed differently. Ultimately, what matters, he says, is that Old Colonists "would have become unified" by agreeing on specific styles, "hold[ing] to those ordinances." But, he reiterates, it's "not that the scriptures say anything about what kind" of clothing should be worn, and Old Colonists mostly like to wear "what [they] are used to." Then he reminds himself that Old Colony clothes do have sacred elements to them: clothing style is how "our forebears decided to be a light to the world. If we dressed like the world, then what light would we be?" No matter where their migrations have taken them, the artifacts have signalled their intention to resist the lure of worldly fashion and consumption.

In their introspections, Old Colonists not only muse about the origins of their ways but also joke about them. Perhaps Old Colony faith is a solemn summoning to consider eternal values, but it's not a belief system that makes Old Colonists dour. Humour infuses both their self-deprecation and their judgment of the world. Veterinarian David Friesen of Progreso doesn't shy away from making light of the Old Colony stance against technology:

> There was a man who went to the doctor with his boy, who was sick. The doctor said, "You have to give him a pill at 5 a.m. and an hour later give him an injection. Then come and see me in a week." "Oh, I don't have a clock, how will I know when to give the medicine?" "Well, then, when the cock crows, give him the pill, and when the milk driver comes give him the injection." When he came to the doctor later that week, the doctor asked how the boy was. The man said, "The boy is dead, and the cock is not doing very well, and the milk

driver is really mad at me." The man was not very clever and misunderstood the doctor. He gave the pill to the cock, and he ran after the milk driver to give him an injection.

It's a joke with a point: Old Colonists need to know that their anti-technological world has not been the most efficient.

They know that in their migrations they have worried too much. They fret that their simple ways should lead to greater trust, and they tell stories of worry infused with hope and always some nostalgia. Thus, having told the joke, David Friesen follows up with a story of a family emergency after moving to Campeche from Zacatecas. They had come south without any money, in part because the family who had purchased their land in the parent colony had not yet paid for it:

> We needed flour, sugar, salt, and we had no money; I was awake all night; then at 11:45 p.m. I thought, "This worried thinking is not going to help. The New Testament says we should not worry about tomorrow." I fell asleep, and then [in the morning] the neighbour came over and ... asked me to come along to the cheese factory, and there I met someone from La Honda [Colony] who had brought money from someone from there [this person owed David money] for me. My heart was light. I came home, and I was so happy.... I went and bought everything we needed.

Later he reflected on "how wrongly I had thought of [the debtor from La Honda]. He had just forgotten." His story is not only a description of pioneer difficulty but also a personal reminder of the security found within community.

At their most vulnerable, Old Colonists talk about the narrow pathway beyond legalism or individualism. Isaac Fehr of Shipyard speaks in English and seemingly is mindful of his evangelical neighbours who offer a superior personal and joyous religion. He admits that he has become impatient with the *Ordnung* and cultivates a more personal faith than the average Old Colonist espouses. But he defends the Old Colony way as offering emotional stability and separation from a life of consumption and self-gratification:

Sometimes I'm not satisfied with [the *Ordnung*], but I wouldn't want all those modern things. Think what will happen if I give all those things to my children, more chance to do bad things like drugs and alcohol. The richer you are, the greater chance to fall out of [the] church; wealth means high risk. My lifestyle is very important to me. I teach it to my children, ... a Christian life that brings me happiness.... I believe very strongly in educating the children about the Bible, very strongly. In my house, God is the first one, I love my wife and children, but they are not the first; we include Jesus in all that we do. The good things about Old Colony life for me is living according to the Bible. I feel like I'm outside the world, no telephone, no TV.... Not having all those bad things—drugs, alcohol, women—is good.... It's a joy living outside the world!.... The preachers don't preach as much as I would want, though.... I'm enjoying the little things that I have so much.

Isaac seems to be prepared to cultivate this joy and maintain the social boundary that encases Shipyard.

His neighbour, Abram Redekopp, utters similar thoughts in English about an inner peace that has come with simplicity, albeit with considerably less piety. He recalls the first days at Shipyard in 1958 with nostalgia: "In the start, people worked together like ants. They carried the flour on their back all the way from the river, and they were all happy, and smoking. Until they started making money, that's when the revolution began." He chooses an unusual word to denote the upheaval that a highly individualized approach to religion and the economy brought to the doorstep of Shipyard. He seems to long for another frontier community.

Conclusion

Old Colonists don't talk about their religious faith easily, but their narratives of migration are a testament to an intentionally religious life. Certainly, they think in terms of a transcendent and immutable God of everyday life, one who rewards and chastises and guides. And it is usually understood that their simple lives represent a form of self-sacrifice, antithetical to a loud and competitive world. The stories of Old Colonists are rarely about the superiority of their particular world; they say that their sacred vows of obedience are for themselves to keep and do not apply to others. They believe strongly that in keeping those vows they have built a particular kind of community.

But they also believe that migration is necessary to safeguard their way of life. Indeed, their stories of migration are especially important to them. They mark a crucial cultural repertoire unknown to Old Orders in Canada and the United States. Old Colonists have moved ever southward—to Belize, Bolivia, East Paraguay, and Campeche, Mexico—at great cost, propelled by visionary church leaders, undergirded by obedient members. The migrations occur because of a religious calling, either to escape the temptation of modernization— all too real when they see neighbours give in to the lure of forbidden technology—or the ongoing need for farmland so that the next generation has the space to maintain the *Ordnung*. Knowing that a move occurred because of faith also means that it can occur again at any time, and this leads to a willingness to consider perpetual dislocation.

Community cohesiveness, simple technology, school freedom, and exemption from most state-run agencies underpin the Old Colony lifeworlds in the new settings. The perpetuation of these worlds occurs because of a complex cultural process in which religion determines action, but action reinforces a particular religious imagining. Even then those worlds are not readily given religious vocabulary, for their very existence is the text on which religion is inscribed.

CHAPTER FOUR

The Genius of Community Survival

"A house burned down, [and] we 'high-speed' rebuilt this house."

Drive south of the sprawling city of Santa Cruz, Bolivia, on the two-lane Highway 9. Half an hour later, at the *Brechas*, where Imperial Oil cut perfectly straight lines and dirt roads through the bushland in the 1950s, turn east. After ten or so kilometres on a bumpy, dusty, red road, you arrive at Riva Palacios Colony. It is the most prominent and historical of the sixty Mennonite colonies in Bolivia. But despite its status as the parent colony (1967) of the Old Colony world in Bolivia, there is no sign announcing the colony's name, no welcome banner, no local hero valorized. And then you discover that all three dozen villages of Riva Palacios are also unmarked, even though a locally produced map indicates that each has both a *Campo* number (a Mexican tradition) and a German-language place name (of West Prussian origin).

Despite a lack of signage marking colony or village, it is clear that this is an Old Colony Mennonite community. There is the horse-and-buggy traffic, the telltale Old Colonist garb of dark dresses and black overalls, the Low German phrases murmured by passersby. There is also a specifically "Mennonite" geographic ordering, with linear space arranged neatly, intentionally, and efficiently. The tractors on steel wheels lumber along on the "lower," more rutted lane, while the parallel "upper," better-graded lane is reserved for visiting semis and taxis. The road is perfectly straight, following a square grid survey pattern, a cultural feature transplanted from Canada to Mexico in the 1920s and then brought to Bolivia in the 1960s. Similarly, the farmyards are also arranged in orderly sequence. Most have a picturesque treed lane leading to a farmyard set against a barn at the far end and, at the side of the yard, a neat brick or concrete house set among ornamental trees and colourful flowers.

How does such a place come to be? It seems to be such a mix of powerful symbols and quiet obscurity. There seems to be an order amid the vagaries of agraria. The roadways and fences seem to be in good repair, internal and external boundaries are maintained, goods and services are produced and exchanged, farm families seem to be faring well, the poor seem to be cared for, a peaceable community seems to exist. What is the genius of this survival?

I am fortunate that on this, my first time in Riva Palacios, I am travelling with my friend Dick Braun of Osler, Saskatchewan, in a red, four-wheel-drive SUV. Dick takes me to visit with his friends, Abram and Aganetha Thiessen, at whose place we enjoy a lunch of hearty chicken noodle soup and freshly baked bread. Abram is an engaging and jocular man. He tells us of his family and farm, he jokes and laments, but along the way he opens up Riva Palacios to us. His narrative outlines an intricate, historically conditioned, self-sufficient, and locally regulated institutional arrangement and local economy. The down payment on his farm came from his meagre salary as a village schoolteacher, a position for which he was hired by the *Darp Schult* ("the village mayor"), who in turn had been elected democratically by the *Schultebott* ("the village council"), consisting of all land-owning farmers. His salary as a teacher came from the school fund, a village tax, half of which is collected from landowners and half from parents, calculated on the number of children in school.

Later, as a farmer, he interacted with other institutions in the colony. His household sells its milk to one of the colony's seven locally organized, cooperative cheese factories, which collects a tax that it sends on to the *Vorsteher*s. The *Vorsteher*s, two colony mayors, use the tax money for colony roads and land for the next generation of farm families, but they also resolve conflicts, negotiate between the colony and outside world, and intervene in domestic disputes. Since the Thiessens were an established family, the *Vorsteher*s approached them one year to see if they would foster a young girl, who now sits at their table. She was brought over by the *Vorsteher*s when her mother died and they decided that her abusive father could not be trusted. They even confiscated his land to hold in trust for the children until they turned twenty-one, thus fulfilling the convention of the *Waisenamt* ("estates commission") and its *Waisenverordnung* (their own eighteenth-century bylaws governing orderly inheritance).

Abram's account is of his family's survival in Bolivia. It is related intricately to a local government that has no legal foundation but tries to ensure social peace and economic success. Abram speaks about institutions that are very old, perhaps a thousand years old, but also of others recently adopted from non-Mennonite societies. He outlines agricultural adaptation, with some aspects transplanted from the semi-arid mountain valleys of northern Mexico, others benefiting from Bolivia's warmer and more humid environment. His narrative touches on shifting global markets, new technologies, and the lure of chemicalized farm methods that have strangely combined old and new ways. But his stories recount a basic principle: technologies must benefit the whole community, not abet the ascendancy of the individual. Indeed, technologies that pit one farm household against another, or lead to the wider world's allure of consumer goods, are not accepted.

In talking about their communities, Old Colony Mennonites blend antiquity and invention, old and new, the certain and the risky. The history of their farm community's survival is always both, a record of what has always been and a conversation on what they have been compelled to do. Old Colonists have survived in strange new worlds by keeping sight of their principles of simplicity, all the while relying on a complex array of old institutions and seasoned farm practices. But their stories also indicate that such a reliance has never been myopic, always also reflecting an openness to some form of adaptation to new circumstances.

Roadways, Fences, and Borderlines

Ask Old Colonists about the temporal foundation of their community and you will hear about a complex, democratically elected colony administration. They can't recall a time when community leaders were not the *Vorsteher*s, elected to staggered terms of two years, a senior First *Vorsteher* and an assistant, the Second *Vorsteher*. In most colonies, these terms have been renewed twice, in some such as Shipyard three times (unless the *Vorsteher* is over sixty), in Nuevo Durango in southern Bolivia without limit. Although most colony offices—the *Brandältester* ("fire commissioner"), the *Waisenmaun* ("estates commissioner"), the *Credit Maun* ("credit man")—are elected at the annual New Year's General Meeting on 31 December, the *Vorstehers* are chosen in a primary system. They are selected by votes conducted in independent meetings in each village, a process presided over by the *Darp Schult*, thus ensuring that no electioneering occurs.

Their work is also complex. At Valle Nuevo in Bolivia, Katherina Fehr, aged forty, lists her husband Jacob's duties as *Vorsteher:* oversee all colony institutions, regulate the cooperatives, work toward social harmony, assure the maintenance of colony infrastructure, and attend to all necessary surveying of land. The *Vorsteher* represents the local community in all external relations, most importantly with outside government agencies. This means that he works to ascertain land titles, address citizenship questions, regulate national identity cards, and register birth and marriage certificates. He also maintains the integrity of internal and external land boundaries.

Always the *Vorstehers* work without the force of law, but they do work with the blessing of the community and ultimately receive their authority from "the church," the *Jemeent*. Significantly, though Old Colonists separate the temporal *Vorsteher*'s office from the sacred, the church, the "*Jemeent,*" they do use the term "*Jemeent*" for the church-sanctioned "community" as a whole. Thus, though each colonist family owns its own land, it is not recognized by legal title but by an informal internal system and it is the *Jemeent* that is said to have legal title on all Colony land, registered as a single deed. On some occasions individual farmers, sometimes two or three, but sometimes dozens, "lend" their names, and allow Colony lands to be registered under their names, but always with the assumption they are doing so on behalf of the colony. In all cases the registration is but a technicality, as farmers buy and sell lands among themselves as if in fact they had title to them; but having the *Jemeent* own the lands also allows it to ensure that they are not sold to non–Old Colonists, and that policies meant to guarantee a degree of equality on the colonies can be enforced.

Johan Dyck of Chavi, Mexico, recalls keeping account of his colony's informal land ownership as one of the most complex features of his work when he was the *Vorsteher*. Johan notes how the system has worked at Chavi in southern Mexico. The colony has about 3,500 hectares, registered on forty-one deeds. Two of the deeds say that he is the owner, and another has his wife's name on it. The deeds all remain with the *Vorsteher*, but in Johan's words, "the person who has bought the land ... from the *Jemeent*, [he] just farms it then.... [Not] like the world.... However, that ... which they have, their piece of land, that is [recorded] with the *Vorsteher*.... [Parent colony] La Batea was exactly the same way. Those who use horse and buggies, they have all their land together [in this way]." Land is thus owned individually, but within a collective spirit, recognizing that individual landownership is never absolute.

At the local level, villages organize themselves as a *Schultebott* and choose a *Schult*, a village mayor. Johan B. Peters of Manitoba Colony, Bolivia, recalls his work of being a *Schult* as multifaceted. It included road maintenance, organization of mutual aid for the poor, and conflict resolution between farmers, when, for example, cattle might cross a fenceline or a land boundary. Many *Schulten*, says Johan, have passed on the conflict at the first opportunity to the more distant *Vorstehers*, who in turn have sometimes asked for ministerial help. Other *Schulten* describe different tasks—ensuring that graves are dug, collecting the two-tiered school tax and hiring the schoolteachers. Jacob Wall of Nuevo Durango, Mexico, adds that the local *Schult* has also hired people to repair roads, kept records of voluntary road work, and negotiated school costs with villages too small to have their own schools.

For both the local *Schult* and the colony *Vorstehers*, the most challenging aspect of their jobs has been tax collection from the recalcitrant few or impoverished families. Peter Friesen of Swift Colony, Bolivia, recalls his term as *Schult* and how collecting the village school tax caused the greatest stress: to "get some villagers to pay their dues" was a task he disliked so much that he "always made up the difference out of [his] own pocket." When he complained about the stress to the church *Ooms*, they offered little help; their lot was even more demanding, they said, since they "don't get paid anything" and are "in it for life." The colony-level land tax used for roadways and drainage—a less onerous tax, on Progreso in Campeche only thirty pesos, for example—is easier to collect, for it is landowners and not labourers who pay it.

Other taxes, based on income, have also been easy to collect. An example of such a tax is the one based on a percentage of gross sales of all commodities that leave the colony borders for the wider national or international market, such as cheese, soybeans, and cattle. It is levied at only 1 to 3 percent, depending on the colony, and used to acquire new sources of land for the colony, pay legal fees of all kinds, and generate funds for social welfare. This tax is paid on an honour basis since farmers must self-report their sales to the *Vorstehers*. It's a good tax for colony officials. Isaac Doerksen of Nuevo Durango, Bolivia, is confident that the system is working well on his colony, where leaders took in $120,000 US in 2010 on the 1 percent gross tax. Of course, farmers might need reminders to pay up, says Isaac, but if they still don't meet their obligctions, he passes word on to the *Ooms*, who then insert reminders into their sermons to stir the consciences of negligent congregants. The most automatic tax is the one collected by the cheese factory, which collects a percentage from every litre of milk shipped.

To make the multi-tiered system work, each colony has chosen a census taker. As such, the deacon of Yalnon, David Wall, not only records "births, deaths, and marriages and movements of residents," but also has kept his eye out for the poor. Of course, his official colony list has not only compelled one to pay taxes but also to be entitled to receive the benefits of belonging to the Old Colony community.

Ancient and New: From Brandschult to Credit Maun

A number of intricate small-scale social networks and self-regulated subinstitutions radiate from the colony *Vorsteher*'s office. Some are recent creations, but most are deeply rooted institutions, based on old Anabaptist principles of mutual aid and fairness.

The "fire insurance organization," the *Brandverordnung*, is one example. The *Brandältester* ("colony fire commissioner") designates a *Brandschult* ("local fire commissioner") in every village to respond expeditiously to any fire. Store owner Heinrich Bueckert of Yalnon explains how it all works: "For the fire insurance, the village

Brandschult has to write down everyone's possessions, like house and contents, food, tractor, buggy, animals. [In case of a fire,] one pays for a percentage of what one has underwritten. Two-thirds of it gets paid out if found not to be responsible, one-third is a loss." It's thus never a simple matter of outright charity: judgment on the fire's cause must be passed, meticulous accounts kept, an entire community's trust maintained. Johan Woelke of Progreso adds that the *Brandältester* is "elected every six years," is always someone trustworthy, and is able to make quick decisions in difficult situations.

The system has worked well. Johan recalls a fire during the time when Progreso was being established by settlers from La Honda: "A house burned down, [and] we 'high-speed' [said in English] rebuilt this house. The people in the colony helped; [as *Brandältester,*] I paid for all materials, there were only a few [families] here [at that time], so we got fire insurance from La Honda [the parent colony]. We got some things from people but [also] a lot of unnecessary things." Within a week, a new house was standing in place of the old structure, built from fire insurance money and voluntary labour readily given.

Entirely new institutions or offices have recently appeared on some colonies. In Nuevo Durango in southern Mexico, for example, the colony has created a *Sociedad,* a Spanish word denoting "a farm supply and marketing cooperative." Its officers are farmers Jacob Peters and Johan Janzen, each designated as a *Credit Maun* ("credit man"), the first word spoken in English, the second in Low German, but mostly it is rendered with the abbreviation CM. The CM oversees all commodity production, including seed purchases and crop marketing. Jacob says that the position of CM arose because in southern Mexico "everything costs so much more, the seed is more expensive, the city is far away, and it was too much work for the *Vorsteher,* so we started with the *Credit Maun* in 2007." The CM is elected at the New Year's meeting; as Jacob explains it, the CM is in essence "the *Vorsteher* over the farming business, lending, buying of seeds, oil, fertilizer, spray, and paying out money to people [after the harvest]." What happens is that "one of us has to go once a week to Mérida [the city] to sell corn, mostly. We buy things in Campeche [another city]. We order, and they deliver, sometimes we call in the orders, and other times we go there, and sometimes they come here to see what we need. We go on [each] Tuesday to buy things, to sell cheese and bring things back." To begin the payment process, "we go get a cheque from the seller and bring it to the bank. We have a bank account for the whole colony. We [then] give out cheques to people, and they go cash them in banks in Hopelchén, Mérida, or Campeche. We try not to travel with too much money."

Other colonies have established cheese factories and general stores as cooperatives. Like the agrarian *Sociedad,* they operate in competition or in collaboration with private firms. Veterinarian David Friesen explains how the cheese cooperatives work in Progreso in southern Mexico: "There is a cheese factory in [villages] 1, 5, and 9 [but] milk tanks in [villages] 2, 4, 5, 8, which are owned by individuals.... The cheese factories buy the milk at 3.3 pesos a litre. The milk tank [owner] buys it at 3.5 pesos a litre and sometimes up to 4 pesos a litre." Farmers thus choose to work with the cooperative or the individual entrepreneur. David sees the main difference as one of convenience: "If they sell to the tank [owner], then the farmers have to bring [the milk] in themselves." It's a flexible system David thinks works well.

The colony cooperative general store has been no simpler an enterprise. In Yalnon, long-time schoolteacher Franz Wall served as the manager of the store for a short time from 2001 to 2002, and like that of the *Credit Maun* his was an elected term that came with a small salary of 600 pesos every fifteen days. In his post, Franz "hired and fired employees, booked the work [schedule], [determined the] percentage charged on goods sold so that the store stayed afloat, and bought goods [for it] in Mérida." But running a cooperative was more complicated than buying at wholesale and selling at a profit. To make the store function well, Franz oversaw its patronage and dividend system: "Each patron has to buy a share" for 30,000 pesos; then "a percentage gets given ... to [each] shareholder after the year-end accounting." In addition, patrons often desire a form of credit. At Yalnon, the store and cheese factory are connected, "so when people bring milk [to the cheese factory] one gets credit at the store," up to a limit of 3,000 pesos. Because it is a cooperative, there have been disagreements, even "rough" ones, as "one person wants it one way and [another person wants it] another way, but it mostly works fine," claims Franz. He could tell stories of conflict, but he is more interested in outlining its success.

Co-ops typically have been sound economic ventures, but they have failed, sometimes amid searing community scandal. In East Paraguay, the Nuevo Durango Cooperativa Multiactiva, established with advice and encouragement from the more progressive Chaco-based Menno Colony, collapsed in 1995 amid talk of being defrauded of 66 million guaranies by a Paraguayan agricultural engineer who sold seeds and fertilizers. To make matters worse, legal fees of another 60 million guaranies doubled the loss, and all of this occurred just as half of the colony's most orthodox members were relocating to Bolivia on account of the encroachment of hydroelectricity. It was a controversy that residents such as Johan Klassen, for a time the manager of Multiactiva, still don't want to talk about.

Making Agraria Work in the Modern World

Farmers historically have had two concerns, coaxing the land to produce and then turning a profit with which to purchase more land so that the next generation can also farm. The way that a farmer assembles the family's land base is an important part of any family's lore. Most Old Colony farmers know intimately the histories of their farms.

Old Colonists have built their farms in one of two basic ways: either incrementally, by assembling small pieces of farmland over time on colonies that long ago reached their limit, or by acquiring a larger parcel on a frontier colony. At Shipyard Colony in Belize, Peter Friesen, who supplements his tiny farm with his mechanic shop, has assembled his thirty-six-acre farm "a little here, a little there." He knows the narrative: "It was coming very slowly, ... [but] it was all cleared. When we got married, I had 12.5 acres already, in 1983 I bought ... six more, and in 1998 [I bought] eight more. I had five years to pay that off. And I think somewhere in the '80s I bought another ten [acres], but I don't remember anymore what year that was." Other farm histories speak of sudden increases. Reverend David Redekopp from the newly established colony of Nuevo Durango in Campeche had access to somewhat larger parcels. His farm consists of "thirty hectares in all; in farmstead land, it's ten hectares; five and a half hectares in pasture; [and] we have nine hectares in the village," land farther away from the homestead but within the original village district. The final parcel of five hectares is "land that belongs to a village but is outside the village." David explains the process by which "first we opened the land here in the village, and then three years later we opened up the land outside the village," in actuality a subcolony of twenty-two families.

Farmers often speak of the joy that they felt when they first acquired their land. Indeed, young landowners seem to be a contented lot. Peter Friesen, recalling the pioneer years at Shipyard in Belize in the late 1950s, says that the "first years were difficult, but it was nice." Johann Peters of Manitoba Colony, Belize, recalls the 1980s when he and his wife as a young married couple acquired their land and how "wonderful it was to work at land clearing with my wife."

They also speak of the need to adapt and invent, to survive within nature by observing it. Old Colonists seem to be intimately in tune with the natural world, albeit as farmers, wondering what nature can produce, how it works, and how it can be predicted. David Friesen of southern Mexico switches seamlessly from the topic of colony institutions to that of farm animals: "Roosters crow when there is a change in the weather," he offers, "and they are very interesting; when one starts, then the next one starts, and so on along the village until they have all told each other." He adds how he learned from a Mexican that, "when a cow or calves lift up their tails and run around, rain is imminent. Watch out, you'll see."

This connection to nature is compelling but hardly signals a break from the old Western penchant for order and the ability to tame. Deacon Jacob Wall of Progreso says that they "have two birds called *chachalacas*, wild birds, that ... have [been] tamed. The boys were in the woods, and they found a nest with eggs, took them home, set them under a hen, and they hatched in a couple of days, and now they are totally tame.... At times they sit on their shoulders or lap when they're cracking seeds to get some." Even the sun is tamed in a way. In Progreso, the elderly Wilhelm Penner, who has trained a parrot, wonders how a rooster cannot be trained: "[The] rooster crows here like the one that Jesus says at 3 a.m., like when Peter lied about Jesus." And if you can't train a rooster not to crow at sunrise, neither can you control the rising of the sun. But you can control time. His wife, Maria,[1] says that "we are on old time; we got tired of moving our clocks back and forth" every time the road between Zacatecas and Campeche was traversed. Wilhelm agrees that "it was disorienting" and then jokes that "this way, then, the sun comes up just at the same time as it did in La Honda, Zacatecas!"

Farmers are aware that in the past they controlled nature too much. Settlers talk with shame of how they turned jungle into rolling plain. Wilhelm Buhler of Riva Palacios regrets that the instinct of plains dwellers such as Mennonites was to bulldoze the bushland, getting a breeze to drive away the mosquitoes and lighten up the landscape. But then dry times came, and dust hung in the air, and at Riva Palacios they embarked on rigorous tree-planting schemes and shelterbelts in addition to lane trees, ornamental shrubs, and shade foliage around the house. Wilhelm Wall of Nuevo Durango in East Paraguay was about thirty when the colony was founded, and he now talks "of climate change and the rise in temperature." He admits "the great error of indiscriminately chopping down all the trees without thinking of erosion by rain and wind," and he embraces government plans to raise the percentage of forested lands on the colony from 3 to 8 percent.

Most often the Old Colony's connectedness to nature has been expressed with reference to what will grow in new places of settlement. The distance from Durango to Campeche in Mexico is only 2,000 kilometres, but the difference from semi-arid plain to rainforest is great. Thus, experimentation has been crucial to farm success. Farmer Johan Woelke of Progreso is adamant that "the cows do not give as much milk here [in the south], barely two cans for eleven cows." He adds that the "calves were able to handle the heat as they grew," but adult cattle brought to the south from the north were not. At the least, farmers have been required to consider new sources of nutrition. Johan's neighbours, farmers Peter Hiebert and David Friesen, describe how native grasses left the cows undernourished and had to be replaced with "new grasses from Cuba [that] boosted milk production and maintained healthier cows." But they also point out that farmers in the south have had to treat their cows for ticks in a way that they did not in the north.

Many southern Mexico farm families have adapted by turning away from their traditional love of dairy farming to vegetable and fruit production. Peter Hiebert says that, since "dairying does not work" in the south, people are compelled to consider other ventures: "One makes charcoal from felled trees, and others raise 'greens'" as they "search for something else." Back in Zacatecas in the north, says Peter, "we had seven milk cows, cattle, pigs a bit, and seven hectares of land," but in Campeche they were able to "start with twenty-three hectares of land," so there was the opportunity to focus on commodity production. Heinrich Bueckert saw his opportunity in watermelons and is now considering papayas. But there the problem is that "the buyer needs two to five hectares of one kind [of crop]" to rationalize the purchase, and such a commitment is simply too risky. Less risky are limes, and to that end Heinrich has planted 700 lime trees that he received from the state agricultural agency for eight pesos each. The only real difficulty is that he has to wait two years before the trees reach maturity. He speaks as if experimenting is fundamental to adapting to a new land.

Some cultural limits have curtailed experimentation. Mennonites have hesitated to grow rice since it seems to be antithetical to their sensibilities as traditional grain and cattle producers, even though it has been supported by religious leaders. Elderly Peter Wiebe of Yalnon explains that "there is ... one village" set up for rice farming, but "few people are moving there.... Most are not interested in farming rice.... [It] must always be done in the mud!... Here they have not farmed rice before.... At first ... preachers moved there," but development "is happening quite slowly." Mennonites have long learned to manage water, removing it from swamps, adding it to parched land; they just haven't learned to work in it.

Old Colonists have also experimented with raising animals, either for food production or for energy sources. In Chavi, former *Vorsteher* Johan Dyck says that he "wants to dig a water pit and raise fish," something that Mennonites have not considered since their sixteenth-century Dutch ancestors plied the North Sea for fish and whales. Stranger still is an idea that David Friesen, the veterinarian from Progreso, relates. There are Mennonites raising deer, he says, a special breed "from Italy" and "a lot bigger" than regional deer. A deer farmer can fetch "8,000 pesos for one" since its meat is especially attractive to "tourists and sold ... internationally." Both less exotic and more practical is an idea on a way to produce a new source of gas, an idea Katherina Dyck from Progreso has heard about. She says that the "*Dietsche* do not want" electricity from the outside world, yet they use gas to power washing machines, refrigerators, ovens, ice boxes, and machine shops. For that reason, she was intrigued to hear about Mennonites "making gas from chicken dung in Belize." Fish production, deer hunting, and manure-derived gas signal the innovative edge of horse-and-buggy Mennonites.

They have also been innovative in simply increasing the sizes of their farms. Like all farmers, Old Colony Mennonites have had to adjust constantly to shifting market demands, varying commodity prices, and fluctuating input costs, all pressuring even the steel-wheel tractor people to embrace scales of economy if they can. Wilhelm Buhler of Riva Palacios farms 100 hectares and milks thirty cows, a large farm by Old Colony standards. Ask him why thirty cows, and he answers wryly and without elaboration that, if his family milked fewer cows, the "milk cheque would be smaller." But he does expound on the size of the family's land base. When Mennonites "first moved to Bolivia," says Wilhelm, "corn was a good-paying crop," but input costs have risen sharply, the cost of diesel tenfold. Then, too, "the price of corn is less now than it was then." Even an Old Colonist has to realize that corn is not profitable unless efficiency in growth is secured.

A more controversial strategy involving a certain embrace of modernity is the limited acceptance of chemicalized farming. At Manitoba Colony in Bolivia, Johan Knelsen says that he and others have "started to spray their fields in the last several years with Round Up ... [purchased] in Santa Cruz." He thinks that their crops would have performed better in other years too if they had been sprayed. Some farmers, such as Johan Klassen in East Paraguay, say bluntly that "agriculture has become a lot easier ... with the numerous new agrichemicals that ... kill all weeds, funguses, or pests." But he is apprehensive, since chemicals will fundamentally change agriculture. It becomes "more complicated each year because the genetically modified soybeans become vulnerable to new pests within a short time, and some weeds become immune to the herbicides, and so there are new seeds and agrochemicals each year." It's a problem all farmers experience who use herbicides, but for the Old Colonists another problem is that chemicalized farming drives a wedge between rich and poor farmers, for the poor ones "cannot afford to grow soybeans on their small pieces of land."

Other farmers say that they have had no choice but to use chemicals and hybrid seeds suggested by outside experts. Heinrich Bueckert of Yalnon celebrates southern Mexico's fertility, but the problem here is worms, so when "a Mexican said what to spray ... I did." But he too is apprehensive about the tropical climate inviting too great a reliance on chemicals. He contrasts the past with the present: "We [once] used very little chemicals, now [we] use so much insecticide, herbicide, and fertilizer. Back then we had a thousand kilograms of watermelons around five trees.... Now one can't grow them [cucumbers] because of too many insects.... The Mexicans said to us when we came not to shoot the white birds because the government brought them in to control the ticks on cattle." Heinrich would like to have the white birds back because he seems to have lost faith in chemicals. His neighbour, Reverend David Redekopp of Nuevo Durango, claims a similar compulsion to use hybrid corn seed, saying that it was easier to keep to the old ways in old Durango in northern Mexico. For example, upon arriving in southern Mexico, they were told to buy *hibrido* seed "because we heard one had to, otherwise it would not produce [in the semi-tropical climate]. I tried planting corn from seed brought from [old] Durango, but no ears appeared." In David's estimation, *hibrido* seed, that symbol of modern farming, has become a necessity in building an anti-modern society in the south.

Some families have resisted the new ways, and women in particular talk about returning to older patterns of farming. Frieda Guenther of Oriente Colony in Bolivia says that they "used to farm soybeans and sorghum" but have shifted back to "pasture land to focus more on milking and ... have been doing better now." Dairy farming is an old craft that relied on women, the traditional milkers, and it still engenders confidence among Mennonite farmers. On Manitoba Colony in Bolivia, Susie Knelsen is uneasy with the temptation to farm "more acres ... because the land is more fertile" and to put in at least two crops a year, "soya and corn in the summer and sorghum and sunflowers and wheat in the winter." Although the Knelsen farm at 250 hectares is one of the largest among Old Colonists in Bolivia, the Knelsens still have ten cows, fifty chickens, and several pigs on their commercialized farm. Why? Because "this is how we have always done it." A total reliance on cash crops is not an option among self-sufficient horse-and-buggy Mennonites.

Confronting Economic Limitations

Nor, given constant land shortages in agrarian communities with high fertility rates, has a reliance on crops been possible. Indeed, it has been a challenge to sustain large families on farms with a limited land base and reliant on primitive technology. Every Old Colonist has a story of how such hurdles can or have been overcome. The oldest strategy has been to supplement household income with non-agricultural forms of revenue. As the stories of three Shipyard Colony farmers demonstrate, Old Colonists think of themselves as historical agents, people with a range of options, including wage labour at the outset of adult life and then shifting to self-employed, household-based mechanics or small-scale manufacturing as the household becomes more established.

Farmers talk with ease about moving in and out of farming, and working with metal or wood or machines. Craft householders, farmers who turn natural products into sellable items, are perhaps the most common. Johan Neufeld explains that he "does a lot of different things to make money," farming a few pigs and cows, growing corn and sorghum, and making furniture, which he hauls every Friday to Belize City, where he "rents a small place" in the central market; what he "does not sell [he] leaves there for the next week." But Old Colonists are also machinists, known for their ability to fix the most challenging technical problems. Peter Friesen, a one-time lumber worker and now a small farmer, "fixes transmissions" with "parts imported from Mexico and the States and Guatemala," thus combining farming and mechanics and ensuring that, "whenever one goes bad, you have the other." Some farmers have procured additional income by capitalizing on specific anti-technology religious teachings of Old Colonists. Abram Redekopp, a one-time bulldozer operator, has linked to his vocations of farming and carpentry a craft reflecting the colony's rejection of electricity; he fixes "propane fridges," and he's "the only one in Belize who does this."

Similar vocational choices for landless Old Colonists have been the crafts linked to horse-and-buggy culture. Every colony has its harness makers. At Riva Palacios in Bolivia, for example, Abram Friesen built a harness shop behind the house one year, and here he still works with two employees. Although "leather is very expensive," he has "made more than a hundred harnesses and would have been able to sell more" if only he had been able to produce them. Other farmers have taken the basic Old Colony artifact, the horse-drawn buggy, and re-fashioned it for broader sales. At Nuevo Durango in southern Mexico, for example, veteran schoolteacher Isaac Wall has a *Schmäd*, "a shop" in which he builds wagons of all sorts, to date "seventeen buggies, the children's buggies, milk wagons—about forty-five." Reflecting a common adaptability, he also builds steel vises "to hold things one needs to work on." It's a skill that he learned when he found he needed a vise to build the buggies but did not have the means to purchase one.

Another set of farmers has gone in the opposite direction and be-come integrated into the wider Bolivian economy. At Riva Palacios, Peter Friesen operates his *Schmäd* based on a craft that he learned from his father in Mexico and one that he will pass on to his son Jacob. But his *Schmäd* is anything but traditional, because Peter uses it to build machines not used by Mennonites. He has developed sawdust blow-ers for mainstream Bolivian sawmill owners who like his machines because "they [don't] … have to pay men to haul the sawdust away in wheelbarrows." He recalls that his household finances were in desper-ate shape until his first sawdust blower contract, a turning point in his enterprise. Most recently, his *Schmäd* won a lucrative contract to make "rice machines [equipped with] Japanese motors for Japanese farmers." Although his *Schmäd* has grown to employ six men, Peter emphasizes that it is still located on his farmyard and will not develop into some kind of factory.

Indeed, the farm and farmyard have been front and centre in the household economy. Still, farmer David Friesen of Yalnon in southern Mexico says that Mennonites should care even more than they do about land and farming. He complains that "50 percent [of

Mennonites] are not cut out for" farming and "would rather work for someone else." The next step, he says, is a move to town, away from the colony and farm, where they will no longer be able to "grow things for ourselves." He can't imagine how the ordinary person in town, in Mexico, the United States, or Canada, survives economic crises. David preaches investment in farmland. For example, "our Jake thought of going to the States to make money, ... but then he had an opportunity to buy twenty hectares of land at 10,000 pesos, that was really cheap." He already had his buggy, a few cows, a house, and some furniture, so with this land purchase he was set. He knew that, if he sold "the cows and house, ... he would spend that money and have nothing in return.... The land [is] now ... worth three to four times as much.... It's always worth it to put money in land." But according to David, it has to be farmland: "Another fellow bought a piece of land at this end of the village for 35,000 pesos. It's just big enough to build a house and have a bit of a garden but not farmland. This was a waste of money because he cannot do anything with it to earn a living. It's not big enough to have cows on it either." Indeed, the only advantage is that the young man "can just be close to his mom." David's derision stems not from his view of kinship ties but from his belief in economically sound households based on farmland.

This expressed value of land has exhibited itself in numerous ways. The *Waisenamt* described above does more than ensure smooth inheritance processes; it also secures the generational succession of land. Levi Reimer of Santa Rita Colony is its *Waisenmaun*. He knows his way through the centuries-old set of bylaws dictating how estates are divided and bequeathed in Old Colony communities. He says that, upon the death of a parent, mother, or father, the farm is divided in half, with one part staying with the surviving spouse and the other half divided equally among all children, boys and girls alike. Levi knows that the process can cause parents distress, but ultimately the children benefit, and so does the community. The effect of this old practice on landholding is multiple. Because every adult is entitled to inherit at least some land, the inheritance system keeps households somewhat equal. It also means that farmland is transferred peacefully from one generation to the next, both technically and culturally. And it has kept the youth on the colony: better to have a hectare that you can see on the colony than the equivalent of two in the city that you can imagine.

Nevertheless, landlessness has been a long-standing problem in Mennonite history. Land hunger fuelled the historic migrations from West Prussia to Russia, from Russia to Manitoba and Kansas, and from western Canada to Mexico. For this reason, Old Colonists have had their commodity tax, using proceeds from it to buy tracts of land in Mexico, Paraguay, and Bolivia to assist the landless. But even this program has fallen short. Maria Wall of Sabinal in northern Mexico says that it was much easier purchasing the second fifty hectares than the first fifty. Every colony has instances of striking inequality, but in semi-arid Sabinal inequality is pronounced. One farm family, the Brauns, own 100 head of beef cattle, including calves, and milk thirty cows. They can also afford the diesel fuel to run the irrigation systems for the pastures. In contrast, Maria's household has only a small plot along the road running through the colony, a road said to be filling up with the landless. With their one cow, says Maria, they "send one can of milk to the cheese factory," but even this is not assured since they "have no pasture." It is an expression of need but also a disclosure of the social status of landlessness.

Some checks on inequality, however, have developed over time in every colony. In Nuevo Durango in southern Bolivia, *Vorsteher* Jacob Harder is about to leave on the eight-hour trip to Santa Cruz to register a land purchase just outside the colony when I meet him. This land will be parcelled out for purchase by eager Old Colony farmers not allowed to purchase land of their own outside colony lands. Nor are they allowed to mortgage their holdings on the colony since doing so will merely exacerbate inequalities among farm families. More specific rules discourage inequality. Well-to-do Manitoba Colony farmer Peter Knelsen, for example, explains that he has come up against colony rules prohibiting him from purchasing more than twenty-five hectares on the new colony of California unless he moves there. *Vorsteher* Johan Dyck of Chavi in southern Mexico has acted retroactively to encourage equality. When Chavi was being settled, farmers were initially limited to purchasing ten hectares of good farmland, and twenty hectares of sandy, hilly land, thus equalizing things. But even then, after clearing the jungle, it became apparent that "we did not all have the same luck," for some of the land that had appeared good before clearing took place turned out to be sandy, so the lucky ones were asked to return some of their good land or "repay a bit to the *Jemeent* ... treasury."

Each colony also developed a program to help the destitute, even if somewhat grudgingly. The poor are pressed to care for themselves, if possible, within colony borders, an attitude that has encouraged out-migration to Canada or the United States. The poor do what they can. At Sabinal, for example, where young Abram Braun injured his spine one year, leaving him in a wheelchair, his wife, Aganetha, says that she "fabric-paints handkerchiefs and sells them in sets of three ... at the fabric store for fifty-five pesos a set"; these handkerchiefs are popular on the colony, especially at Christmastime. Her "husband makes chairs for sale," welding "the frames and then weaving the seat and back with plastic cords," and he "weaves laundry baskets in the same way." As a family, they have also made a small wage by sorting chilies, and selling milk from the eight cows they milk.

Families in dire circumstances—because of death, abandonment, imprisonment, alcoholism—have long come to expect help from the *Armen Kasse,* the "poor man's chest." As Peter Enns of Shipyard explains, "if a man has an accident and the family needs money for an operation, they get the money from a [special] collection in church" without any expectation of repayment. But money is rarely distributed without strings attached. A widow, for example, says Peter, "can go to the deacon," who can approve a credit line for her at the store. And, as Reverend Aron Guenther says of his colony, though "the poor would get help from the *Armen Kasse,*" at least half also receive counselling, "to watch how they spend their money, not live too rich." Aganetha, his wife, offers as an example the quip "not buy too much soda."

If the watchful eye of the deacon has caused some humiliation, so has a household's downward spiral to a point where it needs direct support. Middle-aged widow Aganetha Wall of Yalnon knows first-hand the feeling of poverty: "[At] first we made charcoal, but now that is not enough.... I have three grown boys, but ... no one has money to hire them.... The [cows] give twenty litres, but I let the children drink it. When one is poor, then one has to let them have something.... They have some sugar, milk, and tortilla flour and drink that, and then they have had something. I am also in debt to the store." Poverty is difficult to escape when the entire colony is just beginning, suffering the woes of all pioneers or the travails of a weather-related downturn in the local economy. Widow Katherina Dyck says that she did not "borrow money when [her] calf was starving to death" because "borrowing money is not that easy." Her colony had virtually nothing to spare; it's especially difficult to be poor on a poor colony.

All colonies have embraced a culture of neighbourly care, helping to till the fields of an accident victim or organizing meals for families in need. Sometimes the only obstacle to the smooth functioning of such aid has been the pride of the designated recipient. At Sabinal Colony, widow Justina[2] Klassen, mother of eighteen children, recalls that some years ago Elisabeth[3] Fehr, the wife of a former *Vorsteher*, was laid up. Justina initiated a food ring by sending around a *Satel*, "a sign-up sheet," for all village women to indicate when they could provide the Fehrs with a meal, even though the Fehrs were well-to-do. Embarrassed, the *Vorsteher* stopped the circulation of the sign-up sheet when it came by his house, objecting that "he didn't want the village looking after him." Nor did he want to "give the impression that his [adult] children weren't willing to take care of their mother anymore." Justina ignored the *Vorsteher*'s objections and merely reissued another *Satel*, this time sending it around in the opposite direction to avoid having the *Vorsteher* find out. Evidently, the new method succeeded, and the village women were able to devise a meal distribution plan. Later Justina herself was laid up, and the village women organized themselves so that "each household [took] its turn in bringing her food" for a two-week period. It was a reciprocal action that Justina, for one, did not reject.

Children in need have also been looked after by neighbours and colony officials. Childhood can be an especially difficult time in a society that takes no or little aid from the state. The death of a spouse or alcoholism of a breadwinner has led to severe social problems in a family, and it has not been uncommon for the *Jemeent* to intervene, usually through the *Vorstehers*. When the extended family has been available, a seamless transition has ensued. In a double tragedy one year, Johan and Liesbeth Wall's young married son died from electrocution on Manitoba Colony, and shortly thereafter their young married daughter died in childbirth. Suddenly, the Walls had two sets of grandchildren with only one young parent each. When their widowed son-in-law "went back to live with his parents," the Walls took in the infant granddaughter as their own child. By happenstance, some time later, the Walls' widowed son-in-law married their widowed daughter-in-law, and they had their own children, but they never challenged the role of the Walls as surrogate parents of the little girl.

The process of caring for vulnerable children has been more complicated without kinship networks to address difficult domestic situations. In such cases, children have been divided up by the *Jemeent*. Foster parents readily tell of such instances. At Riva Palacios in Bolivia, Wilhelm and Anna Buhler have two unmarried daughters, Katherine and Anita, but they also have adopted siblings, Fred and Eleanor,[4] from a large family "after their mother died." Anna says that in their case the *Jemeent* intervened because the children's father was deemed "incapable of looking after" them for personal reasons. Because Anna had "always wanted more" children, especially because two of hers had died in infancy, she approached the *Vorsteher*s as soon as she heard that the *Jemeent* was intervening. At first she "put in my request for the youngest girl," but later the Buhlers also adopted one of the boys. In Sabinal in northern Mexico, Wilhelma Penner describes a similar situation. She and her husband took in three children at the request of the *Vorsteher*s after "not a very good man," who had forced his family to "live off of the *Jemeent*," died. As Wilhelma recalls it, "Peter and Elizabeth, a set of twins, were twelve years old, and we took them in, and so we had three 'babies'": that is, the foster twins and the Penners' own "'baby' at home." Then, when the mother died in 2003, the Penners took in a third child, Tina, from the troubled family. It's a system of mutual care that serves the community well.

Disabled children have also been able to expect assistance even though no institutions or special education programs exist for them. One such source is the *Waisenverordnung* that dictates an inheritance double the size for children with disabilities. In addition, a culture of sympathy gives the disabled credit for even a bit of productivity in the agrarian community. Former schoolteacher Franz Wall of Yalnon explains that "there is one man in the colony who is blind and crippled, but he can reason.... The other day I asked him what work he had done that day, and he said he had brought the whey from the street to the barn." In a society that has accepted only a low level of technology, any work-related activity receives a nod of approval.

Healing the Sick

Providing health care has been another concern among Old Colonists. They certainly have made use of modern medicine, travelling to Santa Cruz, Casas Grandes, Hopelchén, Belize City, or other nearby cities to access highly regarded medical practitioners. But doctors have also come to them. In Mexico, home to a foundationary state-run medical system, doctors or nurses often travel out to the colonies. On Nuevo Durango, Campeche, for example, residents revere their local "Dr." Heinrich Peters, not only for his folk medicine, but also for his authority arising from accompanying state-licensed nurses and a doctor on their semi-monthly visits to the colony. But this system does not address emergencies. When accidents occur on this colony, says Aganetha Guenther, trucks are hired to take the injured to a regional hospital. In cases in which they have not been available, someone has been sent to the Mayan village of Ramon Caron, ten kilometres away, to hire a truck.

Given their distance from regional cities, however, most colonies have produced their own "doctors." Some are male, most are female, though often it is a couple who operate a medical centre. And, as with all local know-how, knowledge in the birthing clinics, *farmacias,* or chiropractic rooms has been transferred informally from generation to generation. But the effect of an entrepreneurial spirit cannot be exaggerated. Elisabeth Hildebrandt of Nuevo Durango, East Paraguay, has worked as a chiropractor, midwife, and unlicensed pharmacist since she was seventeen. She learned her healing skills from her father. And, following his example, she has "read a lot in books in German on different types of therapies." In 2003, after the colony's "Dr." Isaac Hildebrandt moved to Bolivia, Elisabeth established her own birthing clinic, Clínica Lucero, as well as a pharmacy. Her income has increased considerably since she began operating her very "own clinic." In the fifteen years since she delivered her first baby, in 1994, she has overseen the births of 1,400 babies, about 100 a year, only half of whom were Mennonite, the other half Paraguayan or Brazilian. She has developed a broad client base, in part because the price of 360,000 guaranies (eighty dollars US) is affordable, but also because she comes from a recognized medical lineage.

Other women, however, have struck out on their own, without having been raised in a "medical" household. Some entries into the medical world were rather simple, some even occurred by happenstance. Sara Hildebrandt[5] of Sabinal, in northern Mexico, is a local dealer for Herbal Life, a diet supplement. She says she used to be overweight, and it badly affected her life since even washing dishes was an effort. So she went to Cuauhtémoc for medical advice, and there a "*Dietsche* woman gave [me] some Herbal Life, and it helped very much." When the woman in Cuauhtémoc asked "if there would be other people on Sabinal that would benefit from Herbal Life," Sara agreed. Today she is the product's agent on her colony. Katherina Teichrob of Valle Nuevo, Bolivia, also entered the medical world by chance, even though she had a long-held interest in the field. She is both a textile store owner and masseuse who goes to Santa Cruz weekly to "buy supplies." She started her business simply because it interested her, always thinking that she "would like to be either a doctor or run a store." Her reflexology massage practice began some fourteen years ago when "some *Dietsche* from Morgenland Colony came to Swift Colony to do reflexology." She then ran with her curiosity and learned the skill from other Mennonites as well as from medical books in the German language. "Doctoring doesn't run in the family," but like her grandmother she "is always full of ideas of things to do." And when she sees an opportunity she takes it.

Some medical practitioners speak of having combined a curiosity with a simple need to make a living. At Yalnon, widow Anna Wiebe recalls both her parents as medical practitioners and her mother as an especially knowledgeable "doctor": "My mother always said that if she wrote a book it would be very thick; she could have told you a lot of things.... She was thirty-five when she started. I think she was seventy-four when she died." But the way that she began the practice with her husband was simple enough: "My parents were always poor, ... schoolteachers for seventeen winters.... Then they became doctors, and ... people would come to them for sicknesses, to sew together wounds and attend births." Working from their three-room house, they operated a thriving business. Sure, in time "they got old and worn out, ... but they were known far and wide.... David and Anna (Penner) Bueckert.... [They had both] doctor rooms and birth rooms.... They learned it [all] on their own." But Anna still wonders if perhaps it was "because they were poor [that] they were sought out" and given recompense.

The idea of working together as partners, combining specific skills and aptitudes under one roof, has been at the foundation of other practices. Franz and Susie Rempel of Valle Nuevo in Bolivia say that they have worked well together, he as a pharmacist and she as a chiropractor and midwife. His busy *farmacia* has its roots in the parent colony, Swift Current, near Santa Cruz, but he admits that he has not "studied medicine anywhere." Rather, "having learned some English," he has been able to read relevant books as well as the "labels on some medication." Susie speaks of having come to her craft out of simple curiosity: she "always wanted to do this kind of work but only started when [the] children were out of *Kindheit* ['childhood']" and has now "been doing it for fifteen years." She "has sewn closed a lot of wounds" and is good at it in part because "it doesn't bother me at all"; she "can handle the blood."

Sometimes the couple-run medical household has taken off because grown children have learned to participate. At Progreso in southern Mexico, Elisabeth and Isaac Dyck work together, she as a midwife and he as a pharmacist. But in addition they employ their grown, unmarried daughters as denturists, and they add to the household income by constructing up to two sets of false teeth per month at a cost of 2,000 pesos ($150 US) per set. The entire family is very busy: the pharmacy has its "office hours," from 8 a.m. to 12 p.m. and from 3 p.m. to 6 p.m., but "this is just a suggestion because people show up at any time of the day." But when a woman goes into labour, Helena "is often on duty in the evening and overnight." Clearly, she relies on a supportive household to carry on her busy life.

Some of the local "doctors," and especially the women, have established themselves simply by being assertive and claiming an authoritative knowledge of medicine. Helena Dyck of Chavi speaks about her calling as the "will of God" but then recites six specific reasons for her skill and reputation, most of which speak of a self-confidence arising from experience. First, having twelve children of her own made her believe that she knew what she was talking about when she spoke about the body. Second, her own *"Muddakje* [affection-ate for 'mother'] has also often done [midwifery and] ... told me many things." Third, she has "a book, ... well, two books, one book that includes all that sort of stuff in High German, ... [including] pictures and explanation, a bit like how that must be done," a book obtained from "old [midwife Hiebert], who ... bequeathed it to us." Fourth, Helena knows her limits: she once tried to deliver twins, and though "one was born here ... the other lay at the top, and they had to send [the mother] away to the city" for a C-section, and even the one born on the colony was "'half a mistake'....yes, that one died." Fifth, she has acquired supplemental training from government-ordered medi-cal workshops: "A couple of weeks ago," for example, "we had to for one day ... go back to school," and she learned "how I am supposed to keep things organized, how things are all arranged in women['s bod-ies], and how the doctors work, when they use precautions, making sure one does not give someone medicine that is too strong.... When to know when a woman is in trouble and needs to be sent away." And sixth, she is simply innately confident. She describes what happens when a woman goes into labour without a shred of self-doubt: "I give the intravenous [for pain] before the baby comes. I mix the medicine with the saline solution. That is medicine to stop the progress of the labour.... I can set it ... for how quickly I want it to drip.... And, if it is not yet time [for the baby to come], then I put her to the side and wait for another week or two."

This innate confidence among local medical practitioners has been noticed and reinforced among neighbours. Frieda Klassen[6] of Sabinal in northern Mexico recalls a time when she suffered either a broken or sprained arm requiring surgery in the hospital in the city. She remembers that her neighbour, "Chiropractor" Katherina Friesen, the mother of fourteen children, approached her and "claimed that she could have fixed [my] arm just as well as the operation." Frieda's daughters doubted the claim, but Frieda herself says that, if only she had known this, she would have given herself to Mrs. Friesen's care.

Within their colonies, Mennonites tell stories of being self-sufficient, offering special respect to those who take care of one another.

Conclusion

Old Colony Mennonites like talking about their complex community networks. Their locally constituted institutions have addressed a wide range of concerns, while their locally structured economies have produced livelihoods close to nature that rely on family and neighbourhood networks. The various forms of mutual aid have included everything from fire insurance to zero-interest loans for the poor and outright gifts to the distressed. The *Waisenamt* has ensured the orderly transfer of property from one generation to the other. A wider colony administration operating by democratic principle and a taxation and land ownership system based on honour has kept the colony functioning peaceably. A local village authority has had charge of roadways and schools and the first line of mutual aid and conflict resolution. All of these systems have their histories, dating to Mennonite sojourns in Canada and earlier in Russia, West Prussia, and the Netherlands.

Of course, social adaptations have occurred in Latin America, but they relate more to new economic and environmental necessities than to any shift from a communitarian concern. The need to produce new commodities in new climates for unfamiliar markets has spawned new forms of cooperation. Where Old Colonists once employed the cooperative model of ownership only for the old village cheese factory, in Paraguay and Mexico in particular, cooperatives have formed to support the production and export of grain commodities. But no one suggests that these cooperatives have shifted the meaning and substance of their horse-and-buggy ways.

Over the years a wide variety of other adaptations secured rural life, within semi-tropical climates. Agricultural adaptation allowed Mennonite migrations from semi-arid to semi-tropical locations. Farm practices changed with advice from local indigenous groups or because of the less welcome policies of intrusive, modern, national government departments. Other economic adaptations reflected the combination of land shortages, high birth rates, and resistance to any form of urbanization. A host of new craft industries arose, requiring mechanical, wood-based, and technological expertise, based not on education but on inventive spirit. Given their worry about urban life, Old Colonists established their own, local medical culture. To that end, hundreds of Old Colony Mennonites, especially women, usually equipped with natural talent, inherited aptitude, and self-education, opened pharmacies and clinics, providing rudimentary medical care.

Their stories of adaptation illustrate a flexibility required to maintain the local community. They show how the Old Colonists' careful innovations have enabled old and even ancient patterns of organization to continue. And that continuity has ensured the reproduction of the social and cultural bases of Old Colony Mennonites in the Americas.

CHAPTER FIVE

Nurturing Family
the Old Colony Way

"[It's] because they love children so much..."

From a knoll beside an abandoned railway track, you can see the entire spread of Sabinal Colony, the only remaining horse-and-buggy Mennonite community in northern Mexico. Situated in an austere desert valley within the eastern Sierra Madre, Sabinal consists of half a dozen villages laid out in a perfect grid featuring grey cement houses, straight fencelines, and an occasional green field. The colony is widely known as a community in need. High fuel prices and a prohibition on the use of electricity have turned this irrigation-dependent community into a place of seemingly perpetual drought. The *National Geographic*'s *Living in a Perfect World* and a Dutch journalist's *The Fehr Family* have memorialized Sabinal's stubborn clinging to old ways. I have travelled by truck from Nuevo Casas Grandes with Ann and Jake Enns, who know Sabinal well. I want to see it firsthand and find it even more bitterly and eerily barren than I could have imagined. I am relieved to learn of Sabinal's plans to transplant to the semi-tropical south in Quintana Roo, a place where primitive farming methods can succeed.

During our twenty-four-hour stay, I hope for answers about how these people have maintained stubborn anti-modern ways and what holds them together in this bleak land.[1] We visit three homes and attend the early-Sunday-morning Old Colony worship service. As we do so, the physical austerity gradually becomes overshadowed by social warmth, and the apparent lifelessness slowly turns to vibrant activity. The reason is simple: intertwined in the very fabric of these communities is the family and the imperative of its reproduction. At the first home, that of Johan and Helena Krahn,[2] the *Vorsteher* and his wife, we sit with Helena and a dozen quiet children, waiting for Johan to arrive from the colony office. When he pulls up in his buggy, eight-year-old Margaretha[3] bolts out to greet him, screeching delightfully that visitors from the city are here; then as he alights she grabs the horse's reins and, without further ado, leads the horse to the water trough. At the second home that we visit, that of David and Esther Krahn,[4] the harness makers, I chat with their son Johan,[5] barely twenty, and he tells me his dream. It's a life with his *Schatze* (literally "treasure," his girlfriend), whom he plans to marry that spring right after Pentecost. He says that he can hardly wait.

We spend the night at the Krahns' home, and early the next morning we travel in silence by buggy to the grey adobe church building. During the hour-long sermon read in High German, the minister breaks away from his text to thank the youth—in Low German—for having gathered at the bedside of Grandmother Friesen to sing songs of comfort to her in her last hour. She is not the only grandmother of whom we hear that day. We planned to return to Nuevo Casas Grandes right after church, but then Helena Hiebert sees us and simply insists that we drop by for *Faspa*. When we arrive to partake of "the Sunday-afternoon meal," we find a farmyard full of Helena's joyful, lively grandchildren playing and in the living room half a dozen brothers and brothers-in-law scheming to make a move to a more well-watered climate in the south.

Little Margaretha, young Johan, the Hiebert brothers, the assertive Helena, the dying grandmother—these people are the grist of life in this place in the desert. Old Colonists find their moorings within family and are compelled by the logic of generational succession. They plan for marriage, embrace lively children, meet to talk about family and land, and revere grandparents. Primary loyalties are fixed in the family, where plans for physical survival are considered, debated and finalized. The family is the backbone of the community; its reproduction ensures continuation of the Old Colony community and way of life. Family is important in all cultural groups—its success can signal upward mobility in middle-class societies, its reunification the highest priority in refugee communities, its privacy a haven in a hurried urban world. But here, among Old Colony Mennonites, success is measured by how fully one has helped the next generation establish their own agrarian, landed households.

This pursuit for generational succession is also what Old Colonists say that family history means. It is about the generations: it recounts the infants, young courters and newly wedded, struggling household-ers, middle-aged matriarchs and patriarchs, and elders and their suf-fering that precedes the end of life. And these stories tell of moments of succession: times of handing off and maturing, of passing on and letting go. They constitute the record of building the foundation of the Old Colony community and its values.

Here is an anti-modern culture that has unfolded in everyday life through the family. It's a social and cultural dialectic that has moved along from one generation to the next, following the inexorable cycle of life—from infancy to old age. And it has been held in place by an overarching commitment to agraria, to simple technologies, to changelessness, to the "way we've always done it." History for Old Colonists is less about change over time than about passing change-lessness along from one generation to the next. In this respect, the family is at the centre of their cultural project.

Infants and New Life

Mothers like to talk about how infants have arrived, one after the other, in steady succession. They are more reticent about speaking about birth control, not allowed by their church, not an unusual prohibition in the history of Christianity and one that Old Colonists have usually obeyed. In the past, families of twelve or more children were common, but more recently the number has dropped to about eight. Elderly Anna Banman of Valle Esperanza, Bolivia, puts it more bluntly than anyone: "The women don't have the *Frieheit* ['permission' in Low German] to have fewer children unless the woman is sick; that might be why some women have fewer children than before." The health of a woman has become more important, ironically because modern medicine makes good health possible. Still, pregnancy is seen as inevitable, an unchangeable natural phenomenon in which no one should interfere. Anna's own "children all came very quickly, one soon after the other, although the last ones were spread out a bit more." Anna has lived a life revered in Old Colony culture.

But birth rates are determined not only by the question of *Frieheit.* There is also the peasant logic that many hands address the problem of many mouths, indeed that households cannot be reproduced without having children. Anna Friesen[6] of Shipyard, Belize, recalls how numerous children affected her household's viability: "I was very poor at home till I was thirteen years old; then my other siblings and I could help, and things started to get better." But Old Colonists also speak of the simple love that they have for children. Grandmother Elisabeth Harder of Sabinal says that the doctor told her daughter to "use birth control" after she bore "four children in very short order." Elisabeth also counselled her daughter against becoming pregnant too quickly, assuring her quietly that fewer conceptions "wouldn't be a problem" since she wouldn't necessarily need to "take something for birth control." Ultimately, however, the "daughter and her husband didn't heed the doctor's advice." Why? "Because they love children so much, they're *Kjinga Frind,*" "friends of children." Most Old Colonists don't think that they need to answer the question of why they have many children; they are a divine gift.

Belonging to large families has brought with it an enhanced social status. Old Colonists like citing facts about large families. Franz Penner of Shipyard recites his blended family's particulars: "I was born in Mexico on March 16, 1930, in the Swift Colony in Chihuahua. I come from a family of twenty. Ten children were born to my father's first wife and then ten more to his second wife, which was my mom. I am the second oldest. My youngest sister was born March 17, 1949; she is only a few months older than my oldest son. My wife and I got married June 1949." It seems to matter to Franz that no gap in the generations exists; his sister became an aunt within months of being born. But mothers also speak about the joy that comes with being a parent to many children. Katherina Teichrob of Bolivia says that she "has always been happy in Valle Nuevo," in large measure because of her nine children ages three to twenty-two, seven girls and two boys. But she felt sorry for her husband when they moved to this new colony on her account. It was a move from more fertile Swift Current near Santa Cruz to this "drier region" of the Oriente, which so far has produced only "poor crops." She isn't sure that he has had as much to live for as she has with her family intact.

If the number of children has been left to nature, so has childbirth itself. Women still give birth naturally, even in societies in which C-sections are common. Indeed, typically the only outside help has come from the local Mennonite midwife, a woman of authority, knowledge, and psychological insight. Increasingly, Old Colony mothers have come to proto-clinics like the one run by midwife Helena Dyck of Chavi in southern Mexico. At the height of her practice, some years ago, Helena delivered fifty-seven babies, but more recently the number has been only about forty. Young mothers have tended to come and go quickly, says Helena: "As soon as they are well enough," they go home. "We keep them here about twelve [hours], that depends on the partner, sometimes longer ... if they are [not] from [our] village." In her career, she has also visited the women before their deliveries: "We have always had it that if they want to have it here then they have to let me come and see them first so I can be prepared, ... get to know the woman ... and send them away ... to the city [if necessary]." Women remember giving birth in previous decades in more precarious conditions. The large families today are testimony of greater access to modern medicine.

The infant's particular place within Old Colony families has been announced by use of the English word *baby,* the name of the youngest child until she or he is bumped from that place by the next birth. Like babies elsewhere, Old Colony infants have their roles to play in cultural continuity. Parents comment on inherited appearances, linking children to kinship lines. Sometimes the baby's appearance invokes kind-hearted humour. Johan Neudorf from Del Sur, Bolivia, knows that he is clever with his joke: "Have you heard of the twins who really looked alike, especially the one?" Franz Wall from Yalnon is similarly funny, but his joke references his own family. He once asked the family doctor why the Wall "children have red hair," unusual among these Mennonites, and the doctor explained that the red hair "comes from Holland." Franz says that the answer makes no more sense than if he were to say that "he is blond from carrying sacks of flour in Durango when he worked for a store."

More obvious linkages of children to their kin networks than their appearances are their names. Children are identified as belonging to particular households and to particular clans upon birth, connecting them indelibly to earlier generations. In Swift Colony, all of Katherina Friesen's twelve children were named after other family members: Lisa, after her maternal grandmother; Marie, after her paternal grandmother; Peter, after his paternal grandfather and father; Margareta, after a paternal aunt; Aganetha, after a maternal aunt; Abram, after his maternal grandfather; Lena, after both maternal and paternal aunts; Tina, after a paternal aunt; Johan, after both maternal and paternal uncles; Katherina, after her mother; Jacob, after both maternal and paternal uncles; and Anne, after a maternal aunt. Katherina confesses that none of her daughters carries her own mother's name, the unusual Wilhelmina. She explains that her mother "was mercilessly teased" about it, and thus she asked Katherina "not [to] name a daughter after her," but instead to honour her with the name Lisa, that of the maternal grandmother.

Old Colonists see childhood as the time to train a child in the humble and simple ways of the elders, and they have specific views on disciplining children. They recall the historic warning of Ältester Bernard Peters that parents obey the gospel and teach their children the "way by which a disciple of Jesus should live."[7] In less opaque language, Abram Redekopp of Shipyard Colony says that he wants his children to "hold on to what they have been taught." He also reads the Bible to them, emphasizing obedience. When he disciplines them, he does so first with a warning, and then, if they don't obey, he spanks them. Other parents have been stricter than Abram, more focused on another text of Ältester Peters based on the apocryphal book of Sirach, that "a horse not broken becometh headstrong: and a child left to himself will be willful."[8] Although Abram agrees with this teaching, he says that it has been "corrupted" by some parents, and he disparages the actions of a neighbour who routinely "abuses his kids" and even "swears" at them. The idea that discipline involves the exercise of dominance of parent over child is dismissed by other Old Colonists who emphasize the importance of a child's sense of submission to a higher social authority. Peter Hiebert of Progreso, Mexico, sums up his view on true discipline by weaving together the roles of the church, school, and family: "We have the church when they are out of school" and before that the "home to teach them what is written in the Bible, and that way they are taught."

Despite their willingness to talk about disciplining children, the overall picture of childhood described by most Old Colonists invokes images of a carefree life on the farm and within nature. There are stories of children outdoors, among animals, being active. Margaretha Rempel of Nuevo Durango, East Paraguay, says that she can still "remember the starlit sky in Mexico on cold winter nights, while we lay in the back of the buggy, wrapped in blankets, staring at the sky while we returned from visiting relatives in another village." And now in East Paraguay she is a mother who enjoys lying in the garden with her own children at night watching the stars and playing "spot-a-satellite." It is a night sky available to children in communities without light pollution from streetlights. The daylight takes children into farmyards, into the worlds of their parents at work, or onto swing sets, or simply into some make-believe world in a corner of the farmyard. The low level of technology on the farm makes it a relatively safe place to play at will, but some form of order is inscribed in children at a young age. Justina Klassen of Sabinal explains that her three-year-old daughter has no fear of a turkey in their yard, "equal to her in size," because she has been taught to "carry a stick and whack the turkey if it comes too close." Justina says that now "children play outside without any worries," anywhere in the yard, or on the swing set.

Reflections on childhood invariably bring recollections of work on the farm. It seems to be a particular point of pride to be able to recount how children learned to work at a young age. Marie Hamm of Riva Palacios in Bolivia says that when her Justina was seven she "was very anxious to start milking" but was told that "she would have to wait until she was twelve": that is, when a girl stops attending school and is expected to begin the apprentice years in the farm household. Heinrich Wolfe of Shipyard attended school, as all boys do, until he was thirteen but recalls that he "started to work when I was six years old, doing chores like milking the cow and all that," and later, presumably at thirteen, he helped his father to sell lumber from a British-owned sawmill at Little Belize. He emphasizes a skill learned and a parental relationship, without a sense that he was shortchanged as a child.

But work is not just about learning skills but also about learning the basics of economic exchange. At the Hiebert residence in Riva Palacios, Isaac (thirteen) and Johan (fifteen)[9] have been raising rabbits for sale in Santa Cruz, charging fifteen bolivianos per rabbit. Young Isaac says that he "feeds them and cleans their pens" and that he "can tell when a doe will deliver because she pulls hair off herself to build a nest as well as collects grass." He would raise doves, but the price for a dove is so low that it doesn't "pay, even if ... sold in fancy restaurants in Santa Cruz." He is aware of both the cost of production and market demand. At the Klassen residence at Sabinal, ten-year-old Maria[10] says that she knows "all about the animals," including how profitable they are. She reports that her family has "three horses and three young ones," which the family intends to sell. Each day she milks only one cow, but she knows how much milk each of the other cows gives. She even corrects her mother and aunt that their two calves were not given to them by their neighbour but purchased for a total of 200 pesos. Isaac and Maria have both been socialized well in ensuring the economic well-being of the farm household.

The years of apprenticeship coincide with the years of *Rommdriewen*, what the Amish famously call *Rumspringa* and the English peasants call "sowing wild oats." It's a time of tolerated youthful wildness, mostly in the unlit village streets, after dark or during daytime on Sunday afternoons. Adults bemoan this time, almost an obligatory disapproval, even though, if pressed, most say that they too experienced their own *Rommdriewen.* Grandmother Anna Thiessen of Colonia Trinidad expresses an old sentiment when she describes *Rommdriewen:* "Like here too, here on a Sunday, one would not go to the corner, that is not pleasant; there are about twenty or thirty boys, not?.... They have a bit of beer and are drinking a bit and have a bit of music, and what kind of trouble do they make? They make no trouble." Her point is that *Rommdriewen* is tolerable if it occurs on the village's own streets; add a car and a drive to the city, and then there would be trouble. And this is the conclusion of Abram Redekopp of Shipyard, Belize. He says that *Rommdriewen* is "a stage in young people's lives when they are very rebellious" but a state that can be tolerated. The problem is that yesteryear's youth were different from today's youth, who want "to hear the loud guitar and rock music and reggae" blaring from "ghetto blasters on their buggies [as they] drive through the *Darp.*" Technology has allowed the world to come to the colonies, and parents have little recourse. Frieda Guenther[11] of Colonia Oriente in Bolivia, however, says that, when she sees youth "drinking alcohol and chewing coca on Wednesdays and Sundays," she wishes that parents would more proactively "teach the children about the Bible." Still, it is Anna's laissez-faire approach and not Frieda's more moralistic vision that has shaped the culture of youth on the colonies over the years.

The idea that *Rommdriewen* is a natural time in the life cycle of every Old Colonist dovetails with the idea that youth naturally organize themselves into social groups. Their leisure time is spent on the street or in some village home. The Klassen children at Sabinal Colony in northern Mexico, for example, have their own social groups: Sarah heads to Village 4 to find her group of sixteen girls, a number that rises to twenty-six at Christmas when the girls "pull tickets" to determine who buys whom a gift; Susanna finds her group in Village 3, her home village; and Agatha meets "with another group of [single] women over thirty ... from a variety of villages." The younger two girls find their counterparts on the street. But being on the street is generally not worrisome for the parents. In fact, middle-aged Johan Woelke at Progreso in southern Mexico recalls with gratitude the day that his son, depressed and lonely, was invited by other youth to join them in fun: we "saw some girls and boys come down the street toward our place, and we thought, 'We'll see what it gives,' and they got him to laugh!... The next day he came and asked how he could help in building our house." To have been on the street in this instance was to have become accepted by the youth of the colony.

For all the talk of strictness in the colonies, of needing to break the innate rebelliousness of the child, childhood is recalled as a surprisingly relaxed time. Adults remember being trained mostly by example, in worlds close to nature, and without the pressures of a middle-class adolescence: that is, the idea that vulnerable teenagers need special activities to rein in youthful energies. Letting the teenagers go for a time, within some limits, has long been seen as natural conditioning for eventual participation in adult life.

Courtship and Camaraderie

The time of being on the street is somewhat controversial, however, because it also coincides with the time of increasing sexual desire and curiosity. Girls and boys tend to move in gender-specific groups, but rumours do circulate of sexual impropriety and perniciousness. Still, the street is mostly the avenue for a centuries-old and, in some ways, tightly regulated courting ritual. Certainly, Mennonite leaders in nineteenth-century Russia and early-twentieth-century Canada complained about unruly youth on village streets, acting "like the world" in wooing partners, singing irreverent Low German love songs, and participating in subversive acts of charivari. But the street has played an important role in courtship.

Indeed, time and again, oldtimers talk about first meeting their spouses on the street. Sometimes it happened when "strange" boys from another village came "cruising" in their buggies or when familiar neighbourhood boys gathered in "herds" at street corners. Aganetha Wall of Yalnon, Mexico, explains the process from her experience: "The girls go onto the street in the afternoon [of a Sunday] with the boys, and they find out whom they like, and then if it happens that they like each other then they discuss meeting in the evening. The boy comes to the girl's house, and she asks her parents if they can visit, and they visit in the summer room…. [And then] you .:. find out if you get along…. Our children are all happy; they all found partners in this colony [that way]." What began as an open practice, meeting on the street, quickly became regulated once partners had been selected.

Other oldtimers recall first meeting their future spouses while working in neighbouring households as servants or day labourers. Peter Jantzen of East Paraguay says that he began dating his future wife, Elisabeth Hildebrandt, when he was working for her parents. Elisabeth Harder of Sabinal talks about meeting her future husband, Franz, during the corn harvest. She tells a story of quiet romance. She was engaged to Heinrich Braun, but then tragically "he and his eleven-year-old brother were killed by lightning." Over a two-year period, she "saw other boys but [never] felt right about any of them." Then came a day when she and her two closest girlfriends and several boys worked in the corn harvest, cutting down rows of corn, each allotted a row. At some point, she "noticed that a good bit of [her] row had been cut down already," and she was told by another worker that "it was Franz Harder who had done that." She doesn't say when the courtship began; what matters is that this act of kindness led to her marriage to Franz in 1973.

Old Colonists usually describe a dating ritual lasting at least a year, most dates taking place at the girl's house and being regulated by parental rules. Peter Friesen of Shipyard recalls that his future wife was "nineteen years [old] when we started visiting [according to some] very strict hours. On Sunday two hours from 7 to 9 p.m.…. After that, I got one hour on Wednesday, in the evening, from 7 to 8 [p.m.]." Always the location of dating was clearly demarcated: "Visiting took place inside the house, in the kitchen. It was just the two of us, but her mom and dad would be in another room." Other Old Colonists suggest that the sanctioned place could also include the summer kitchen, or even the girl's bedroom, understood to be a public space. And dating, says Peter, consisted of talking: "We would talk about all kinds of things, what we did during the week, making huge plans and never getting anywhere." Yet, in his case, the events did lead somewhere. As he puts it, "we dated for one year and got baptized in that same year, both of us at one time, … and got married November 15, 1980."

Like dating couples everywhere, some Old Colonists do recall pushing acceptable courting standards. David Penner says that, when his family moved to Shipyard from Canada in 1966, he as a sixteen-year-old spent much time in Neuendorf, that is, Camp 17, as he and his friends "found the most girls" there. He recalls that his brother was especially drawn to one of Peter Dyck's three daughters, so they "would sneak up to the house and shine flashlights into the house," enough to aggravate the father, who "chased us away." David doesn't offer whether a lasting relationship resulted from the flashlight affair. But Sara Fehr, now of Valle Esperanza, Bolivia, who broke a convention while still living in Mexico in 1968 by talking to a boy in a car, did find a lasting partner in her indiscretion. In fact, as she recalls it, her future husband cruised their village one Sunday afternoon in a car filled with boys from a distant village, and this act led to a courtship and eventually to her marriage to him at age eighteen.

Couples describe how their rituals of courtship included other rites of passage. There was the spring baptism, then within weeks the *Falafnis*, "the engagement party," and then the wedding. Oldtimers recall it as a tightly scripted sequence of events. Anna Wiebe of Progreso says that she met her future husband "once a week, just on Sundays," and courted him for a year and a half, then had the *Falafnis* in

"Rosenort, at my parents' [house]," and then the "church [ceremony] was at Hochstadt." The *Falafnis* is recalled as an exciting day. Young Jacob Schmidt[12] of Rio Verde, East Paraguay, explains *Falafnis* as an event at which he meets his close friends, indeed "everyone" is there, aunts and uncles, all the youth, eating and visiting. No dancing or music, of course, though, warns Jacob, "there are always those who try something," perhaps even some of the old charivari when young men find ways to embarrass the bridal couple. If things have been done according to script, the *Falafnis* marks the first time that the couple are seen together in public. For Isaac Wieler of Swift Colony, his "*Falafnis* was the first time" that he and his fiancée saw one another by day, for they "had always visited only in the evenings." He says that, when he "saw his bride at their *Falafnis,* she was even more beautiful in the daylight than at night."

The story of marriage unfolds in careful language, for Mennonites historically have not cultivated romantic vocabulary. Old Colonists joke that there is no Low German translation for "I love you." In fact, when boys have gone looking for girls, it's spoken about euphemistically. Helena Dyck of Chavi says that her brother travelled from Campeche to Chihuahua "to go somewhere different and find something.... Yes, he found something," and married shortly thereafter. True, sometimes Old Colonists use rather passionate language. Isaac Dyck of Progreso says that he and his wife met "like a wolf and a rabbit" after she came to his colony to help celebrate a *Falafnis.* Then, just as quickly, he returns to a pedestrian narrative: "We visited for a year, and then I asked if she would marry me.... I was baptized in 1979 and my wife in 1980." Yet enough sad stories recount the unhappiness of physical separation to suggest the presence of romantic love. Isaac's neighbour Jacob Warkentin[13] recalls his son's depression after being forced to leave his girlfriend when the family moved south from La Honda. Then, when they had a house fire in which he lost a gift "from his girlfriend from La Honda, he cried for days without stopping and wouldn't eat or sleep." The loss of memorabilia apparently broke his heart. Jacob recalls that a Mexican doctor prescribed "some pills but [warned that] the pills are only one part of his healing. The other part ... if he wants to ... is with God's help." Romantic love might have few words in Low German, but the sentiment of romance is not foreign even to pragmatic Old Colonists.

The dynamic years of dating have usually ended in orderly fashion with the establishment of the conjugal household. For all the worry about possible indiscretions during the *Rommdriewen* years, surprisingly few cases of pre-nuptially conceived children seem to exist. Indeed, Old Colonists ascribe premarital sex to car-driving colonies where the automobile—private and mobile in the darkness—becomes the arena for steamy dating. Sexual purity is given special significance because the wedding has always been preceded by the sacrament of adult baptism. The pathway to baptism includes reciting the catechism, but also the momentous hour of "confession" at *Donnadach*. It is a confession to the ministers behind closed doors of all the sins that the baptismal candidate has ever committed. Full disclosure usually occurs because the result is complete forgiveness by the ministers, whereas the penalty for covering up a sin can lead to eternal damnation. A gendered outcome of the confession is that women who confess to premarital sex must wear a special headcovering at baptism. At Shipyard, Heinrich Wolfe explains that young women "wear white kerchiefs until they are married; then they turn to black because they are not pure anymore. If a woman gets pregnant [or has sex] before she gets married, she has to wear a [special] black kerchief during her wedding, making [it] clear that she is not a virgin anymore. She is supposed to be in deep shame, and everybody can see." The act of premarital sex might be forgiven, but for the young woman it is nevertheless exacting. Old Colonists cannot explain the tradition of shaming the occasionally transgressing woman but not the transgressing man.

Even during the week between *Falafnis* and the church wedding, when custom dictates that the young couple visit as many aunts and uncles, ministers, and elderly people as possible, transgressions remain minimal. These social outings occur during the daytime and are highly public. Isaac Fehr of Shipyard jokes that the long week of visiting is so stressful that, if "you still like each other" after it, "then you get married on Sunday."

The wedding itself is but a short event on the Sunday following the *Falafnis* and week of "bridal couple" visiting. It is a ceremony added to the end of a regular church service, followed by another afternoon of feasting. Isaac Fehr recalls that, when "we decided to get married, her parents agreed, [but] it was mainly a decision between me and my wife. I only arranged a meeting with the minister to talk about our situation, [and] he gave a few warnings, not to divorce, [for example]. We were wearing our church clothes, nothing special." David Penner, also of Shipyard, offers only a few more details of a short ceremony. He describes it as occurring toward the end of "the worship service [when] it is announced that a wedding will occur." Attention turns to the bridal couple, who have taken their place on two chairs in front of the pulpit. "The minister turns to them, they receive a short sermon, offer their vows, and then sometime during a long final hymn they walk out of church," making their way "through the women's entrance.... It's just the custom." An afternoon of eating and visiting at the paternal home ends the multi-step process of courtship and marriage.

Marriage and the New Household

Marriage stories inevitably lead to accounts of setting up the new agrarian household. Parents speak about wanting to give their newly wed children "at least something" with which to start their own households. The disparity in what young married couples receive from their parents is remarkable for a people committed to equality. Abram Thiessen of Riva Palacios says that his children will receive little, perhaps only $500: "We have nine children, less than my parents, who had seventeen, so we don't worry.... We know some things [about making a living], and our children know things, so we make things work." The children of Franz and Agatha Wall of Yalnon received more. Franz enumerates the list—"a cow, a horse, five hens, a couple of piglets, and a rooster"—and Agatha adds that "we also gave them a bed, sheets, pillows, etc., household items, glass cabinet," though these gifts were given over time. Isaac Wall of Nuevo Durango, East Paraguay, received even more: twelve hectares from his parents, and two cows from his wife Elisabeth Schmidt's parents, an economic base that allowed them to acquire another six hectares and thirteen more cows. Class differences are apparent in how often both the bride and the groom receive land or how often neither does.

The precise size of the bequeathal has usually determined in which parental household the young couple will live during their first year of marriage or indeed in which village they will ultimately establish their own household. It has usually been a patrilocal move if the groom's parents have been the more well-to-do and a matrilocal move if the bride's parents have been. David Redekopp's home in Nuevo Durango, Mexico, is typical: David has "eight children, two of whom are married; one couple live at home, but our son lives at his in-laws; they are moving them to their own place; we couldn't give them land." It's not unlike other families, he says, in which often the child is given only "one cow [and] a china cabinet," but "our boy's wife got the land, where they built, from her parents, they got two hectares." This small land base was enough to determine their place of residence.

The couple have usually built their own small house after a year of marriage, often next to the parental home in which they have spent their first year. Still, they speak of their desire to have their own land and separate farmyard. Johan Peters recalls that the opportunity of owning land on Bolivia's newly established Manitoba Colony in 1983 as a young married couple was the most joyful time of his and his wife's lives. Middle-aged Susanna Bergen[14] of Valle Nuevo still longs for such a day. She says that her "husband works in the store Monday to Saturday; he leaves after breakfast and comes home when it's dark, ... [and she] would like it if he were at home working.... It's good when he's at home." But one can't work "at home" if there is no land.

The new household on the colony has been not only the economic base for a new generation but also its nexus of faith. In a non-proselytizing faith, it is only by having children and seeing them accept the parental teachings that the faith grows in number. This pressure to pass on the faith, of course, varies from household to household. It is so great for Lena Funk[15] of Valle Nuevo that she muses about singleness: "People get married because to remain single would be lonely, ... but it might be better to be single because then you don't have to worry about your children, whether they will stay in the Old Colony church." But singleness among Old Colonists in Latin America, for any reason, has been uncommon, and parents do speak positively about the challenge of passing on the faith. Peter Friesen of Shipyard begins his story by celebrating the companionship of his marriage: "Life after getting married was not difficult to me, not at all, it still feels like a honeymoon!... We were [accepted by each other's] family.

We make our decisions together." But his marriage narrative moves on quickly to children and faith: "We had eight children; now we have five because three died. And we have five grandchildren. To be realistic, I do things in smaller ways, but I take time for my children.... I teach [them] about our way of life.... It's their culture.... I think they are strong enough to keep modernity [and its technologies] out.... My parents taught me about farming, garage work, faith, and [they] were an example by their church [participation]. 'Keep to the Ten Commandments, work six days, give one to the Lord.'" The intergenerational tie clearly relates to material goods but also to the passing on of religious values and identities.

Intergenerationality also means close identification with a wider kin network. As Chapter 7 indicates, every Old Colonist has a story of the scattering of kin but also a story of siblings coalescing in one or two regions. And they tell stories of the extended family gathering. The most elaborate of such gatherings are those on holy days—the three days each at Christmas and Easter, but also the one-day events of Epiphany and Pentecost. These days are recalled as times of attending church services, but they are also family times, blending the sacred and the temporal. Old Colonists recall Christmas gift giving as being as elaborate as they could afford, with gifts varying from the sacred to the practical to the surprisingly secular. Katherina Friesen of Swift Colony in Bolivia reports that each of her "daughters and daughters-in-law [received] black fabric for a dress for [the past] Christmas, while last year they all got brown fabric; the men all got fabric for a shirt and fifty bolivianos; the grandchildren all got two place settings of cutlery." But gifts have not only been meant to help maintain the household. Katherina says that she once saw "an advertisement for chocolates in the newspaper ... [and] decided that if they weren't too expensive [she] would buy them for [the] children for Easter." A similar blend of sacred holidays and secular symbols is expressed at the Buhlers' place in Riva Palacios, where one Christmas one daughter "received ... cloth for a dress, a sandwich maker, trinkets, cutlery, and dishes," while another "received from her boyfriend a waffle iron, blender, tea set, Santa Claus figurine, among other things." All is not dour behind the grey and brown walls of the Old Colony home!

Even when families have been poor, celebrations such as birthdays have marked joyful occasions, times of either small or grand kin gatherings. Widow Katherina Woelke of Progreso recalls the time that her family gathered for a surprise birthday party for her son Johan: "He lives in a village farther away" but was home on his birthday, so "I suggested to one of the boys that he get some pop and ice [from the store] and not let [his brother] know about it. So we were all sitting around, and one was saying, 'Oh, it would be nice to have some cold pop,' and then someone brought it out. We said it was for his birthday. Oh, he was surprised!" It was a small pleasure for a simple home but one meaningful enough to warrant a story. Gatherings involving grandparents have been more elaborate events, with many grandchildren playing in the farmyard. Peter Friesen of Shipyard recalls how they "were very poor in Mexico," but it was a fact of life made palatable because "we had a huge family ... [with] over 200 people ... there for our gatherings." Meals were served in sequence, the older generations first, and usually, as is the Old Colony custom, they were consumed in silence. "My grandparents and us, we would just sit at a table and eat; there were not really any direct conversations." Storytelling began after the meal.

Community values lie at the foundation of Old Colony society, but the sense is conveyed by kinship. It reminds members that life is about social belonging and not personal achievement, about communitarian solidarity and not individual ascendancy.

Women, Homemaking, and the Household

Family has been gendered, consisting obviously of women and men, of boys and girls, but also of culturally conditioned masculinities and femininities. Old Colony society is patriarchal; only men have ever voted in church elections, held church offices, and been recognized as household heads. Despite this official categorization, however, the role of women on a mixed farm is one of surprising complementarity. Men and women work together on the farm, and on many days they are the only adults whom they see. Where roles differ, with men away at the city market and women parenting small children at home, a mutual respect marks their roles: the farm cannot function without the market, and the Old Colony world dies without children.

Marriages are not perfect, especially in the stress-filled homes of the landless. Certainly, as in all societies, and especially in communities, clubs, or congregations closed to outside scrutiny, there are various forms of abuse and occasionally reports of physical violence against women. But questions of such abuse receive similar answers: abuse, and even violence, have happened but are not tolerated. To the point-blank question "are you aware if there is wife abuse happening in your colony?" Aron Guenther of Nuevo Durango in Mexico responds "not that we are aware, but it would not be tolerated. We have heard of it in [another colony] a bit but not here."[16] To a similar question, Levi Reimer of Santa Rita, Bolivia, says that he has always treated his wife with respect; should anyone doubt him, they should ask her; but such behaviour, he says, would not be tolerated. Aron and Levi mean that the offending party would be summoned to *Donnadach* and compelled to mend his ways. It can also mean vigilante action or, in exceptional cases, involvement of local police, especially in cases dealing with members on the peripheries of colonies. Old Colonists have their horrific stories of occasional crime. Jacob Schellenberg[17] of Rio Verde, East Paraguay, tells a story that he says is exceptional but speaks of an informal reaction to the worst case of which he has heard:

> The wife of a colony member who was working in Mariscal Estigarribia near Fernheim Colony [in the distant Chaco region] died, leaving a number of children. Her husband claimed she jumped out of the speeding car intending suicide. That the woman had to suffer domestic violence before [is] no secret in Rio Verde. The police wondered why her corpse didn't exhibit any [lacerations]. A coroner found out she was killed by a hammer blow in the neck…. Friends and close relatives of the man believe … in his innocence, but many others believe … in his guilt…. It was reported that the police had driven nails under the man's fingernails in order to press a confession.

It is an action that even the pacifist Old Colonists accept, says Jacob, for "he that will not hear must feel."

Just how much agency a woman has had in the conjugal unit is difficult to ascertain in a peasant society in which talk about sexuality, or indeed the body, is universally taboo. Still, stories suggest both, that abuse has happened and that women have possessed agency in matters of sexuality. A young husband at Colonia Del Sur says that a story told by a resident Canadian that Old Colony men expect to have sex with their wives three times a day is incredible—perhaps "three times a week, but then only if we both want it," he responds.[18] A middle-aged man at Rio Verde in East Paraguay says that his Latino doctor, attempting to determine the cause of his depression, asked him if his "wife was good to him at night"; his answer was in the affirmative, with a hint of appreciation for his wife's acceptance of him.[19] A more concerted act of female agency is conveyed in a story told by a Riva Palacios woman of her neighbours, an estranged couple who inhabited the same house but slept in different bedrooms. One night the wife sensed a "strange man" climb into bed with her. Defending herself, she bit him. The man bolted, remaining unidentified. Suspicious that he might have been her husband, the wife peeked in the bathhouse the next day as he was bathing and confirmed from the bite marks that indeed he was the culprit.[20] The public telling of this story signals a willingness to talk about broken marriages, but perhaps it also affirms a woman's agency in matters of sexuality.

Significantly, such stories are told within the company of other women. The church perhaps has been an imperfect instrument of protection for women, but the informal sisterhoods, the female networks, have been called on by women, in multiple ways. Connections among sisters have been especially important. On a March 2009 Sunday in Riva Palacios, Bolivia, Marie Hamm's sisters brought their families over for a spontaneous *Faspa* and family gathering. The women gathered in the kitchen did more than prepare food; they visited intensely, on a range of matters, including travel, the farm economy, and social boundaries. Elisabeth[21] said that she had made sweetened pastry, *Kringel,* for her son-in-law's song leader's practice; Tina was scolded for not grabbing "the opportunity to travel to Mexico" with her husband; Sara interjected that she would love to travel, to Canada, or La Paz, where "you can get things very cheaply"; one of the sisters introduced the problem of the "low price for milk" that farmers are receiving; another relayed news of the death of an Old Colony woman in Toronto who went "into the world." The conversation moved into and out of Riva Palacios and in the process nurtured the bonds among the sisters. On other occasions, such informal sisterhoods have spontaneously focused on a local need and reached out to other women.

The stories women tell, however, focus first and foremost on their children, and tending to the central task of any Old Colonist woman, strengthening the self-sufficient household. Doing so has involved a seemingly endless round of baking, cooking, sewing, and washing. Susanna Bergen[22] from Valle Nuevo puts her vocation in the simplest of terms: "An Old Colony house is so busy with all the work" that has to be done. And it is a lifelong calling, every day and every year. Susanna Friesen[23] from Shipyard says that, when she "was thirteen or fourteen years old, that's when I started to help baking; baking I do every other day; every Monday and Friday I do laundry." She says that her life has been made easier in that "my laundry machine has an electric motor," powered by a farm-based generator. Other technological changes have also helped to reduce the workload. Peter Wiebe of Yalnon says that a gas oven has replaced their old wood stove and that a solar panel has replaced the old kerosene lamp. But these are limited technologies, and large families and competition among women for the reputation of the cleanest and most efficient house mean that there is little time for leisure. Katherina Friesen of Swift Colony says that she cannot compete with Riva Palacios resident Gertruda Klassen,[24] whose "house is always immaculate"; Gertruda's daughter retorts that, according to her mother, it is Katherina's house that "is always very neat and tidy."

Women have also been the sewers of clothes, some with precise patterns passed on from generations past, others adapted to fit new climates of the south. The dresses of Old Colony women must meet their community's expectations, says Susanna Friesen of Shipyard. But some such expectations seem to have no religious significance. Susanna describes dresses that "are supposed to have thirty pleats in the skirt, fifteen to the left and fifteen to the right," and the top has "three pleats, and there are twelve buttons in the back," but the expectation is clearly a matter of custom. Her explanation that the women should have two sets of dresses does have religious significance, for the dresses include "dark dresses with flowers" for workdays, and "on Sunday dresses [that] are totally dark." Similarly, clothing patterns that have been handed down from one generation to the other, may or may not matter religiously. Eighteen-year-old Anna Peters of Oriente in Bolivia says that, when her grandmother was a girl, certain fashions were forbidden; they had to "wear dresses with aprons" and "weren't allowed to have the fringes on their headscarves." Over time it seems the dress code opened up as the aprons disappeared and fringes appeared, although no one can tell just when the change occurred, or why. Women in Bolivia do know why the cotton dresses that they used to wear in Mexico were exchanged for polyester dresses: they were "nicer," cooler and more pleasant in the heat of South America. Thus, while "people in the colony think they are keeping things the same," says Anna, in fact "things are changing." Sometimes the changes seem to have some religious bearing; usually they merely reflect changing likes and dislikes, or new climates and social conditions.

A woman's duty has been not only to maintain values of simplicity, with plain dress, but also to maintain uncut and covered hair according to scriptural teachings and the *Ordnung*. This duty is not easily attended to without electricity and readily accessible hot water. Shipyard resident Susanna Friesen talks about the deep traditions regarding the care of women's hair and the work that comes with those traditions: "Girls and women put new braids in their hair ... on Wednesday and Saturday [when] they wash their hair.... Then we ... comb [oil] through our hair. We help each other braid our hair.... The Bible tells us it is wrong [for us to cut our hair]. Some women have their hair down on the ground when they sit on a chair, having it open!" No matter the actual length of hair, it's a form of beauty nicely rolled up under a covering, signifying humility and obedience.

As in most peasant societies, women's identities are indelibly wrapped into their roles as producers of food. A challenge for Old Colony women is to cook without electricity in a tropical climate. Justina Rempel[25] of Oriente in Bolivia "misses the pork of Mexico," where "when they slaughtered a pig it got cold enough so that you had enough time to cure and smoke hams and sausage.... Not so in Bolivia." In the latter country, partly because of the hot climate, says Maria Hamm of Riva Palacios, they have adopted the "butcher ring." Every second week one household within the ring butchers a pig, and the Hamms "get ten kilograms of meat." It's just one of the adaptations that Old Colony women have made in increasingly hot climates.

Greater awareness of health issues also means that in Bolivia Old Colony households have begun emphasizing vegetables. Katherina Wolfe of Neuland says that in Bolivia they "eat more salad" than they did back in Mexico in the 1960s; Anna Banman of Valle Esperanza agrees, saying that she "wants to have a garden beside her house so that she can have fresh vegetables." Similar changes have occurred in southern Mexico in recent years. Aganetha Wall of Yalnon says that "people grow peanuts, sweet peppers, sunflowers, squash, potatoes, carrots for their own consumption and do canning of meat and veggies and fruit." But in most instances, foodways have reflected an amalgam of northern and southern Mexico. A meal at the Penner home in Progreso in 2009 included "homemade pasta," *Kjielkje,* as well as "gravy and farmer sausage and lime juice and coffee and papaya." A meal prepared by Aganetha Bueckert in Yalnon was made with a pressure cooker, a mélange of "corn, meat, green beans, potatoes, chilies, and salt"—in the words of Aganetha, a "meal in a jar." She says that it is a Mennonite foodway, which their neighbours, "the Mayans, also do not understand." Old Colonists have adapted their foodways, but they still think of them as distinctively Mennonite.

Old Colony women have been not only homemakers but also householders, participating in farm activities in which their lives have intersected directly with the lives of men in the farmyard. Women's roles have included tending chickens and milking cows. As Leona Sawatsky, a single woman of twenty-eight from Valle Esperanza, Bolivia, puts it, "in her home milking is a womanly concern," meaning that it is natural that she, herself, should be thinking of buying some cows; but she has hesitated, as "the milk price has dropped." Women not only tend to cows but also manage them, and they know them. Elisabeth Harder of Sabinal jokes that, though she doesn't milk cows, she can recognize all of their cows "from their back ends" as she makes her way past them "to feed the calves and the chickens." With her knowledge she joins her husband in planning the dairy sector of the farm. Old Colony women readily talk about and debate farm matters, especially when it regards dairying. David Friesen of Progreso recalls a time when they could not afford to build a house for their daughter and husband because "we only had two cows." His idea to "sell one cow to help pay for it" was vetoed by his wife, who countered with, "then we'll only have one left." She did agree, however, with his revised plan to "sell one and ... buy five yearlings instead." This was a good idea, says David, for soon the yearlings became "cows, and all five had nice calves, and the cows gave milk, and like that we got ahead."

Similar debates on dairy procedures take place among women. In 2009, two sisters, Margaret Rempel[26] and Tina Fehr, of Riva Palacios, debated how best to wean calves. Margaret has always favoured "designating some milk cows to feed calves," with "four calves for every ... cow," saving the work of first milking "all the cows and then feeding [some of the milk back to] the calves." In addition, her method has "contributed to the calves' health, for if calves suck they are healthier and don't need as much medicating." Tina disagrees, stating that "it would be more work and involve more effort to allow the calves to suck," and certainly it would be less pleasant as they would "bawl endlessly," and "you'd have to keep your eye on the scrawnier calves to make sure they were well fed." Two quieter Fehr sisters present agree with the way that Tina does it; it's more scientific and profitable.

The agency of women in mixed farming has translated into numerous cases of entrepreneurship, especially ventures related to traditional female concerns. As noted in Chapter 4, often these concerns have been linked to health, but more often women's supplemental work has complemented their routine of mothering and homemaking. Women, especially those from poorer families, have often found work as seamstresses. Anna Guenther of Nuevo Durango, Mexico, says that, when her sister's husband died with "high blood pressure and bad kidneys" at age thirty-five, leaving four children, her sister was forced to become the sole breadwinner. She did so "by sewing," living simply in "a tin house," milking one cow, and sending "her children ... to work as soon as they could." Significantly, seamstresses say that their work has complemented their Old Colony ways. Katherine Wolfe recalls life in Zacatecas when she put embroidery away "to have one child after another—fifteen children I have had." But then she returned to craft work that could turn a profit: "I got a sewing machine.... I sat day and night at it. When pea jackets became fashionable, then I made a lot of those for others."

But Anna also advanced Old Colony culture by producing "a lot of men's suits," required for their baptism, the day when they "become a member of the *Jemeent*." At Sabinal, Aganetha Wall[27] has sewed some 200 black overalls for Old Colony men each year, earning 120 pesos per pair. She is proud of the white label "Made in Bolivia" that she sews on each pair, emulating a factory label. She has even helped Mennonites to realize that "they could sew them themselves," and in the process she has driven a regional Mexican factory out of business. Other women have advanced Old Colony goals by reducing prices for children's clothing: thus, though Anna Guenther of Colonia Trinidad charges "thirty pesos for a large shirt and fifteen pesos for a small shirt, we do not ask very much for the dresses for the little girls; we sew for those mothers with small children who do not have time to do it themselves; we do it for next to nothing." An Old Colony sisterhood has served both to help the poorest in the community survive and to maintain a degree of colony-based self-sufficiency.

The Elderly and Venerable

Old age has been much more than the dusk of one's life. It has also come with the knowledge that one is a father or mother of a whole lineage, the genesis of a new generation, and the provider of an identity for it. Jacob Wall of Nuevo Durango, Mexico, describes the colony registry in his possession, not only showing a list of names but also revealing a culture that venerates the family line. It lists settlers by name, birth date, and always names of the father and mother—with her maiden name given as her surname. Every person in the colony thus has a double—maternal and paternal—genealogical identity. Nuevo Durango resident Dietrich Wiebe, listed as having been born on "1957 March 28" is also registered as the son of "Peter Wiebe and Margaretha Braun." Meanwhile, his wife, listed as "Anna Bueckert, date of birth, 1958 October 16," is registered as the child of "David Bueckert and Anna Penner." This system of recognizing both maternal and paternal lines is also articulated, of course, when men announce their mothers' maiden names in the form of their middle names. Ironically, a middle name is not often used in public by women who are simply known as the *Frau* of a particular male head of a household. Nevertheless, the emphasis even then is on lineage and participation in a particular household, not on the authority of a particular man.

To have grown old well is to have produced a lineage and earned respect. Isaac Fehr of Shipyard says that he was taught "to say *jie* instead of *du*," that is a formal "you" rather than an informal "you," to an older person, a significant designation for a person worthy of respect. But this demarcation has not made becoming old and letting go easy. Old Colony elderly tell stories of physical decline, and as they do, it is clear that physical limitations are especially difficult in a low-technology society dependent on physical activity and the outdoors, without any form of state aid. Anna Bergen,[28] eighty-one, of Riva Palacios, says that she is poor and not well, having developed "high blood pressure and diabetes," and her husband has lost his clarity of thought. But even in their old age, they need to milk their eleven-cow herd, Anna tending to six cows, her husband to five. Other oldtimers recall the psychological difficulty of stepping down from active farm work. Johan Woelke of Progreso rented out his last seven hectares one year after embarrassingly slipping off his tractor. As he lay on the ground, he "looked around to see if someone saw" and decided right there to "rent it out; I just was not able to do the work myself anymore; I was getting too old.... So I rented to my son" for a fifth of the yield. It was a decline that he could accept for he also was assured that the farm would stay in the family.

Tradition dictates that the elderly couple sell their farmstead to their youngest child and move into a small house nearby. Isaac and Marie Wieler of Swift Current, Bolivia, for example, are eighty-two and eighty-one, respectively, and some time ago they moved into a small house built for them by their children, next to the house that they themselves had built many years earlier, the one that their son Johan had moved into. Old age has also been the time when grandparents have passed on old ways to the next generation. Isaac Fehr of Shipyard recalls with gratitude when his grandmother made "delicious meals, ... potatoes with gravy, beans, pie, and noodles," or the new foodways of the south, such as "cocoa, peanuts, coconut," in the process doing "what she could" to make a poor household survive.

But he especially recalls how she "told many stories, ... taught us poems and songs, ... Low German songs, church songs." It is this repertoire—of temporal Low German street songs and High German sacred hymns—that he will pass on to the next generation.

The elderly speak sadly about incapacitation, when they began moving "from child to child," living for a time in the household of each of their children. Yet they became conditioned incrementally to this situation. At first, it was dependence on their children for shelter. Elderly Franz Wiebe of Bolivia says that his "youngest daughter was part of the first group that settled in Neuland" and that she and her family made sure that when her parents "arrived they already had a roof." At times, that "roof" has been a stand-alone cottage; at other times, it has been care provided within the adult child's house. In Swift Colony, Katherina Friesen cared for her father and her mother-in-law, both suffering from Alzheimer's. She says that it "was very difficult," for her "father would wander off," and locking him in the house made "him very angry." Eventually, they "built an extra room with an attached bathroom to accommodate" him and then cared for both him and his wife until they died, both at age ninety-one. It was a level of care that Katherina thought natural to provide.

When horse-and-buggy people talk about separation, they usually refer to the end of life or the moving away of children. The marriage unit is especially strong in agraria since spouses work together each day, seeking similar cultural goals, with their identities intertwined. Sara Fehr from Valle Esperanza says simply that "it was difficult to lose [my] husband; he [always] said 'as long as we are together,' but now he's gone—it's too soon." Indeed, family histories emphasize the day of the death of a loved one over any step of upward mobility, migration, or natural disaster. Usually, the death of a spouse is not merely mentioned; rather, the description of any physical suffering is given in detail.

Life after the death of a loved one is made easier by being able to connect to close kin within a close-knit community. Widow Frieda Bergen[29] of Manitoba Colony says that her husband's death marked a hard period; she kept the big farmhouse, but whenever she "had enough of being alone" she harnessed the horse to the buggy and headed off to see family members nearby. Widow Sara Fehr of Valle Esperenza has taken an extra step to connect with her children located farther away. She has acquired property in three different colonies—seven hectares in her current colony, another "twenty-five hectares in another colony, then another twenty-five in Yacuiba"—but has recently decided to "sell the first twenty-five and move to Yacuiba because ... [her] children ... live there." She will live there alone, beside her children, unless she remarries. Remarriage among Old Colonists has been common, and widowers in particular have gone to great lengths to find mates with whom to spend the last few years. It is possible that Sara will move again.

The death of the surviving partner has usually occurred in the household of one of the children. Death can be terrifying, but Old Colonists in particular have honed a theology of death that prepares them for it. They make no grand claim about what will happen after death, no declaration that they will soon be in paradise; rather, they speak of a quiet trust in a just and final divine judgment, a belief coupled with an absolute belief in eternity. They speak of pilgrimage, of having been sojourners, of earthly life as a journey towards eternal life. And they speak easily about the details of the day of death. Katherina Dyck of Progreso narrates her father's passing soon after her mother's death:

> [After mother's death,] father moved in with the children.
> First to [my sister] Anna's, then [my brother] Abram's, and
> at last at ours. He had stayed alive as long as he wanted to,
> and he just died. He had a lot of pain the last day; one did not
> know what to do. He lifted his hands and said, 'Oh, wife.' And
> he said, 'Now what, now how?' He lay on his left side, then
> turned and said, 'Now what, now how?' Then he turned on
> his right side and folded his hands and had a peaceful face and
> went to sleep. He had had problems, he had to have his right
> leg cut off at the ankle, then to the knee, and then his left leg
> to the knee because his veins got too thick. He smoked and
> couldn't leave [tobacco] alone until they cut off his right leg....

Every Old Colonist has a narrative of dying told and retold by the children. More important than any obituary listing personal accomplishment are the details of the place of death, the last words, the degree of physical pain, the psychological condition at the moment of death. What matters is how well the grandparent has exited life, and handed off property and legacy to the next generation.

The funeral is almost as simple as the celebration of birth, the wedding ceremony, or the establishment of the first household. Adult children tell of the process in which the female undertaker and an assistant come for the body of the aged matriarch or patriarch and take it for washing and wrapping. At Swift Colony, says Katherina Friesen, the woman in charge for years has been Mrs. Isaac Rempel, who today works with an assistant. Katherina describes how Mrs. Rempel goes about preparing for the funeral: "The first thing they do is wash the body and then lay it on a series of benches that are slightly sloped. Then [they] cradle the body with two sheets of tin and then put ice all around and on it, ... then wrap it in sheets to keep it colder, ... then wash the body again and dress it with a white shirt and then ... wrap a white sheet around it. Women used to wear their black caps, but now they wear white ones.... There are women who make the caps." The only difference between dressing men and women is that men wear no headcovering, and the white sheets are taken in to make them resemble loose-fitting pants.

When the body, dressed in white, is ready for the coffin, says Katherina, loved ones and neighbours gather around and sing the traditional Old Colony *Langwiese* hymns, slowly and earnestly. The entire funeral process is long and emotional, with an open casket, and family sitting around it in silence for hours. The funeral service includes a sermon containing words of comfort and a warning to extend one's love to family and neighbours while time allows, long silent prayers on bent knees, and more lengthy hymns. Each village has a graveyard. There is a spoken prayer only at the graveside. After the funeral, says Isaac Fehr of Shipyard, there is a simple *Faspa*—the sweet *Kringel* pastry, coffee, and sugar cubes—the same fare as that served at weddings.

Conclusion

The outsider might see Old Colonists as a peculiarly dressed people who travel by horse and buggy, but Old Colonists think of themselves first as a people connected to one another by kin and household. They tell stories about the family, emphasizing generational succession, in both cultural and economic terms. They talk about naming practices, how children bear the surnames of both mother and father. They recall times of cousins meeting in clan gatherings, of siblings acting in primordial loyalty to one another, of in-laws bonding quickly with parallel families upon marriage. The elderly recount clan genealogies, the ways in which they are all connected intergenerationally. They recall working with their parents and hearing their grandparents' stories. They tell stories of birth and death, of nurturing the young, and of care of the elderly. They celebrate the creation of new households and hope that they are established on adequate land.

In the process, they describe a social organism, the family, which has relayed the ideas most sacred to Old Colony communities. The high number of children born echoes the teaching that they are to leave fertility control to nature. The rudimentary private school education reflects the belief that children learn best by watching their parents build the farm household and nurture communitarian relations. The tolerated time of *Rommdriewen* ends with finding a spouse, sacralized by the rite of adult baptism. The well-established agrarian household is the best guarantee of a life of rural simplicity. Not only solemn rites but also informal, earthy, even humorous, quotidian lore has maintained these loyalties, as have the kin-honed rituals of Christmas or Easter meals or birthday gatherings.

Importantly, the family has been an arena in which gender roles are played out, shaped by internal dynamics of work, play, and ritual. Women and men speak of their historically conditioned roles. They recall debates about how to build the rural household or which specific economic strategy to pursue. Family members describe how kinship networks undergird healthy domestic relations and how instances of abuse are met by church censure, even excommunication. Effective intervention has sometimes been stymied, however, by the reluctance, as in all peasant societies, to speak openly about sexuality and by misplaced teachings on forgiveness and patriarchal privilege.

The soul of Old Colony life has been expressed in social relations and institutions. But the sacred calling to live anti-modern lives cannot be understood without also recognizing the compelling nature of kin and family loyalty. Overshadowed by the overt artifacts of Old Colony identity, the family nevertheless has at once strengthened social bonds within the community and enhanced age-old teachings.

CHAPTER SIX

Boundaries, Race, and the Moral Economy

*"We have such cards when it is necessary to deal
with the world..."*

Rio Verde Colony lies three hours north of Asunción on Highway 3, halfway between the Paraguayan capital and the Brazilian border town of Pedro Juan Cabarello. The colony has just recently accepted electricity and trucks, with only the Ältester and a few faithful horse-and-buggy people refusing these amenities. By rented car, Paul Redekop, a fellow professor from Canada, and I leave the week-long 2009 Mennonite World Conference, held once every six years, this year in Asunción. I knew that few Mennonites in embroidered kerchiefs or black overalls would be in attendance among the 6,000 delegates coming from countries around the world, conversing in one of the official conference languages—English, French, and Spanish. We exit the sprawling city and drive north toward the Old Colony communities in the countryside, places where residents feel more comfortable than in the multinational setting of a world conference.

When we get to Rio Verde, we find the opposite of a quaint and pastoral Mennonite place. Indeed, we find immediate evidence of a fundamental divide between evangelicals and traditionalists. Highway service station owner Franz Loewen, who has left the Old Colony church to pursue business with a Paraguayan clientele, is the first Mennonite whom we meet. Dressed in a baseball cap and loud red shirt, he is outgoing and eager. He shows us around the station but most eagerly guides us to a suit of offices in the back housing a radio station with which his Evangelical Mennonite Church reaches out to Catholics and Old Colonists alike with an evangelical message about a personal relationship with Jesus. Franz is confident that both his business and the mission that he supports will thrive.

The home of Old Colony Ältester Johan Schmidt, our next destination, is well away from the highway, back along a dusty red clay road. When we pull up to his farm, a quiet-spoken, kindly man wearing the telltale collarless black shirt of an *Oom* appears from the barn. He invites us into the visiting room of his house, as elsewhere, the master bedroom, where we sit on white plastic chairs. Johan asks about the gathering in Asunción and recalls a very good sermon that he once heard a Spanish Paraguayan preach at the rehab centre that Old Colonists support. But his quiet curiosity turns into sad concern when he speaks of his Rio Verde Colony: the "world" has arrived, mostly in the form of cars and trucks used by members disobeying the *Ordnung*. Recently, the rebels have even ignored the agreement that Sunday would be reserved for the horse and buggy. The stress of this conflict has forced him to seek advice from his highly supportive Paraguayan doctor. Johan says that life would be easier in Bolivia, where the boundary between the Old Colony and the world is more clearly marked.

If a social boundary separates the Mennonites gathering in Asunción from the Rio Verde Mennonites, yet another boundary separates Johan the Ältester from Franz the evangelical entrepreneur. Both men are descendants of Old Colonists who left Canada in 1922, but three generations later they represent stark differences within the Low German–speaking Mennonite world in Latin America. Johan believes that a Christian must live apart from the world in order to be a light to it; Franz thinks that one cannot be a light to the world unless one lives in the middle of it. Other boundaries separate Johan from his Latino doctor and the Hispanic preacher whom he likes, itinerant workers, soldiers patrolling the highway, or Brazilian soybean farmers who drive up land prices. Each boundary further defines Johan and his Old Colony Mennonites. Theorists argue that social boundaries don't separate cultures as much as shape them when people bump into them or cross them. They define who the people are and determine how they see themselves, whom they meet, and on what conditions. Of course, visitors to the colonies also cross this boundary. There are cattle dealers, truck drivers, and government agents, as well as missionaries, journalists, and curious academics. Each visit reinforces Old Colony identity in some way.

Perhaps Anna Harms of Colonia Trinidad in Mexico is correct in saying that her world is very small: "Nah, I don't know anything about others, I only know the *Dietsche* and how sometimes one reads things in the [*Mennonitische*] *Post*." But this intentional ignorance of a person sequestered from the wider world is only part of the picture. Abram Dyck, *Vorsteher* of neighbouring Chavi Colony, is also right when he says that, "yes, we cannot exist without dealing with the world; we have to use it.... We would like it to be without troubles; however, it doesn't work like that, and so we have to concern ourselves with it." Old Colonists might have tried escaping from modernity in their exodus from Canada in 1922, but the irony is that you can only escape it by dealing with it.

Consumption, Trade, and Ties to the City

It is rather obvious that Old Colonists maintain rigid social boundaries. The very mode of transportation, the horse and buggy, and the rules against rubber tires on tractors, and even bicycles, ensure social distance. Susie Knelsen of Manitoba Colony in Bolivia says that they live separated from the world "this way because it says so in the Bible." But she adds a practical side to a religious abstraction, noting that Old Colonists "don't have cars because then the young people can go into the towns and make trouble." Susie means that they would find ways of bringing worldly values from the towns to the colony. But new technologies, especially new forms of communication, are making this social distance harder to maintain. Jacob Wall of Shipyard in Belize says that "cell phones are not allowed, but, yes, most people have one, they just don't tell each other." His problem with having a cell phone is unambiguous: it "makes the connection to the outside world too easy."

Old Colonists worry a great deal about the slippery slope into the modern world. Wilhelm Penner of Progreso in southern Mexico says that he is part of a local consortium of four neighbours who share a gasoline-powered generator: "On Monday, we start it up so they can all do laundry. The cistern is pumped full, and this is used for the neighbours too. We [also] use batteries and charge them up." They find electricity beneficial for the basics of household activity; still, they reject electricity brought in by power lines from state-run companies: "We do not want to be beholden to the world, because the electricity comes from them. Like the road to Hopelchén, we maintain that so we do not have to be beholden to the government. There are some colonies that have accepted [electricity], those who have rubber on their tractors and drive trucks.... If we took the electricity, then we could have [air conditioning and] colder rooms. But it's against our rules, and we mean to keep them." It's the same logic uttered in more truncated form by David Friesen of Progreso. The simple explanation for objection to electricity is that "all sorts of things would come in that the youth would want." What he means are radios, televisions, musical instruments, computers, and all manner of gadgets that would undermine Old Colonists' ethos of simplicity.

But social distance is never absolute, and over the years Old Colony Mennonites have visited the regional city regularly. Their way of life has always made allowance for a judicious interaction with the marketplace. It's the source of financial resources to purchase land and the products needed to keep alive their agrarian ways.

It's not hard to find Old Colonists who talk about the importance of connections to the city. Justina Hiebert[1] of Sabinal in northern Mexico says that "Juárez would be just two hours away if the road through the mountains was decent. You can see the lights of Juárez in the night from Sabinal. Selling cheese would be more profitable if Juárez was [closer]; now [we] have to first go to Nuevo Casas Grandes and from there to Juárez." She wouldn't mind if the city was closer. Making matters worse, adds Justina, the road to Nuevo Casas Grandes is in disrepair, and it takes more than two hours to get to it. "The president of Mexico should travel on it," she laments, and it would be improved at once. Franz Wall of Yalnon is grateful for the enhanced connection from his colony to Campeche City. At first, it was not easy to go to the city, but "now with the bus it is an hour and forty-five minutes to Campeche. At first, we had to go by foot to the nearest 'ranch' [town]" to catch the bus. But three years earlier, with the blessing of colony officials, the bus company extended service to the colony itself.

Old Colony Mennonites engage in a wide range of activities in cities, though with strict guidelines that all such interactions ultimately serve to strengthen and not undermine colony life. The most easily sanctioned crossings into the wider world include those undertaken on behalf of the colony or groups of neighbours. Isaac Rempel of Oriente in Bolivia "takes cattle to sell in Santa Cruz; people will come and drop off their cattle, and once [there are] enough" he goes to Santa Cruz, where he "will spend the night in the city if necessary." Isaac Reimer sells cheese for the Yalnon Colony to Mérida's restaurants and to corner stores, usually about fifteen kilograms. If he doesn't sell it all in one day, then he will simply stay overnight and finish selling it the next day. He insists that he needs this urban connection since the commissions that he makes on the cheese sales help him to survive, for he is "very poor, ... with only a little house and a yard with a fence, no land." No one visits the city without a good purpose.

A measure of the ease with which many Mennonites negotiate the city is the self-confidence with which they have entered its gates. Katherina Woelke of Progreso speaks self-assuredly about the economic effect of Old Colony Mennonites on the city of Hopelchén since they first arrived in the 1980s: "It has received a lot of money from [trading with] the Mennonites. They were poorly educated [but] ... would tell us how to [farm]. [Use a] stick [for planting] and a few kernels. But now they have seen [how we] ... get credit to buy seed and fertilizer [in the city]. The government agent came to see what we had done.... His people had never opened up this many hectares in ten years. Hopelchén has improved; they have taken many a peso from the Mennonites." When they go to the city, Old Colonists congregate in a place that has become their own. In Santa Cruz, the meeting place is Calle 6 Agosto, where hotels and travel agencies operate in Low German; in Hopelchén, it is at Farmacia Margarita, owned by Omar and Luz Maria Mazz Tapia. These places are only fleetingly Old Colony locations, there by the workday and then gone after hours or on weekends.

It's a big step that separates the regional city from the international field. Nevertheless, the culture of trade has taken Old Colonists to surprising places well beyond their local towns. Jacob Klassen of Valle Nuevo has twice gone to Paraguay, once in 2002 on a trip organized by North American–based Mennonite Central Committee's Santa Cruz office, Centro Menno, to visit the more progressive Mennonite colonies of the Chaco; a delegation of about eighteen Old Colony men, one each from a different colony, toured businesses and cooperatives in the Mennonite colonies to consider new farming methods.

More often Old Colonists' business opportunities within South America have taken them outside the Mennonite world. Anna Banman of Valle Esperanza recalls going "to Brazil twenty-five years ago," by train (a common form of travel for Mennonites), with her husband, where he "bought combine harvesters to sell in the colony," and she recalls that they "stayed in Brazil two to three days; stayed in a hotel ... [and] ate ... good food in the restaurant." The pursuit of improved genetics for their fields and herds takes Old Colonists even farther afield. Through intermediaries working to secure better breeding stock, some Old Colonists have come to know an even larger world, one that they have heard of but likely will never visit. Abram Wiebe of Trinidad in southern Mexico, for example, explains that "we are always 'trading,' ... trying to get better milk cows. We can order them from [New] Zealand.... They come all on a ship, from afar.... One month they travel." He adds that such far-off sources are not necessarily better than those closer to home: in this instance, most of the New Zealand cattle died prematurely in the heat of southern Mexico.

Old Colony women talk about which boundaries have been crossed safely and brought gain to the colonies. Frieda Wiebe[2] of Neuland says that "it's been difficult to start anew in Bolivia," but things have improved since they "have a bus to the city once a week." But this link is shaped by the patriarchal structure, negotiated by their Spanish-speaking husbands. Katherina Friesen of Swift Colony recalls being "invited to go to Santa Cruz ... [to] visit [a] sick granddaughter in the hospital," but she would not go to Santa Cruz just "like this." She doesn't think that she would "manage on my own"; she would need her husband even in a restaurant, for she speaks little Spanish. From Katherina's perspective, Old Colony women can travel so much more easily the width of the colony than leave its boundaries: "Taking a taxi across the colony to visit this granddaughter, if she were sick at home, wouldn't be a problem, ... as long as the taxi driver is reliable." Most women know which taxi drivers and bus lines to trust. And they are willing to use them if colony life is strengthened in the process.

The Government and Nation

The basic rule for boundary crossing is clear: doing so must benefit the Old Colony way of life in some way. To that end, Old Colonists have honed a long-standing tradition of regulated interactions with various social groups.

At the top of these various groups is the government. Here social boundaries are well established, indeed reflecting the centuries-old Anabaptist two-kingdom theology and practice of separation of church and state. Old Colony Mennonites have an old system in which they seek favour with government heads, refuse to vote, and then work as best they can at lower levels. They inherited this system from their ancestors, revealed in the way that Dutch-descended Mennonites still tell stories of how Katherine the Great "invited" Mennonites to Russia in the late eighteenth century and then how President Obregón provided them with their charter of privileges in 1921, enabling the move to Mexico. In the second half of the twentieth century, this story was repeated in British Honduras (Belize) and Bolivia, and with variations in Argentina.

But as the following accounts demonstrate, the relationship with the modern state is never merely a matter of its acknowledging Old Colony schools, military exemption, and self-organization. As a constant reminder of this complex relationship, Old Colonists as Mexican citizens, for example, are compelled to carry national identity cards, or voters' cards, even though they do not vote. Abram Dyck of Chavi says that "we have such cards when it is necessary to deal with the world.... If one does not have one, you can't start anything.... Now they require more than ... a birth certificate or a marriage certificate, they first have to have a voter's card." The cards are simply a matter of practicality, of course, and do not denote a sense of cultural citizenship.

But even this situation is more complex than continued separation. Old Colonists might not vote, but they do have political leanings, and they tend toward the conservative end of the political spectrum. It is their instinct to support governments that leave them alone and allow them to take care of their own social concerns; it's a simple equation that left-leaning governments are less willing than right-wing administrations to do so. Abram Peters of Rio Verde recalls how in April 1969, when the first group of fourteen Old Colony families landed in Asunción, "a committee was waiting for us." The ultra-right-wing "President Stroessner, [who] liked the Mennonites a lot, ... had arranged that we were brought to a hotel where we were invited to a very nice meal; the first day [in the hotel] and the meals were free." In Bolivia, the government of Evo Morales, the leftist indigenous president, is seen through a different lens. Jacob Friesen of Manitoba Colony is rather apprehensive about Morales. He recalls reading a newspaper "about Morales' hunger strike to carry through a [new electoral] law in the latest *Mennonitische Post*" and thinks that "it's foolish." You work to achieve results, you don't strike.

Elderly Anna Banman of Valle Esperanza has other pointed, somewhat racialized ideas, about Morales. As a Colla, an indigenous person, his views on "land claims are a little more strict," and she worries that he might incite the indigenous to move against the Mennonites. She also worries that he lacks the resolve to fight crime: "He hasn't made drugs illegal" and instead has lobbied internationally to make the use of coca leaves legal. But then, as she notes, "Morales is a Colla," not a Camba, as Bolivian presidents historically have been, and he naturally supports policies favouring indigenous cultures. She nevertheless muses that "in December is another election.... We will see how many will support him." But Mennonites keep these ideas within their colonies; the government is to be obeyed, not tampered with, within the tradition of their faith.

Old Colonists can disapprove of national laws, even disregard those that they deem hostile to their traditional concerns. Mennonites know that their forebears came to Latin America in 1922 to protect their German-language schools, and they have repeatedly withstood state attempts to have them assimilate to Spanish ways by simply refusing to comply with national laws. Peter Bergen of Valle Nuevo in Bolivia puts the idea of civil disobedience rather nonchalantly: "The Bolivian government has said [that we] should have one hour of Spanish a day in the school, but [we] haven't followed this; ... it would be good to learn Spanish in the school, but [we] learn German." Ironically, this attitude does not mean that they disrespect state authorities; they are classic examples of folks who see themselves as loyal subjects but not good citizens. They seem to have less faith in laws than legislators; indeed, their histories are replete with stories of having appealed to national leaders. Heinrich Loewen of Rio Verde in Paraguay recalls an act of deference toward a national leader during his decade-long post as the Old Colony's representative to the Mexican Embassy in Asunción. He recalls how he once "spoke to President [Vicente] Fox during his visit to Paraguay," after which "it took [but] one day to arrange a new passport" for Mexican-born Mennonites living in Paraguay or those wishing to travel to Paraguay. Old Colony Mennonites have a strange confidence in matters related to national governments.

Indeed, Old Colonists can play politics at the highest levels. They know that, as hard-working agricultural settlers, they have something of value to offer to the state. And, where one official might oppose them, another might well favour them. Wilhelm Unger of Colonia Trinidad in southern Mexico says that the "governor of Campeche [has turned] against the Mennonites, and so the governor of Quintana Roo asked if he could have them." The simple reason for his approval of Mennonites, says Wilhelm, is "because of how [we] improved the land." This sense that the state recognizes the value of Mennonite settlers seems to boost Old Colony confidence. Peter Wiebe of Progreso says that he personally knows high-ranking officials, and when Mennonite land scouts from Durango state visited Chiapas state in the 1980s they found a hostile governor who "renounced us in everything." But the Mennonites were not worried, says Peter, for at the same time "the governor of Durango did not want us to leave" and offered to "take care of our land needs." When the Durango governor was unable to do so, he told the Mennonites that "he was a friend of the governor of Campeche" and would call him to facilitate land purchases in the south: "That's how it moved forward." The old mythology of a head of state inviting Mennonites to settle in his land lingers in Old Colony culture.

Old Colonists do have issues with governments, mostly with local officials and regional agricultural regulations. They have regularly bumped into the state over issues of environmental regulation and animal health, most often because they appear to interfere with Mennonites' intentions to farm whatever lands they can purchase and to remain independent of the government.

This means that they sometimes feel justified in flouting state regulations. Jacob Peters of Nuevo Durango in southern Mexico says that the first step in settlement was to "get land ready," but "we had to get permits to break the land ... [from] Campeche.... It was difficult.... The first permit was for [only] seventy hectares ... in 2001 [on the] west side of Campo 1." He admits that they sometimes took measures into their own hands but that state officials turned a blind eye to their indiscretion. The land that they cleared, for example, "did not include the farmsteads that were done without permits," but the "officials left them alone," and they ignored the fact that "before we got here some of the Mayans had opened up some of the land" for them. Jacob also confesses that a "second permit" for forty-eight hectares of cleared land was exceeded, but again officials didn't say anything. He muses that "they knew it was being used for farming, and they forgave us that. They flew planes over and did not do anything." His confidence reflects the idea that Old Colonists have been called to farm in difficult circumstances in which large, commercial farmers would fail.

This idea shapes their responses to any encroachment on their colonies by local officials wishing to regulate their relationship to the land. Abram Wall of Sabinal is distressed that a "new colony [El Vado] being established near Sabinal" in semi-arid northern Mexico has been refused permission to dig wells by officials influenced by the town of Ascensión. He can't understand how the state can deny farmland a chance to blossom. As his neighbour Katherina Friesen puts it, the Sabinal people think that the state favours the non-farming activities of neighbouring non-Mennonites. As she sees it, the town of "Ascensión doesn't allow [Sabinal] to dig any more wells because it claims Sabinal is taking all its water." But Katherina suspects that "in reality it's the mine in the mountains that is depleting the water." Similar protests are uttered by women in southern Mexico, where officials have insisted that farmers obtain permits for making charcoal, a process that they have learned from Mayan neighbours and a craft that offered a lifeline to the poorest of Mennonites, especially during the settlement years.

Government veterinarians are similarly seen to interfere with Mennonite agendas—and for rather corrupt reasons. David Friesen of Progreso might say matter-of-factly that "there are men from 'out of the world' who are supposed to come here today to test the animals to see if they have the flu that can be passed on to humans." But his neighbour, Katherina Dyck, is blunt about her desire to be left alone and tend to her cattle as she has learned along the way: "I wish they would leave us alone.... If a cow is sick, half a litre of vinegar is supposed to stop diarrhea." She is indignant, senses corruption, and even has her conspiracy theory that state-appointed veterinarians falsely diagnose perfectly healthy cows. She says that "it's funny to me that it's only the best cows that get the sickness and have to be sold for a low price." She tells a story of a widow who "had to sell all of hers, and she went to a large dairy, and there were her cows" alive and well. Katherina is frustrated that officials can declare a cow ill, and then "we either have to sell them for cheap, let them be slaughtered, or shoot them dead." It all means that she simply doesn't get the chance to build up a decent herd.

Old Colonists, especially in relatively developed Mexico, are also concerned about accepting government aid, any form of which they dub *seguro* ("state-funded social security"). They fear that such aid could ensnare them in too cozy a relationship with the state. Still, some Old Colonists have been driven by abject poverty to take the aid. Widow Anna Thiessen of Trinidad says that she would get medical *seguro* available at the Hopelchén hospital if she could only get to the city and if she could speak Spanish. She understands that "Mrs. Kethler, she has [medical *seguro*], she has so many troubles, she can barely walk, and she said how expensive it always was, and now she can do it for free." In the meantime, Anna is thankful for the state aid that she does receive. She announces with some assurance that "at seventy years I get something like old-age pension....In February, I will get ... 1,000 pesos [a month], that will help me [out] yet."

But most Old Colonists in southern Mexico oppose such aid from the state. True, Helena Dyck of Chavi is thankful for a state food program in which "two times a month one will get a [big] bag of food from the government." But it is controversial and has led to a great deal of debate. "There are those who do not sign up for it, they do not want to have anything to do with it.... One person has such an idea and another such, not? One is scared [of being] ... too closely linked with the world, that it will create something disastrous. And the other will think it won't be as bad." She too is uncertain. Reverend Franz Schmidt of Progreso is more unequivocal and speaks the official church line: "People here do not have *seguro*. They [the government] have asked us to, but ... we have the *seguro* from God. We leave ourselves in God's hands. We would be too tied up with the world if we would accept that.... There is a *seguro* hospital, and [without *seguro*] we cannot get treated if we go there. One man had intestinal problems, and the *seguro* hospital took him, but why I do not know." Refusing *seguro* is potentially costly, but as Franz sees it the cost is worth the independence of Old Colony communities.

It's a different matter with regard to mandated state immunization programs or emergency aid, both of which have been accepted,
though always with residual Old Colony defensiveness. Johan Dyck
of Chavi says that he works with the government in immunization
programs for a simple reason: "Oh, that ... has always been, for years,
here in Mexico anyway, the government always comes around and
immunizes children. And now ... the *Vorstehers* have been ordered to
take control, ... [be] in contact with the immunizers, and ... drive
them around the villages." Some Old Colonists have resisted the
program, but Johan has a counter-argument that they as Mennonites
cannot remain unnoticed and might as well cooperate with officials
who are simply doing their duties. They were "helping people with
medical assistance" and "wonder[ing] if we would also stand with
them. Well, then, what?" Why would Old Colonists not wish to
cooperate?

With similar logic, Old Colony Mennonites have accepted state
emergency aid and occasionally even police and military protection.
Peter Wiebe of Progreso describes the scene during the 2002 hurricane
in Campeche: "108 people had to go to a two-storey house at the north
end of Campo 1.... The soldiers came as far as the paved road just
past the woods from Yalnon and then took boats to Number 1 to get
the people and bring them to Yalnon, where they had relations.... The
soldiers had gone to the ranch [the nearby Mexican town] because
everything was under water everywhere, and then they saw there
were houses there (Campo 1), and they came in the boats and went
around the houses and found them." Wilhelmina Penner[3] of Progreso
even recalls the Mennonites' acceptance of advanced technology in
the rescue: "In 2002, a helicopter brought food here, when the [flood]
water was here. We ate in the pantry and slept in the second floor; they
[the soldiers] brought the bedding upstairs." The state can help out in
emergencies as long as it doesn't have a staying presence.

Farmers in southern Mexico are more sure about government farm
aid and seem to know well how various state programs work. Peter
Hiebert of Progreso says that things have changed, and now "we get
seguro, but it doesn't pay for everything"; for example, "30 percent gets
taken off ... [since] we are still indebted to the bank." David Friesen of
Progreso has a different term for it and embraces it even more readily.

He says that "we got 'Apollo' ... money from the government to help small farmers," and at "960 pesos a hectare [eighty American dollars] for every year ... that's a big help," but given the drought "this year it won't be enough. [Fortunately,] the bank will hold our debt over" to the next year. He is even open to considering closer ties: the "Mexican government [arm] FIRA [Fideicomisos Instituidos en Relación con la Agricultura] got all us farmers into a bus and showed us all sorts of new things like grass that gave more strength and milk." He seems to be impressed that farmers who accept these reforms are "aided by taxes from the government." But clearly David is not ready to commit himself to this level of engagement in state programs.

Nor has their openness to state protection translated into an identi-fication with the nation-state. Many Old Colony Mennonites have been preoccupied with the process of procuring passports, always concerned that the process requires them to register with state officials. In the distant past, Mennonites did not even register their marriages with the state, meaning that many of their children were technically considered "illegitimate" and hence ineligible for Canadian passports granted to children born to Canadian parents abroad. Reverend Franz Schmidt of Progreso says that this practice has changed, and today "all who marry in this colony register with the government, and babies are also registered." But he feels the need to offer a rationale for it: "We did not used to register, but then we read how Maria and Joseph went to [Bethlehem], and from then on we did." His story references an event three generations earlier when Mennonites in Canada refused to sign up for the 1917 wartime national labour registration until a government official argued that according to Luke 2 even Mary and Joseph had answered Caesar's census.

Mennonites in Mexico have even gone so far as to register for military service cards for the sole purpose of securing passports. Peter Wiebe of Progreso says that the cards are forwarded to Mexico City, where government officials stamp them as *libre*, indicating Mennonite military "exemption," thus enabling the issuing of passports. Some Mexican officials frightened the Mennonites, saying that "those who made a military card ... had to become a soldier," but Peter says "that was totally dishonest. It wasn't necessary.... It was stamped *libre*." Men-nonite sojourners might be vulnerable, but they do know their rights.

Neighbours, the Mexa, and the Native

The social boundary between Old Colony Mennonites and their Latin American neighbours has long been reinforced by race. Among the Amish and Old Order Mennonites in North America, all English speakers, no matter their ethnic backgrounds, are simply referred to as "the English." Old Colony Mennonites in Latin America face a cultural landscape at once more simplistic and more complicated. They see a basic divide. On the one side are the Mennonites, the *Dietsche,* literally "Germans" but meaning Low German–speaking Mennonites. They are aware that they differ from Germans in Germany: Elisabeth Dyck of Progreso says that, though "we can read High German in the Bible and [know it] from church, when someone comes from Germany, I can't speak with them…. It's all closed off." She says that even with the Amish from the United States "we speak Spanish, not High German." On the other side is the Latino person or, in Mennonite parlance, the *Mexa:* that is, any Spanish-speaking person of Hispanic background, not only in Mexico, but also in Belize, Paraguay, and Bolivia. This broad dichotomy leads to the ironic outcome that Mennonite immigrants from Mexico refer to their hosts in South America with a term denoting their own country of origin. Bolivian taxi drivers who hear the term directed at them have retorted that, if anyone is a *Mexa,* it is a Mennonite from Mexico. Making matters even more complicated, Mennonites readily divide their Latino neighbours from indigenous groups, whom they refer to as the *Einhaema,* the *Einheimische,* or "native peoples."

The social border between the *Dietsche* and the *Mexa* is clearly defined, and Mennonites' refusal to teach Spanish reinforces the division. True, men know a basic market Spanish, and many women know the language. Justina Hiebert[4] of Sabinal says that she "learns easily and is very interested in interacting with Mexicans" and hence has "learned Spanish, even better than her husband." Anna Banman of Valle Esperanza in Bolivia says that she "learned Spanish … as a little girl" since her "father had hired Bolivian workers, and when it was cold they stayed inside their house," and "one of the older Bolivian workers was quite interested in teaching" them Spanish, and today she "is more comfortable speaking Spanish than High German." But Justina and Anna seem to be in a minority of women. More typical is Katherina

Fehr of Valle Nuevo, who says that she "doesn't know Spanish," so she "will go to the dentist ... [who] knows some German," or she will get her husband to translate for her. She doesn't "want the children to learn Spanish in school; if they know Spanish when they're young, it will make it easier for them to go into the world."

Mennonites, in turn, are aware that they are perceived as "other" people by neighbours. Peter Friesen of Shipyard says, "I am aware of how people from the outside see me, and I talked to a few about it. Some will come and tell me what they think about me and my way of life when I am in town," calling out, "'hey, you are a Mennonite,' and then I explain my heritage," but, "no, I don't feel offended." Most Mennonites might not be eager to explain their heritage to perfect strangers, but they are keenly aware of their distinctive identity.

They are also keenly aware that they are "newcomers," even interlopers. They have purchased most of their land from faceless estate owners. Isaac Wall lists the vendors for Yalnon: "The first piece [was] in a private sale from Carlos Cardinas Montero, ... a Mexican living in Baja California. Then Chichmuk was bought, for Yalnon, which was far off, ... from a Valtazar Rios. He was a Mexican; he bought land here and then sold it again. Chavi had also bought land from the Valtazar Rios, it was also his." But there is no sense of having built relationships with previous owners. And, as for their actual neighbours, a recurring theme in Old Colony conversation is the hostile initial impression that natives had of Mennonite settlers. Johan Knelsen of Shipyard says that in British Honduras in 1958 "the *Mexa* had the impression based on rumours that the Mennonites were going to kill them. Soon this settled down, and the *Mexa* became very friendly toward the Mennonites." He remembers a moment on the historic 1958 trip into British Honduras: "[We were] sitting in a bus in Orange Walk, and it was getting dark outside. Then a lot of black people came with their white eyes and their white teeth, and they looked into the bus full of Mennonites. Neither of them [or we] had seen anyone like that before." A similar story tells of the beginning of the colony in Campeche in the 1980s. Peter Wiebe of Progreso recalls that "the first time we came here, that was with Carlos Cardenas [the land dealer], ... and went into the [Mayan] village, and they fled from us.... They said they had closed the door and gotten their guns out [chuckles] because of what kind of people were arriving here." He says that at one point "[I] took out my birth certificate," and they realized, "oh, this is a Mexican! He is just like me or you! He is a Mexican."

This sense of being a people from the outside is reinforced by stories about the legal complexity of purchasing land. Cornelius Guenther recalls the beginning of Nuevo Durango in Mexico. He explains that in 1998 the parent colony of Yalnon began the process of establishing a subcolony by purchasing land from fourteen different owners whose lands formed a contiguous unit. The only problem was that a Mayan widow whose lot was at the centre of the envisaged Mennonite colony declined the purchase price, according to Cornelius, because she "knew she was in the middle" and could extract a higher price. Not able to conceive of a colony without her parcel, the Yalnon *Vorstehers* approached the Ijido, Mayan residents of government-created land reserves, who were able and "ready to sell" following a historic change to Article 27 of the Mexican constitution. However, given that this parcel was too large for Yalnon, its leaders invited the prospective settlers from the old Durango Colony in the north to make a joint purchase. Quickly, a delegation came south, and hence Nuevo Durango was established. But now the Mennonites encountered Mexican law forbidding the specific process that they had envisoned. Clearly, says Cornelius, "we had to know the laws; then we went to the city of Durango to the land office, and then we hired [Mr.] Vargas, who does [land] deals, and asked how it had to work" and whether he would "go to Mexico City to find out how the land was registered." They had learned that another Mennonite colony, Tamaulipas, had acquired land without proper legal dealings and after three years of hard work had been told to "get off the land." This time the Mennonites followed proper channels and set up a "meeting with the *Ejido* and ... two other government officials to oversee the meeting and witness the signatures of all the *Ejido* and stamp and sign it themselves to make it official."

But having acknowledged these moments of tension with their neighbours, Old Colony Mennonites also emphasize their ability to work with people of other ethno-religious traditions. In fact, they typically speak of their Catholic or Mayan neighbours with respect. Isaac Fehr of Shipyard says that "the difference between us and

non-Mennonites or non–Old Colony Mennonites I see is not important. We work together on material things; there is no competition
on matters of faith." In fact, when "some natives say 'why don't you
drive trucks?'" he jokes with them, saying, "if we do, [you] will all
lose [your] jobs." He adds that in northern Mexico, when Mennonites
turned from their horses and buggies, "a lot of taxi drivers lost their
jobs." Isaac says that "I want other people to know that decency and
respect are very important in the Old Colony way of life. We can live
in peace with each other, we with them and they with us."

Other Old Colonists are more specific about their relationships
with their neighbours, recalling small acts of kindness along the way.
Peter Enns of Shipyard relates a terrible accident in which his brother
was killed and his two sons severely burned when a machine that they
were working on exploded. Neighbours rented a small plane to fly
them to the hospital for a cost of over $12,000 US, paid for by dona-
tions from various Mennonite communities. But Peter emphasizes
that Belizean neighbours also "made donations ... because the father
of the boys who had died was well known among them as well." Mennonites also tell stories of how they came to the rescue of their Latino
neighbours. David Friesen of Progreso recalls precisely that on 28
July 1966 a tornado struck the parent colony of Durango and region.
He recalls that his parents were travelling in another part of Mexico
and that he and his brother had stayed at home to care for the cows.
Fortunately, they escaped the tornado, but then "the *Einheimische*
came and asked us for help" since their village had been destroyed
and "they were missing [a] child, so we helped look for it, I and my
brother, ... and [we] found something lying under some rubble, and it
was the body of a baby; that I will not soon forget."

Knowledge has also been shared across this social boundary.
Most often the information is related to nature and its way in the
rainforest. Wilhelm Penner of Progreso relates how Mennonites
learned about the danger of sink holes: "The Mexicans say there
was a hole where the water would go, and then all of a sudden it
was, whoosh, gone, when the hole opened." But Mayan neighbours
there also taught Mennonites about farming in the heat and humid-
ity of the south. Aron Guenther of Nuevo Durango in southern
Mexico says that as "northerners" they needed to be taught to put

"poison" (pesticides/fungicides) in the corn to protect it from insects and mould and that they learned the process from Mayans. But he catches himself, insisting that Mayans "have learned much from us too," for "they used to be a people that planted using a stick and ... closing it up with their foot.... Now most farm with equipment and have built themselves up like we have."

The indigenous or Hispanic workers are not faceless or feckless and have won the respect of Mennonites. Helena Wieler of Colonia Trinidad says that the Mayans who produce charcoal for the Wielers stand up for themselves and negotiate if necessary; in fact, "they can make things very difficult" for the owners. For example, after building "a hole house, for the charcoal, ... they [will say] ... 'I made a hole; then I get paid so and so much,'" and if they are unhappy with their pay they will simply "say 'then we will do it differently ... [by] piecework, as to how much charcoal it gives,'" and if they then get their way they also "do better work right away." Helena has come to respect her Mayan neighbours for other reasons: "They are strong. Oh, yes," and "they are very nice." In fact, these "Mayans are way better than those Mexicans" whom she experienced in northern Mexico. She elaborates that she and her husband prefer to hire Mayan workers over young Mennonites, the *Dietsche:* "My husband doesn't seem to know how to work with *Dietsche,* the *Dietsche* around here themselves have so much work, we rather just make do with Mexicans"; the fact is that "the *Dietsche* aren't worthwhile ... if there are Mexicans [available].... He knows how to deal with [them] better."

This approach also holds true not only for vegetable gardening but also for construction, in which Mennonites have traditionally taken pride. In Bolivia, says Marie Wieler of Swift Colony, most housebuilders are Bolivian. The reason is simple: they "do a much better job than Mennonites." She adds that "at first Mennonites did all the construction, but that has changed; many Mennonites now hire Bolivians." Another factor, no doubt, is that the Latino worker is seen as sturdier and more self-sufficient. Sara Unger of Colonia Trinidad says that, when they cracked stones to build the foundation, they hired two rather self-reliant Mexicans: "We would give them water, and when it got late we would give them food to eat," but "it did not seem they wanted to eat; they had just a lump of cornmeal and water;

I think about it, how they were scared of us; they ... feared our food," but after "a long time ... they ate our food."

This racialized border affects not only economic exchange but also other neighbourly interactions. There are numerous stories of co-operation between Mennonites and their Latin American neighbours, but they are often laced with a sense of lingering cultural distance. Anna Thiessen of Trinidad has one such story:

> [We once] heard something bawling and bawling, and a cow
> came running, and I thought I knew whose cow that was,
> it was from that village, and it reached the lane, and there
> came a large group of [Mayan] workers, I wanted to go here
> and ... ask ... if they would do a favour for me and go and
> tell that village that that beast belonged to [them].... I might
> not be able to speak Spanish.... Well, yes, I can, but very
> barely, but they understood.... [I] gestured a bit too.... And
> they asked if they should try to corral it with a bicycle and
> drive it back home. I said that didn't matter to me. So they
> tried it yet, and it went into the corn, and they took off, and it
> didn't take long and a tractor came charging up and got it.

The cultural divide hinted at by Anna is not seen, of course, as something that should be changed; Old Colonists know that their tradition teaches them to live different lives than their neighbours. In Bolivia, Justina and Katherina Reimer[5] of Manitoba Colony, sisters aged seventeen and eighteen, recall how Bolivian workers introduced soccer to the colony. One year the "Bolivians started playing soccer on the Reimers' yard ... every Sunday," and Mennonite boys began playing alongside them. Eventually, "the Ältester came ... and said they weren't allowed to play.... Now the Bolivians don't let the Mennonites play with them. The [Mennonite] girls played soccer once with the boys in the *campo*, but it was after dark." At Sabinal, in northern Mexico, Mexican youth have tempted Mennonites in a different way. Elisabeth Harder of Sabinal says that they "used to have a dugout at the back of their yard for irrigation" in which they swam a lot; sometimes she and her "husband went swimming at midnight after all the children were in bed." But then many "Mexicans came swimming there as well. They would sometimes bring their picnics and sometimes also alcohol," and worse, "sometimes Mexican girls came very scantily dressed," which simply wasn't good for her boys. Finally, she "told her husband to clean it all up because they couldn't manage it any longer."

Such a level of conflict pales in comparison to times when Mennonite settlers contravened into indigenous peoples' historical land claims. It has been a worry woven into a narrative of the Mennonites from Chihuahua from the late 1920s to the present. The term *Agaristas,* referring to peasants who revolted in the mid-1920s by occupying lands that they considered their own, including from time to time Mennonite farms in northern Mexico, has evolved into a general term for such protesters throughout the Americas. *Vorsteher* Abram Dyck of Chavi claims that the occupiers were poor folks simply trying to extort money from the peaceful Mennonites. He recalls how it happened to his parents in La Honda: "The *Dietsche* came to live there.... Then [as the landscape] started to look productive, they [the *Agaristas*] started to see if they could get it back. That's how it was in La Batea and La Honda [in the 1970s], and that's how it worked here. It seems everywhere that we try to get land the *Agaristas* want to get onto it." As Abram sees it, it was the Mennonites who had purchased lands from legally recognized landowners and held title to the lands who were the victims. They were but simple farmers facing problems not of their own making. If there was a clear culprit, then it was the local government for allowing corruption.

The conflict is especially pronounced in Bolivia, where indigenous people have actively campaigned for land rights. Their demands have included an indigenous territory, in the eastern lowlands of the country under the auspices of Confederación de Pueblos Indígenas del Oriente Boliviano. There were large demonstrations, including epic marches and sporadic land occupation, sometimes involving land farmed by Mennonites. Usually, Mennonites caught in this political uprising have simply moved. Franz Rempel of Valle Nuevo explains how one of his daughters and her young family who moved to a new colony in the northern state of Beni "had trouble keeping their land because there were conflicting indigenous land claims, so she moved to the colony where her brother was," while "the sons who bought the land in Beni moved back to Swift."

In more serious situations, it has been a matter not simply of indigenous ownership claims but also of imprecise land titles. At Colonia California Mennonites discovered that lands that they had purchased had overlapping land titles. Daniel Neudorf explains that, when they "started clearing the land" at the new colony, he "was arrested with several others because ... the sale of the land had been illegal. Having paid seven dollars per hectare for the land [should have secured] clear title." At first, they were imprisoned in Santa Cruz and then ordered "for a year ... to leave the land while the lawyers fought over it." They discovered that the Mennonites had been duped into paying for the land to a person merely claiming to be the owner. Eventually, they had to pay an additional fifteen dollars per hectare. But no sooner had this problem been solved than in early 2009 Indigenous protesters "moved onto [the] land": they "were part of the MAS [Movement for Socialism] group—and this group doesn't like foreign farmers." The Mennonites who usually teach against any form of suing over business dealings, in this case retained legal representation to try to evict the occupiers, but as Daniel puts it, "they're still fighting it in the courts."

Mennonites in Latin America, where policing is often inconsistent, have also faced the reality of crime, especially in crime-plagued northern Mexico. Old Colonists do have stories of crime from earlier times. Reverend Franz Schmidt of Progreso recalls a story from Durango involving his parents, "how a Mexican had broken in, he was at the window, and the parents had run away. The Mexican had known [my father] had sold something that day and wanted his money." But it is not just a story of the past. Indeed, Jacob Bergen of Yalnon says that it seems over time as if "the government always gets weaker and the bands stronger." Especially the Mennonites from northern Mexico have had to deal with crime linked to the brisk drug trade of the region, including kidnappings, holdups, and extortions. Peter Klassen of Sabinal reports that "thievery has increased on the colony," mostly because the drug trade became less than lucrative after the Felipe Calderón government moved against the drug cartels. But "there's still drug activity going on [in] the ranches" nearby, and "Mexicans drive through the colony, and an airplane regularly lands at one of the ranches." From the perspective of isolated Sabinal, this is code for the unusual and the suspicious.

As pacifists, Mennonites usually respond to crime through simple acquiescence and strategies to avoid potential trouble. Sometimes their reputation as honest, ordinary farm folk has been enough to get them out of trouble. Elisabeth Harder says that on one "occasion several Mennonites from Sabinal … rented a truck and were held up by some Mexicans," but "when the Mexicans … realized they were holding up Mennonites they … said they knew who these people were and let them go." But the Mennonite reputation for taking it on the chin can also backfire. Sara Friesen of Sabinal recalls that the Mexican bus driver who lived in the colony "on rented property with his second wife and young children" who allegedly became involved in stealing calves. She is also certain that, assisted by his brothers, he twice held up the very bus that he later drove. Of course, the Mennonites didn't report him, and they're thankful that "now that he drives the bus all the trouble has stopped on the route."

When crime becomes more serious, Old Colonists have gone to the police, but even then many think that the best strategy is to remain quiet, to bend, forgive, and move on. For Mennonites, the question of responding to crime can be contentious, even within a household. David Friesen of Progreso recounts a story in which colony people entrusted him with 60,000 pesos with which to purchase building materials. He explains that on the bus to the city he was robbed by a group of men who, he is convinced, somehow drugged him, putting him in a deep sleep. When he woke up, he discovered that "the bag was cut at the bottom, and … our money was gone," but so were the men, including "the bus helper." When David reported the incident to officials at the bus company, they confronted the driver, and David overheard them saying "you were lying, and the *Dietsche* man was telling the truth." Clearly, he had the support of the bus company and subsequently that of the police. But he wavered:

> The police asked us three times if we wanted to press charges against the bus driver. He said it would go very badly for [the driver] if we did…. I sat back and thought it could give us a lot of problems if we did. They may come after us later. God had a hand in this, and we were going to leave it in the loving God's hands…. I had to go to all the people who had given us money and told them what happened. Some wanted it

back, some just erased the debts. Those who wanted it I paid
back…. It took a while, but I did.

It is a submission to suffering, recounting the biblical instruction to
turn the other cheek, deeply rooted in the Old Colony ethos, combined with uncertainty about safety in an increasingly violent Mexico.

"Other" Churches, Sincere Catholics, and Suspect Evangelicals

Old Colony Mennonites are a non-proselytizing, sectarian group, and
as such they have their gradations of separation: some groups can
be friends, whereas other groups must be kept at a distance. But just
whom they keep at a distance and whom they accept can be bewildering. It matters less when someone is culturally close as opposed to
culturally threatening. The most contentious are missionaries who
undermine the solidarity and commitment of Old Colonists with their
promises that evangelicalism will naturally lead to spiritual renewal.
Old Colonists cannot understand how accepting a more personal
and individual faith can be good when it means breaking the sacred
baptismal vows and embracing a modern way of life.

The most threatening missionaries have sometimes been other
conservative Mennonites, also black kerchiefed, agrarian, plain people
who remain within the community but not the Old Colony church.
Among the most disruptive groups from an Old Colony perspective
are the Kleine Gemeinde Mennonites, once a small marginal group
within the Mennonite world. Established in Latin America only in
1948, they have become more evangelical in the past decades with
a missionary-like presence in many Old Colony communities. Their
appeal lies in their emphasis on a more personal faith, allowing cars
and electricity, but still holding to some traditional values. It was the
establishment of the Kleine Gemeinde at La Honda Colony in Zacatecas state in the 1980s that drove that colony's horse-and-buggy faithful north to Sabinal. *Vorsteher* David Klassen says that Sabinal began
because of land shortages, true to an extent, but then Helena, his wife,[6]
interjects with "and then the *Kjleen Jemeenta* [Kleine Gemeinde Church
in Low German] came in there." The story is repeated elsewhere: an

Old Colony member finds the restriction against trucks economically restrictive, and pressure builds until a few members disobey. They are then excommunicated and invite a more progressive church, such as the Kleine Gemeinde, to establish a small group of dissenters.

Reaction to the Kleine Gemeinde can be rather strident. On Manitoba Colony in Bolivia, Old Colony faithful gathered one year to dismantle a Kleine Gemeinde church building built by dissidents. At Las Palmas, says Johan Fehr, "there are many Kleine Gemeinde," so the "colony … put up a fence so that one end of the colony would be Old Colony and the other Kleine Gemeinde." But this barrier hasn't worked, and people continue to join the Kleine Gemeinde. Johan says that the fence is not "an effective way to deal with the issue," and many Las Palmas members have been excommunicated. Now there are not enough "*Ooms* for Las Palmas." As he sees it, the Old Colony church "isn't taking proper care of the colony," so even more "turn to the Kleine Gemeinde."

Youth especially are attracted to another evangelical body, the Evangelical Mennonite Mission Church (EMMC), consisting of Low German–speaking missionaries from Canada, distantly related to the Old Colony. The temptation is especially strong for unbaptized youth since they know that, should they join the EMMC before they are baptized in the Old Colony church and make their solemn vows of obedience, they would not be shunned by their parents. Heinrich Elias of Shipyard talks about being of two minds on the issue:

> [I go to] both the Old Colony and the EMMC church, and
> I am not baptized yet. I want to, but I don't know yet in
> which church. Yeah, it's hard sometimes, people talk be-
> cause they see me going to the EMMC church too, while my
> parents are Old Colony. It gives problems with the Ältester
> of the Old Colony church. He wants me to go to his church
> and comes and talks to my dad about it. But there is nothing
> he can do because I am not baptized yet, so according to
> the *Ordnung* I don't do anything wrong. My father supports
> me, though, and I am very fortunate with that. Since I
> was small, I was already interested in modern things, my
> parents let me [be] free.

The other reason for the EMMC's appeal to youth is that the church is more progressive than the Kleine Gemeinde. EMMC women, for example, are allowed to cut their hair, wear jewellery, and set aside headcoverings, and young people generally are encouraged to use musical instruments, play sports, and seek higher education.

As the Old Colony sees it, poor people are also especially vulnerable to missionaries. Jacob Friesen of Manitoba Colony says that "many from Charagua, a poorer, drier region close to the Chaco, are moving to the nearby Kleine Gemeinde because they want to use modern technology." Their sense is that the economic disadvantages of steel-wheeled tractors and horse-and-buggy transportation, or not working outside the colony, are too great. Jacob says that the converts are also drawn by the promise of "small plots" of land and the chance to "hire themselves out" to Bolivians. Yet, he insists, "few leave from Manitoba Colony." Evidently, his colony's economy is strong.

Shunning is directed at those who break their vows and join the Kleine Gemeinde or EMMC and especially those few who join Jehovah's Witnesses or Mormons. But not everyone agrees on how strict shunning should be. Speaking in English, Peter Friesen of Shipyard says that "in our garage [service station] ... we never had excommunicated Mennonites, [but] later, in the '80s, we did start to have some." But he says that it doesn't matter:

> I don't struggle with people that are not Old Colony or not
> Mennonite. Among them, I have close friends.... About
> excommunicated people? It's just [a matter of] not praying
> together, and [we] don't shake hands. But we offer them
> help and food. Yes, there is a division about this between the
> preachers. Some want total shunning, others not. Some say
> "be a good example to them."... Because of my business, ... I
> don't struggle with that. Of course we are different. Like the
> Kleine Gemeinde, they use modern things like rubber tires
> and music, TV. We don't have all that. I treat everybody the
> same, also Mexicans or dark [i.e. black] people. But in order
> to keep the community, you have to keep the culture. Mixed
> marriages are not good.

Clearly, the exact degree of separation remains in question.

Attitudes to other non-proselytizing groups, such as neighbouring Catholics, in contrast, are surprisingly open. Heinrich Elias of Shipyard says that "because of my work I have contact with many different people," and he insists that "there are good and bad people, among non-Christians and Christians," and that he has "a lot of friends who are not Mennonite, they are Spanish and English." He understands that they don't agree with the old ways of Old Colonists. But that doesn't matter, for as he sees it "I think all people have their own opinion and are supposed to live their own lives. You are responsible and decide about how you live your life. I believe in working together in the community." Heinrich's view is commonly held: Old Colonists have made their vows at baptism to uphold their church, members of other denominations will have made theirs, and they should uphold what they have promised at baptism or confirmation.

Several communities have encountered Amish service workers from the United States, a group with whom they share a basic set of communitarian ideals. Justina Hiebert, always eager for visitors, notes that American Amish have visited Sabinal in northern Mexico. But the visits have been controversial. She says that "some on the colony are very opposed to having the Amish visit," for it is "difficult for the Amish and the Sabinalers to understand each other." The Amish seem to be more open to reforms than the strictest Old Colonists and have accepted the national language in their country as the language of instruction in their schools. Still, Justina finds comfort in associating with the Amish since she is the only one of her siblings "who still keeps to the old ways," doesn't drive trucks, and "doesn't feel good about the family division." Besides, one is supposed to be hospitable. Elisabeth Harder also appreciates the Amish and can't understand opposition to them: it's "not as if the Amish are trying to change Sabinal in any way," and they do "conduct their affairs better than Old Colony [people] in some ways.... The Amish also have a better way of managing their young people. They have activities for them—volleyball or baseball. These are supervised, and the young people wouldn't just hang out and drink too much." Evidently, the Amish haven't told Old Colonists about the practice of *Rumspringa* among their youth in the United States or their own social problems.

One group who appear regularly but pose little threat are Jeho-vah's Witnesses, seen by Old Colonists as an eternity-denying cult. Anna Buhler of Riva Palacios says that Jehovah's Witnesses "come very regularly," and Old Colonists are torn between a "sense of hos-pitality" and a "desire to have nothing to do with them." When they come, Anna listens politely as they read Low German pamphlets to her. At Riva Palacios, members of a Wall family have converted, but they have changed so radically that they are no longer recognized as Mennonites. Anna says that "recently ... this Wall widow's daughter [was] in the store. She [was] driving a very little car and looked noth-ing *Dietsch* at all." Anna Wall of Sabinal says that Jehovah's Witnesses, or *Biebel Läsa* ("Bible readers"), as she calls them, "come around very often," but usually they "come on Saturdays when there's still a lot of Saturday work to be done," and she just ignores them. She finds it incredible that they don't "even believe in hell when it states so clearly that there is a hell."

It has been easier to relate to modern groups who apparently are quite different but have no intention of converting the Old Colony. The North American–based social development agency Mennonite Central Committee (MCC) might have been spurned by Old Colony leadership back in the 1950s for its paternalistic approach, but things have changed in recent decades. Old Colonists have come to speak in generally positive terms about the MCC. Aganetha Klassen of Chavi says that the cistern that the MCC helped to erect "has been worth so much, you just do not know. Imagine carrying water from [where my well is] all the way to our farm with just a wagon and a barrel." The strategy of capacity building rather than overt reform seems to have won the MCC a second chance. In fact, David Friesen of Progreso speaks in rather nonchalant terms about his colony's link to the MCC. He says that Village 15 in Progreso "was lent 100,000 pesos by the Amish and MCC to set up a well. The people had to pay it back. It was built on a hill, and pipes were led to every house. Many want to move there. There are eleven couples there now." There is nothing controversial about connecting to groups wishing only to offer practical help.

The same attitude holds true for tourists from Europe, often driven by curiosity about German-speaking Old Colonists. Certainly, the graduate work of members of our team—Anna Sofia Hedberg of Sweden, Jakob Huttner of Germany, and Anne Kok of the Netherlands—speaks to an openness to any curious visitor from Europe. But many Old Colonists also read more than the Bible and hymn book. Leona Sawatsky of Valle Esperanza reports on a book that she once read about Germany in which the "main character ended up going ... to Israel to see Jesus," so "when a girl from Germany, through the Peter Giesbrechts, came to visit them" Leona "asked the girl what Germany was like." She wanted to know if the book's descriptions of it were correct but later thought that "this girl must have been laughing ... because of questions" based in such ignorance.

The closest groups are of course other horse-and-buggy Mennonites, though even they can be kept at a distance. Susie Knelsen of Manitoba Colony says that "some colonies are *Aufjefollene*," that is, "religiously lost," such as car-driving Old Colony communities. Then there are the Sommerfelders, at Sommerfeld, near Santa Cruz, not a threat since they too are a horse-and-buggy community that came to Bolivia in 1967. Still, they allow rubber tires on tractors and thus more often travel by tractor and trailer, and they have other peculiarities frowned on by Old Colonists. Abram Hamm of Riva Palacios is "not impressed that [the Sommerfelders] smoke on the churchyard," even though he acknowledges that he's "seen Old Colony people smoke in Santa Cruz ... even though it's preached against." Nor does he think it right "that usually the Ältester and his wife go to church with just a tractor, both of them sitting on it.... An Ältester of all people should use horse-and-buggy to go to church." The Sommerfelder Ältester, Peter Wiebe, makes no apology for driving his tractor to church; he isn't using a car, which would divide the community, especially along class lines. He is not willing to accept Old Colonist youth who might wish to join the Sommerfelders merely to embrace higher degrees of modernity. Boundaries are often enforced from either side of the line.

Conclusion

Social boundaries have separated Old Colonists from their neighbours, but as social theory has it boundaries do not make a culture by enclosing it. Rather, cultures are created as members cross back and forth and with each crossing remind themselves of their particular identity. Certainly, Old Colonists have sought isolation, and they have worked hard to keep their boundaries in place by being self-sufficient—caring for their own poor, teaching their own children, and organizing their own land ownership system. Over time most Old Colony communities have defied certain national laws, simply refusing to teach Spanish in their schools, for example, and leaving members to learn basic Spanish on their own. Some knowledge of Spanish has been required since Old Colonists have traded with city people, sought medical help or legal representation, and relied on the services of taxi and truck drivers, construction and field workers, cattle traders and government officials who have visited the colonies. But only basic Spanish has been required.

These cross-boundary interactions have often been friendly, but never too personal, allowing for little intermarriage and few close friendships with outsiders. The aim of Old Colonists has been to build their own communities according to their *Ordnung*, with only a judicious interaction with outsiders. From behind those boundaries, though, Old Colonists have been non-judgmental of other faiths; they have insisted on the principle that you keep to the ways that you have been taught. Not surprisingly, they have found evangelical and other proselytizing faiths highly problematic, and they don't understand why they aren't left alone, just as they leave other faiths to their own. This is the same approach that they take to the state: Old Colonists have asked for little other than the right to live out their old ways, in peace and security, and even then they would rather suffer some indignation than regularly be patrolled by the police; they will work hard, pay their taxes, and obey most laws, but they want to take care of their own problems through their own ways of non-violence.

Old Colony appearances can be deceiving. Their histories describe a "traditional" people, but they also suggest a constant and dynamic interaction with the very social organism that stands as its greatest threat. A steady and sustained interaction with the outside world has long been at the foundation of their particular anti-modernity.

CHAPTER SEVEN

The "Othering" of
English North America

"[She has] gone into the world... [and] died in Toronto."

A former teacher and now a farmer, Isaac Klassen of Yacuiba, Bolivia, has travelled 10,000 kilometres to visit us in Manitoba, Canada. Officially he is here to attend a Mennonite Central Committee networking meeting as the lone voice from a horse-and-buggy Old Colony community from the Global South. He stands out among professional service workers with his telltale black overalls and long-sleeved, buttoned-up shirt, but he holds his own with a wry sense of humour and strong sense of self. Having completed the multi-day meeting, Isaac visits our farm just outside Steinbach, a return visit for mine to his farm in Bolivia in 2009. We take the red farm truck and stop on the gravel road on the boundary between sections 11 and 12 of Township 7-6E and walk into the wheat fields.

I like telling Isaac how western Canada is divided into perfectly square townships, each with thirty-six sections, a system his grandparents will have memorized. I tell him about farming in the north: we plant by the end of the first week of May, thus allowing for a late-August harvest while the days are still long and the sun still hot. And it must all happen within Manitoba's 100-day frost-free growing season, using the pent-up precipitation of the long winter's snowfall and the eighteen-hour sunlit days of June. But Isaac has heard this account before. It is knowledge wrapped up in stories that his grandparents from Winkler told long after they migrated to Mexico in 1922. The things that he finds strange about Canada have happened since his ancestors left for Latin America. He asks me about my life. How much does the Toyota truck cost? What do I make of Bible School teachings about the end times? How did I raise my teenagers in modern Steinbach?

Does everyone in Steinbach have a television set? He thinks that there is nothing good about TV and that he needs to be a strong and loving father to keep his sons from going out into the world.

Isaac's questions implicitly place Canada at the doorstep of the world. Most horse-and-buggy Mennonites in Latin America seem to have a story to tell about Canada, which their ancestors left three generations earlier. Indeed, their lives in the south have been anchored by stories of life in the north. They have the old accounts of their grandparents' betrayal in the 1920s. But mostly they have their own stories of more recent times in modern Canada or increasingly in the United States. They look north to the United States or Canada in various ways: some have travelled for business, others for social reasons; some speculate about life in the old homeland; many tell stories of those who went north and never came back. Many of the stories speak of necessary links to the north, but most return to the idea that the north breaks apart families and undermines true ways.

The United States and Canada do represent somewhat different locations in Old Colonist stories. Canada has been the traditional escape from poverty, the United States a more recent destination. Canada has been the choice of those able to obtain Canadian passports, the United States a place for those willing to risk the life of undocumented sojourners. Given the sparser Old Colony population in the United States, those heading there speak of an especially difficult and sometimes fear-driven life, one clearly meant for a quick fix to economic weakness at home in the south. Canada has a richer array of Low German–language institutions and churches into which Old Colony travellers could tie.

But both of the English-dominated countries of the north usually represent a downfall for Old Colonist traditionalists and their life goals of obedience to old vows, simplicity, and isolation. Both represent radical cultural dislocation. Their consumer cultures, wage labour economies, and porous social boundaries have not complemented horse-and-buggy ways. Yet, in contrasting their worlds to life in the north, Old Colonists residing in the south define who they are as a people. The north represents an "other" world. In this respect, it does serve a purpose in maintaining old ways in the south.

Tales of Travelling North

Old Colonists' interactions with the world of North America are described in numerous ways. As noted in Chapter 6, business links are easy to talk about. The links to the north solicit little emotion or controversy. Usually, they are portrayed as sanctioned forays into the English world to acquire approved technologies—tractors, combines, soybean planters—with which to bolster and not undermine colony life in the south. Old Colonist farm equipment dealers, in particular, talk about making regular trips to Canada and the u.s. They describe how they assemble their wares onto flatbed semis for shipment to Mexico or Belize or into cargo containers for seaport destinations in South America.

It doesn't matter just where they have gone; their trips to the north are seen as having complemented true society in the south. Wilhelm Buhler of Riva Palacios, Bolivia, has just returned from the United States, from where he shipped four steel containers, each one filled with four combines, several lawn mower tractors, and other equipment, sending them down the west coast and over the Andes from Iquique in northern Chile. Wilhelm recites the six Midwest states that he has visited as well as the various countries: Canada, Mexico, Paraguay, Chile, Argentina, Brazil, and even England. He has worked closely with his father-in-law and a brother-in-law, Johan Fehr. Other purchasers have worked alone, but also with keen minds for the local markets that they serve.

Johan Wall of Manitoba Colony, Bolivia, who spent boyhood years in public elementary schools in Alberta, Saskatchewan, and Manitoba, and speaks a rudimentary English, recounts his trips, to Nebraska once and to Ontario twice. Each time he "filled a container with a combine" but also added "extras [such as] dishes, bedding, textiles, etc.," in high demand among colony women. He also knows that Bolivian Old Colony men "really want John Deere equipment ... [as] John Deere ... can do more work.... Equipment from Bolivia is not as good." Upon his return home, he has simply called an auction. On his most recent trip, he borrowed $27,000 and, having purchased well, made a good profit at the auction.

These stories tell of an ironic strategy; goods acquired in the north have not only sustained agriculture in general but also served the particularities of Old Colony agriculture as established by the *Ordnung*.

Peter Knelsen of Manitoba Colony, Bolivia, has rejected the combines available in Bolivia because they "are made in Japan or China and are self-propelled." Such self-propelled combines are not allowed by the church's teaching on simplicity, unless they are altered, either by replacing rubber tires with steel wheels or by removing their transmissions and pulling them with steel-wheeled tractors. The easiest solution is to purchase small pull-type combines. They are readily available in Canada and the United States, where rapidly increasing farm sizes have made them obsolete. Religious scruples do not explain all of the particulars of his travel. Peter tells the story, for example, of travelling to Birmingham, England, to purchase a Fordson tractor for the sole reason that "I had not been there yet." But ultimately his narrative ends where all such stories end: after purchasing his British tractor in the company of his English-speaking son-in-law (who has sojourned in Ontario), Peter packed it up, shipped it down the Thames, across the Atlantic, through Panama Canal, from Iquique to Santa Cruz, and then east beyond the Rio Grande to Manitoba Colony. There, after being equipped with steel wheels, it has taken its place alongside his second tractor, one that he purchased in Brazil.

Women also have their versions of such colony-enhancing purchasing trips. Frieda Bergen,[1] also of Manitoba Colony, has been to Canada twice, in 2005 and 2007: the first time to have her husband find seasonal work to "pay off debt," the second time enabling her husband to buy farm equipment. During these trips, Frieda did her own purchasing, including "craft supplies for woodwork, cutouts of roosters, children riding horses," and materials with which "to make miniature sleighs," all complementing Old Colony children's pastimes, perhaps even imagining the old homeland of Canada. Other women have brought back tools specifically meant to address domestic work issues. Maria Klassen of Riva Palacios recalls how one year "Peter Friesen's niece" and her husband, the Knelsens, came back from Leamington, Ontario, for a visit, bringing with them two sewing machines that they wished to sell. Maria was impressed by how the young Mrs. Knelsen, at first declaring that only men should hawk wares in public, nevertheless presented her sewing machines in front of a "large group of people," boldly describing their merits. The real benefit of the sewing machines, of course, was that they guaranteed Old Colony self-sufficiency in making and mending clothing.

Such visits to the north have not only sustained old ways but also seriously undermined them. Indeed, many Old Colonists can recount how they have lost loved ones to Canada and the United States. Transnational kinship networks usually consist of at least some adult children or siblings who have left the southern colonies to find work in the north. Helena Wieler of Colonia Trinidad in southern Mexico employs common parlance when she describes her extended family's places of residence. They are "spread out across the whole world," certainly the worlds of Canada, Mexico, and the United States she knows, and then she traces their places of residence—"one in Canada, a couple in Seminole [Texas], one in Cuauhtémoc [Mexico], and one in Virginias [northern Mexico], and I am here, ... [and] Jacob is also here." But even then it is neither this neat nor this static. After rendering her list, her mother, Anna Thiessen, clarifies that those at "Virginias all moved away: some to the States [and] to Canada and like that." And she explains why it matters: having been abandoned by so many of her children in the north, she and her husband moved from Virginias in northern Mexico to Trinidad in southern Mexico to re-establish ties with at least some of their children and grandchildren.

This story has many variations, even within a single colony. Elisabeth Hiebert of Progreso in Campeche has seven siblings, all in the south except for one who lives in Ontario. But her neighbour, Martin Martens, has eight of his twelve siblings in Canada. He lists them and their places of residence by birth order: "The oldest three live in Manitoba—Johan in Winkler, Cornelius (Neil) Martens at Monarch, Isaac Martens near Gretna. [Then there is] Jake in Oklahoma; Susana Martens, Winkler [Canada]; David, Zacatecas [Mexico]; Sara, Canada, [in] Plum Coulee; Abram in Chortitz [Canada]; two sisters in La Honda [Zacatecas]; and George and Justina in Altona [Canada]." His family network links a dozen points in three countries, not in orderly fashion by country but with reference to family order and in such a way as to tie disparate places together intricately.

A third Progreso resident, Isaac Dyck, introduces another common subnarrative of migration north by invoking the phrase "all alone." Indeed, stories of the diaspora in Canada and the United States often end in a lament about loneliness and social distress. He says that the migration north has been so intensive in his kin group that his wife is the only one from her family left in the south. She "has two sisters in Canada, one is living with a Mexican, [and] three brothers in Canada," and even "her mother is in Canada." Elisabeth is abandoned on all sides, an experience made worse by the sister who has abandoned their ways for a common-law relationship with a non-Mennonite. Isaac has a similar if slightly more complicated story: ten of his twelve siblings are in Mexico, three "are here [in Progreso], five in San Luis [Patosi], one is in La Batea, one in La Honda, and two in Canada. There are ten boys and two girls." But his narrative includes another separation as it moves seamlessly from dispersion to widowhood and ends by repeating Elisabeth's lament: "My mother is here. Father died in 1985 in Zacatecas. When father died, then she was alone with boys at home. Now she is alone."

The Dycks do not want this loneliness for their recently widowed sister Helen, still in Zacatecas in central Mexico, so they have travelled north to help her come south and plan to return to help settle her affairs and make the relocation permanent. Occasionally, however, the family network has simply become impossible to rebuild. Justina[2] Hiebert of Sabinal in northern Mexico utters a familiar refrain; she "has no family [here], and this is very hard" for her. She "has brothers and sisters in Canada, Durango, Campeche, Bolivia, and Capulin," the three places in Mexico listed helter-skelter among foreign countries as if the colonies are countries themselves. In fact, the "only relative on Sabinal was the late Isaac Klassen," says Justina. " At Christmas, [we] get together with the Klassens. [My] husband is the guardian for the Isaac Klassen children." No matter that this tie arises from some kinship link and community duty, Justina clearly sees it as a substandard social arrangement.

Yet the Dycks and the Hieberts are the lucky ones. The dispersion has sometimes caused significant mental strain, especially when it has separated husband and wife. Katherina Woelke of Progreso speaks sadly about her brother, "in a [mental home] in La Honda with Mexicans. It makes one cry to think he is in a place with worldly people. He's not right in the head. His wife and he went to Canada, and he didn't have the right papers, and he was sent back to Mexico, and she stayed, and he ate a lot of nerve pills and went funny in the head." What makes his case especially difficult is that, though he has returned to the south, it is not back to the safety of his old community.

But feelings of dislocation can also be expressed by those who move. Their stories are sometimes of endless mobility, though often they end with a move meant to end any further move. Martin Martens of Progreso tells a story of repeated migration between Canada and Mexico. He says that his family always "lived in Mexico over the winter because it was cheaper and went to Canada for the summer; there's only a few [years] they didn't, until I was grown up." Then, recalling his childhood, he retraces the specifics of the migration: "When I was three years old, ... we went with a [driver of a] four-door car, Dodge, with twelve people. I remember sleeping in the back window behind the seat. When I think back, we never had an accident, all those years we drove back and forth, we were really lucky."

Even after Martin reached adulthood, married in La Honda, and moved to Progreso in search of land in 1989, his "parents kept driving to Canada until the children all grew up and moved away." But fifteen years later the ties to Canada resumed when in 2004 his father died: "One and a half years [after dad died] ... mom remarried a Heinrich Wiebe from Winkler. They phoned each other, and they knew friends of one another, and then that dad [Heinrich] came to Mexico and visited a bit, and then they got married and moved to Canada. When they moved to Canada, we lived in their house for one and a half years." But the dispersion continued unabated when, having lost his mother to Canada, Martin and his wife moved back from La Honda in central Mexico to Campeche in southern Mexico. Martin explains that "my wife's parents and all her siblings were here [in Progreso in the south] and thought we should come back [south]. We had an auction of my mom's possessions. We rented a trailer with another widow, and we brought our possessions with us. That was in November 2008. We left some things back in La Honda." Martin does not offer why they didn't move everything; perhaps no move is permanent after all.

He might have brought some order to his world, but for others the migration between the north and the south is just part of an endless culture of mobility, on again and off again, often for no expressed reason. Susanna Bergen of Valle Nuevo in Bolivia says that they have only "twenty-five hectares; it's too little ... to live on," so she thinks that they will need to move. She says that they "don't want to move to [the new colony of] Asunción because the land there is too wet, and poor people can't make a living there because they can't get anything from the land." But it wouldn't be her first move. She "was two years old when her parents moved to Bolivia from Mexico," about the same time that her "grandparents moved to Canada." Aside from this symmetry of moving north and moving south, she doesn't know much about these migrations. She doesn't "know where in Canada the [grandparents] moved to," and she doesn't "know why the parents decided to move to Bolivia." She was too young, too "innocent, to know," and hasn't bothered to ask anyone. She does know that she and her husband moved to Valle Nuevo east across the Rio Grande because they didn't "own ... land in Swift Current," the 1960s-era parent colony near Santa Cruz. But now, with "ten children—seven girls and three boys—between the ages of twenty-one and two," they will need to move again. But they have not decided whether to move to Colonia Asunción, in the heart of Bolivia, and then she adds more uncertainty to her narrative by offering that Canada also beckons.

Franz Penner of Shipyard in Belize explains an Old Colony world, measured by varied distances, in both geographical and religious terms. Places far away are announced with reference to the countries, places close by with reference to specific communities, and the farthest distance might in fact be religious separation, especially if exacerbated by excommunication and shunning. As Franz says, "my first wife and I, we had sixteen children born to us, all still alive as far as I know! Nine boys and seven girls. Three live in Canada, two in Bolivia, two in Indian Creek [Belize], and the rest in Shipyard. Sometimes the ones from abroad come and visit. The ones [here] in Shipyard are all Old Colony except for one son. He is excommunicated and lives just outside the community. Because of his excommunication, we have less contact [with him]. The relationship between us is fair enough." The most difficult separation is of course one measured by both geographical and religious difference. Unfortunately, the first all too often entails the second.

Escape to Canada

Those who do the actual sojourning in the north sometimes speak less about separation than about a search for security. And of the two places, Canada is more secure than the United States. Certainly, some of the aims of those having been to Canada, or those wishing to go, could be achieved in either country. But casual talk of economically stable life elsewhere has more often invoked Canada, the ancestral home of Old Colonists.

Some Old Colonists talk about Canada as a friendly escape hatch from the restrictive church *Ordnung* in the south. Johan Knelsen of Shipyard recalls how in the 1970s recently settled Canadian Old Colonists at ill-fated Richmond Hill, Belize, split over the issue of steel wheels on tractors. He recalls that the progressives who supported a switch to rubber tires returned to Canada, and those insisting on steel wheels relocated to nearby Shipyard. Numerous stories recount more recent aggravations. Sara Kornelsen[3] of Manitoba Colony in Bolivia speaks of "a brother who moved to Canada six years ago" and then "came back once with his wife, and considered coming to Manitoba Colony because he liked it, but the wife didn't want to." But then the story becomes more complicated. Sara says that the couple "had had problems with the [old] Riva Palacios Colony and had been excommunicated." She doesn't give the reason for the rupture, but it seems to be linked to her final thought: "The wife didn't want to come back [to Bolivia] because there were so many rules." Ironically, one of the central rules is that it is wrong to leave the communitarian world of the south for the individualistic one of the north.

A much more common reason given for having moved to Canada is poverty. Abram Penner[4] of Oriente in Bolivia wants to move to Canada to get away "from all the rules in the colony," but it's not simply a matter of religion, for he is "poor here" and hopes "to do better in Canada." His wife offers more details on how poverty has affected the family. She says that Abram wants to get away from the stigma of *Utschaufe,* literally "working out": that is, working for wages, even though he is employed as a bulldozer operator, a labourer of some status. Teenaged daughter Anna adds another layer of analysis, for she thinks that her father "feels the pressure to provide for his family ... because he came from a well-to-do family in [the parent colony] Riva Palacios and isn't used to being poor." She doesn't mind being poor as long as she finds happiness; for her father, poverty spells humiliation in a society that is surprisingly divided along class lines. Heinrich Buekert of Yalnon in southern Mexico says that no one wants to go to Canada; rather, they are compelled to go there. It is a simple formula: "People have to go into debt to plant a crop, and then if it does not give a good harvest then they are in trouble. And then people feel that they have to go to Canada to find work to pay off debts or earn money." It's a double setback, simultaneously working as a lowly labourer and doing so to pay off debts from farm failures.

A third aspect of Canada that some Old Colonists laud is its government-funded social safety net. Some recall it as a place where children or siblings have fared well, even though life in Canada has entailed state incursion into family life. Sara Fehr of Valle Esperanza in Bolivia says that she "doesn't know if [our] son will come back to Bolivia because in Canada they get better pay—$2,000 per month, plus [family allowance] cheques for their children." Others see a benefit in Canada's publicly funded medical services. Riva Palacios resident Marie Hamm gave birth to her youngest daughters, now six and seven, in Canada, and she knows them as her "Canadian girls." She recalls in particular how the eldest one required medical attention from the time that she was a baby, with regular trips from Leamington, where they lived, to see specialists in London, Ontario. The whole affair was covered by the province: in fact, her only cost was "$100 to hire a *Dietscha* to [drive them] and translate."

Those who have chosen Canada over the United States speak most often about the citizenship to which they are entitled as grandchildren of Canadian emigrants. Maria Dyck of Colonia Trinidad says that crime in Mexico has driven them back into the arms of the Old Colony. But the outside world has not been entirely hostile. Maria, for example, has lived in Canada with her parents and thus obtained citizenship, and then when she married Bernard he followed her to Canada and obtained his citizenship. Now both are working at securing Canadian citizenship for their firstborn, a son. They returned from Canada in 2008 with enough funds for their own farm, so "we could have cattle and horses." It's a tough return: "We are living at my parents; there are other children at home, so we are helping them too. They have a big house. We planned on getting our own place. If you start big, they say you break more quickly, so we're starting small and will then grow bigger." However measured their strategy of growth, it was made possible by Canadian passports.

Many Old Colonists spend a great deal of time talking about this pursuit of Canadian citizenship, even of clarifying their birthright as children of Canadian citizens with a bit of triumph. Often they recount the arduous process of ascertaining their parentage and then processing the papers. Anna Harms of Colonia Trinidad in southern Mexico recites the basis of her claim to Canadian citizenship: "through my parents, and my husband has [it] through me. And then we had all our children there ... when this ... Marvin Dueck [from MCC Canada] was there. And then when [our children's] citizen[ship] was going to run out, and ours too, then he [Dueck] was also there at the school at Peter Rempel's, and he just asked if I had a 'birth abroad' [certificate]. I had. Then he said they won't run out, they remained [valid]. Then it was finished." But citizenship isn't the answer to social problems, as others see it. Indeed, it can merely be the beginning of a long moral demise.

In fact, citizenship of any kind has often been viewed by Old Colonists as unnecessary, reflecting an almost nihilistic view of the nation-state. Many Old Colonists came to Bolivia from Mexico in the 1960s, for example, without giving much thought to citizenship. Under the Evo Morales government, Mennonites born in Mexico were asked to demonstrate their citizenship and obtain Mexican passports. To that end, Johan Fehr and another member of Riva Palacios flew to Mexico in 2009 to collect over 1,000 birth certificates, for all those born in Mexico before the 1967 migration to Bolivia. But even Walter Banman,[5] who has travelled widely in North America on business trips, thinks that "the *Jemeent* made a mistake in getting involved because now everyone will be able to get a passport easily, and then they'll travel to Mexico, Canada, and the United States" at will, "just what the *Jemeent* does not want to have happen." As Walter sees it, his own business trips north aid colony life, but general travel north could undermine it.

A Corrupting Canada

The idea that Canada can be a country of more pitfalls than promises seems to be common among Old Colonists in the south. Many Old Colonists tell stories of difficult times in the English-speaking country, one at once luring with its worldly ways and hostile to Old Colony teachings. The stories range from mildly derisive talk of bad winters to more serious concerns with assimilation. Aganetha Klassen of Chavi in southern Mexico recalls how her husband, Johan, reacted to Canada one year when they went to visit her parents there. Unsuccessful in getting his citizenship papers, he could not work and simply "hated sitting inside all winter"; Johan concurs: "Oh, I got tired of that."

Most Old Colonists, however, have been much more concerned with the cultural climate. A perennial concern has been assimilation to English ways. Susanna Wall of Nuevo Durango has heard that "many *Dietsche* have moved from Durango [her old home in northern Mexico] to Canada and do not teach their children Low German," and she is adamant "that [this] should not be." She lauds families, like "the Dycks, [who] came from Alberta, and their children could speak very good Low German." But a more serious concern is when assimilation involves more than losing the mother tongue. Even then some see it as an adjustment that they can control. Teenaged Aganetha Penner[6] of Oriente in Bolivia "doesn't want to get married yet" and would like to see the wider world, perhaps "work for MCC," for others, and not just for her own family. She recalls fondly having been "offered a job by Centro Menno two years ago" in Santa Cruz, but her mom thought that she "was too young." She might go to Canada, and with this her mother agrees, "learn English and then come back," even though life in Canada might entail living *plietsch*, on the sly, for example, accepting Canadian "hairstyles with no braids" and simply not letting anyone back in Bolivia know.

But such limited assimilation has often not been achieved. Some folks see Canada as little more than a cultural trap. Peter Bergen of Valle Nuevo in Bolivia says that Canada is attractive but worries what happens to people who move there. The fact is that "it's different in Canada; if there were colonies there, like in Bolivia, then ... more people would move there" without concern. Yet Canada is not Bolivia, and often it has spelled a significant cultural break from the close-knit community back in Latin America. Sara Rempel[7] of Riva Palacios has heard of a Mennonite woman from Bolivia who, having "gone into the world, ... has died in Toronto." Sadly, she wasn't a part of the *Jemeent*, a fact that significantly added to the tragedy of her death. She says that the Old Colony church in Bolivia was unable to give her a decent funeral; perhaps the "church would help her husband, but in the area he really needed it, his 'nerves,' the church wouldn't be able to help." Members who have given themselves to Canada have removed themselves from the arena of care of the Old Colony church in Bolivia.

This feeling of being unsettled among the poor migrating north has been exacerbated by secrecy and controversy. Such moves are rarely sanctioned by church leaders, who generally view them as akin to breaking baptismal vows. Heinrich Wolfe of Shipyard, born in Canada, relates this story: "In 1980, [we moved] back to … Burns Lake [British Columbia]. We were very poor in Belize; dad made two dollars a day. We kept it a secret that we were planning on moving back to Canada; … otherwise, you got excommunicated. Somebody else sold all our stuff when we were back in Canada already, but I don't think we ever got the money for it." Indeed, the question of money or debt can add to uncertainty, with those moving north often bearing the additional stigma of people escaping from financial obligations in the south.

People who leave the colony for the north have indeed sometimes been linked to crime. Elderly Aganetha Barkman[8] of Valle Esperanza in Bolivia says that her "niece in Canada … lives with a man who was paid to bring drugs into Canada. But he took the money … but then didn't buy the drugs," meaning that the drug lords "came after him." He has become a fugitive. When Frieda Schmidt[9] of Valle Nuevo speaks of her four siblings in Canada, she emphasizes the sister who moved to Alberta and raises the theme of exile. Her story is a sad one: "Because of their debt in Bolivia, if they had stayed, they would've gone to jail; now they have trouble in Alberta, her husband drinks, and they still have debt; they've lived in Canada for sixteen years but have never returned to visit because they are too poor." As Frieda sees it, life in Canada spells dislocation; home is in Bolivia.

Others know Canada as a frightening place—expensive, English, and interventionist. Abram Hamm of Riva Palacios recalls something as simple as taking a taxi as an ordeal. He wasn't "able to speak English," and he wasn't "familiar with taxis in Canada. It was a fifteen-kilometre drive and … cost … $65.50"; he was "horrified." Some Old Colonists retell stories of how the Canadian government has undermined family cohesiveness. It is a country that allows the state to intervene in the discipline of children and even marriage relationships, says Johan Woelke of Progreso. He has heard of some extreme cases. Canada, he says, has "a terrible government that takes kids away from parents who punish their children.... Lots of people divorce, and that's not right. More men get sent to jail than women if they argue, even if it's also the woman's fault." And then without explanation he adds that "when we die we won't take a cent with us, rich or poor." Johan can't see how stable family life can take root in a country that regulates spousal relations. And indelibly he links governments, divorce, and wealth, a package of Western culture that horse-and-buggy people oppose.

Other Old Colonists have found local and even school administration in Canada problematic. Stories abound of Old Colonist migrants not integrating well in the Canadian school system. Elisabeth Harder at Sabinal recalls her childhood in British Columbia as fraught with conflict, filtered by an education system privileging middle-class values of individual rights over any sense of family solidarity. She recalls having often been "teased for being *Dietsch*" and receiving little support from school officials. She has since decided to always dress her "children like the *Moud* [fashion] of the place where they live; it is too difficult being different." She recalls specifically an incident from her schooldays when she and her siblings were on their "way home from school" and "a boy rode his bicycle into ... younger sister Nettie. She fell and scraped her knees very badly."

Elisabeth and her brother decided to take matters into their own hands and stand in solidarity as a family. They "raced home and ... wait[ed] for the boy as he rode by." Stopping him, Elisabeth "held his head by the hair, and [my] brother slapped him across the face.... Mother had warned [us] not to do something like this, and [we] told her 'wait until you see Nettie's knees.'" Their mother believed them and according to Elisabeth just "stood and watched.... The next day in school the teacher ... strapped all three of [us]; the boy claimed it was an accident." Elisabeth recalls having received only tepid support from the teacher. The boy was asked "whether the street was so narrow that he couldn't just have ridden past the girl instead of at her." But even then their father was called in to account for the children's actions. Appearing before the school board, he was "asked whether he had punished his children; he said he hadn't, he'd just had a talking with them." Luckily, recalls Elisabeth, "that was good enough for the school board." The incident changed the family. After this, "Father bought a record player so that his children would stay at home rather than hang out on the streets. [We] listened to Wilf Carter, Kitty Wells, and one Elvis Presley record [was] allowed.... Father ... listened to them first to make sure they were okay." In any case, he considered that pop stars could produce a safer environment for his children than hypocritical teachers and feckless school boards.

Contrasted to family services and school boards, border officials elicit greater fear. Indeed, distressing stories of being caught between Canadian and American border officials are not uncommon, and even the experience with American officials is often conflated with the experience in Canada generally. Sara Unger of Colonia Trinidad in southern Mexico recalls the year that she and her husband, Wilhelm, travelled to Canada to visit their children, an uneventful time except that they ran into serious trouble at the American border on the way home since her visa had expired two days earlier. They were delayed because a broken windshield had forced them back at the border. The repair took two days, and when they returned to the border Sara was taken aside and forced to "sit in a big room with lots of chairs" by herself. The officials would not let her into the United States, nor would they let her back into Canada. Her choices were to "sit in jail," sign a form promising not to try to cross the border again for a certain number of years, or purchase a ticket right there to return to Cancún, a short day's drive to her colony, before they would let her go. Sara didn't want to sit in jail, for "what would they do to me?" Nor did she want to write off her ability to cross the border, because she had children in Canada, so she bought her ticket to Cancún. She did not want to fly by herself with just English people, but she had no choice.

Canada might be the land of their grandparents, but it has often not received its lost sons and daughters in kindly fashion. Perhaps the most hostile aspect of Canada has not been the times that it has been unfriendly to Old Colony Mennonites but the times that it has successfully lured them into its lap of English-language, consumption-based society.

"Unsettled" in the United States

In recent decades, as Canadian passports have been harder to obtain, and with the American border as porous as ever, an increasing number of Old Colonists have headed into the land once traversed by their parents and grandparents. Abram Wiebe of Colonia Trinidad says that, because he has a registration of birth abroad card from the Canadian government, his son Johan plans "to apply for Canadian citizenship for himself and children." But in the meantime the "plan is to go to the United States to work again as they have in the past to earn enough money to live here. They would like to come to Canada to do the same," even take advantage of government-funded child benefits, but they are not Canadian citizens. They will join the thousands of Old Colonists who have found their way to Mennonite clusters in western Texas, Oklahoma, and Kansas, or in some cases in places well beyond this nucleus of Mexican Mennonite settlements. Like Canada, the United States has been seen as a stopgap measure against poverty in the south. But life in the United States has been fraught with uncertainty as Old Colonists join the throngs of undocumented migrants from Latin America attempting to obtain financial resources with which to rebuild lives in the Global South.

Like those choosing Canada, those electing the United States are almost always driven by poverty. The move north is often a "grapes of wrath" migration, a difficult fleeing from southern privation, amid worry of what leaving old ways in the south will mean. Anna Harms of Colonia Trinidad in southern Mexico pits her deep desire that her children live the Old Colony way against the economic reality that "they do not know what they are supposed to do here." There simply seems to be no option for them in the south. The reality that Anna faces is that the Mexican government has intervened and forced poor Old Colonists "to stop making charcoal" from felled jungle, their only form of livelihood. To make matters worse, her eldest son, Jake, recently married, has "only ... a cow," because the parents of his wife "were so poor they could never give them a cow," resulting in a rather tenuous new household. To make matters worse, in the tropical heat of southern Mexico, the "one cow ... did not always give milk." Thus, Jake and his wife moved to a place near Juárez on the American border where he found work in a Mennonite general store. Anna's other children have also been forced to address economic pressures with an openness to migration. Anna adds that "our Johan [now] works on a farm in the States," while, still in Mexico, "our Trudy also works for ... a low wage." But she is also thinking of moving north since she and her husband "don't have a place of their own."

The poor have also been the most vulnerable to crime, especially in northern Mexico. Heinrich and Maria Dyck of Colonia Trinidad take turns describing their reasons for sojourning in Texas during the time that they lived in the Buenos Aires Colony in northern Mexico. One reason was that "everything was too expensive, [the cattle] feed [was so scarce that we] could not get enough money from milk." But to make matters worse, "the drug people came in and started farming marijuana, also in Buenos Aires. The drug groups fight among themselves and then shoot each other. The Mennonites cannot drive around at night because they are afraid of getting shot. Many have been held up at gunpoint and had money stolen and lives threatened." Sometimes it is safest to cross into the United States and lie low for a while.

The United States is often only the most recent of destinations along a difficult pathway. Sara Fehr of Valle Esperanza in Bolivia recites the figures for her family: "Seven children, thirty-nine grandchildren, three grandchildren died, and the oldest is fifteen.... Thirteen siblings, but three siblings died at birth." But then the narrative becomes more complicated. Although most of the "children are in various colonies throughout Bolivia," having "moved because they needed land as Valle Esperanza was full," two have moved north, in two distinct stages. The oldest son, thirty-nine, initially moved to the new colony of Valle Esperanza, attracting his parents to move there as well, but then he pulled up stakes and "moved to Elmer, Ontario, four years ago; first he worked in a greenhouse, but now he works in a dairy." But more recently the favoured destination has been the United States. Sara adds that a daughter also "moved with her husband to Kansas this past December. They had been working in Mexico, and they moved to Kansas because they wanted the work." Sara is unhappy about this move, concluding simply that it is "too bad."

Her main concern seems to be the volatility of life as an undocumented alien in the United States. Such a sojourn has been possible for many Old Colonists only because of the chain migration of relatives creating a kinship network able to absorb newcomers from the south. Frieda Wiebe[10] of Neuland in Bolivia has siblings in Winkler (Canada) and Rio Verde (Paraguay), well-established Mennonite communities, but she also has a brother in Oklahoma. He moved there "because he was poor and needed work," and even this move was made possible because "there are other *Dietsche* there." Still, an illegal stay in the United States presents a host of problems. Margaretha Friesen of Progreso in southern Mexico answers, with a chuckle, the question of how living in the United States is possible without a visa: "It works but with fear.... One always has to be ... unsettled, one always has to be afraid, afraid of the authorities. That part, that is not pleasant there. For that reason, it would be better for one in Canada. There one doesn't have to be so afraid."

Another problem is that getting into the United States is also falling into a trap because it is extremely difficult to negotiate the border and even return home for visits. Katherina Dyck of Progreso is pleased that her daughter Marie and her husband, Jacob Martens, live in Village 6; that her son Abram and his wife, Greet, live in Village 15; and that her younger children, "Franz, a well builder, Aganetha, Sush, Agatha, and Kjnals are at home." But she is deeply worried about her son Peter and his wife. First they "were in the States to pay off debt ... work[ing] illegally," but then things became more difficult since he "had to leave for his wife's father's funeral in Mexico." As a result, they then had "to pay the debt they incurred to go to Mexico for the funeral. That is hard on them." Travel is stressful, especially if one doesn't have the papers to do so safely. Maria Dyck of Colonia Trinidad hears from her children in Bolivia and the United States when they phone. But they do not come in person: Bolivia is too far away, and those in the United States want to stay there because it would be difficult to return if they went to Mexico for a visit. She adds that, though the men have been able to obtain work permits, "they want to make papers" for their wives, for without proper documentation "their wives, who are Mexican [citizens], ... will not be able to get back in[to the United States]."

A main problem with the United States is its immense capitalist power to assimilate people. Given their proximity to the American border, Old Colonists at Sabinal in particular are concerned with the vortex of American culture. Gerhard Hamm[11] points out how the Old Colonist man from Sabinal depicted in the National Geographic documentary *A Perfect World* succumbed to assimilation. He says that the young man "at the end who walks across the bridge" from Chihuahua to Texas was paid to play his role, pretending to be a Sabinal horse-and-buggy Mennonite escaping to the north. Locals know him as an actor. He was being truthful in the filmed re-enactment only in the sense that he was already a car-driving person enmeshed "in the trouble in Cuauhtémoc among the Mennonites there," a vague reference meant to distance him from true Old Colonist. Walking north across that bridge certainly symbolized what could happen to a person leaving Old Colony ways. Marie Froese of Colonia Trinidad is similarly vague about the dangers of assimilation. She recalls her family's life in the United States as one stretched out between two cities in Texas: "One was in Leveland and another in Morton.... We always lived in Leveland, Texas. And another lived in [Morton]. We were all scattered ... in the city" "among other English."

Margaretha Friesen of Progreso might talk about the fear of living as an undocumented person in the United States, but she is as fearful of acculturation as of deportation. She says that life in the United States has been made bearable by the presence of a Reinländer Mennonite church, an offshoot of the Old Colony church. Its worship services and church practices are "a bit more [based] in the 'past,' like the way that we had it" in Mexico. But she is still worried that her children in the United States might lose their way. In fact, she describes her children there with a lament: "Oh, but they are again there [in the States]. The one who got married here." Despite the Reinländer church, she is concerned: "Well, we would have said ... that they do not do right if they stay there. One knows how one has learned, and one has I guess also [taught them] ... , just told [them], how it should be." Her words might be vague, but her thinking is precise.

Susanna Hiebert of Sabinal also dislikes the idea of her children and grandchildren living in the United States and possibly falling prey to American ways, but she thinks that they have no choice but to live there for at least a while. Recently, she and her husband travelled to Hobbs, New Mexico (just across the border from the Mexican Mennonite community at Seminole, Texas), to see their son and his family, who live there illegally. They found them residing in a house trailer, and to her dismay, after longing for her grandchildren, they didn't recognize her. Despite their undocumented status and inability to speak English, her son had a good job on a farm there with a good boss and an acceptable salary of twelve dollars per hour. She accepts the fact that her "seven grandchildren go to an English school and ... [is] very impressed that they get breakfast and lunch there." Still, the United States was a last resort for her son and his family. The only reason that they moved there was because he "had a string of bad luck [here at Sabinal], and eventually it got to the point where he just couldn't make it. One year he tried [growing] chilis, another onions, another cotton. It rained so much the year he tried cotton that all the cotton balls floated away. He now has very much debt at the cotton gin on Buena Vista Colony." She was the one who told him that he should take his family and leave Sabinal, even though they had moved there in the first place so that the Rempels could live together as one extended family. She says that "it was too difficult to watch [the] children and grandchildren live such difficult lives."

Economically difficult times in the south have forced many Old Colonists into culturally treacherous places in the United States. Old Colony mothers do not easily instruct their adult sons to take their families north. It is the north that harbours the very cultural artifacts that the Old Colony has been resisting for generations. Only when northern resources are harnessed for southern survival are sojourns away from the colonies justified.

Rediscovering Salvation in the South

Not surprisingly, given their current locations, Old Colonists in the south tend to speak with gratitude when recounting their return from the north. Indeed, they emphasize that their time in Canada or the United States was meant to be temporary, or they are thankful today that it was. Sometimes the temporary nature of the move north is expressed by material items: land owned, cattle inherited, or even heirlooms maintained. When one of Elisabeth Hiebert's married daughters moved to Kansas, she and her husband "sold almost everything at an auction." But as Elisabeth explains, her daughter found two "chests of drawers," each received as a gift from a respective parent, "too precious to sell," and asked to store them in her parents' basement.

In other cases, the temporary nature of the sojourn is inscribed in the way that the narrative is cast. Peter Rempel and his young family were in the United States for thirteen months in 2007 and 2008 for a simple reason—"to earn money so that [we] could come back to live in Mexico." But Aganetha, says Peter, "can understand a lot of English" because "they came from Seminole, Texas, in 2004," and earlier they were in South Carolina "for one month to work for the Amish." Of course, their location in Campeche itself is less than stationary: after they came back from the United States in 2004, they lived in Village 103 and after 2008 in Village 101. And they recall vividly that they had both been "teachers in Chihuahua, both at the same time, as a married couple, one ... teaching in one village, the other in another," itself a vocation without the potential for more than a subsistence salary.

Others do speak of having considered staying for a longer period by using a common phrase, *tou wiet*, literally meaning "too far" but referring to a lifestyle drifting away from traditional values to middle-class consumption. Justina Giesbrecht says that most of her siblings are with her and her husband in Valle Nuevo, but "one sibling is in Gnadenhof, another sister's husband died, and she remarried to an Argentinean and lives in Argentina for the past ten years." But her siblings did not always stay with the old ways: "A brother and a sister of [my] husband lived in California for three years; they recently came back to Bolivia because they have land in Bolivia and because things in the United States were *tou wiet* for them." It is almost identical to the reason that Margaretha Friesen of Progreso gives for some of her husband's siblings' recent decisions. She is from a family of fourteen and easily lists their various locations: Campeche, Buenos Aires [in northern Mexico], and "three in the States." It's a similar story with her husband's family of eleven, except that she almost forgets about his married sibling and spouse in the United States: "Oh, yes, one pair in the States, but now in January they want to move to Bolivia.... It is also *tou wiet* for them with the way it is in the States."

Tou wiet are not the words that Maria Froese of Colonia Trinidad in southern Mexico employs, but they are what she means when she says that they came south because "my husband was tired of the

States." The narrative has a common flow: "We had to leave Mexico because we were so poor, we just couldn't live anymore. We ... went to Canada to work, and it seemed like it was too far away to be in Canada to work, one couldn't go and visit one's siblings so easily.... So then we went to the States. And now he was tired of the States, to go and work for others, and he desired to work for himself, and we moved here, [where] ... we farm and he repairs ... for others.... We have only... twenty-four hectares I think." Maria continues to describe the farm on which they grow "corn cobs ... to feed our cattle ... and to sell." But ultimately she returns to the core reason for the move and just what her husband meant when he said that he was "tired" of the north. In Campeche, they can "return to more of the way that one was taught, ... and my husband thought he would like to [go] to where [it was] like how we had learned. Trucks, we thought, didn't belong to us. So we are here. We'll see how long we can [live] here."

Not everyone in the south is as resolute as Justina, Maria, and Margaretha. Some who have returned to the south speak of a cultural gap between Canada and Latin America, filling the migrant with ambivalence. Some speak of living between cultures. Franz Wall of Yalnon in southern Mexico has positive memories of his family's sojourn in Canada. It was a time when "the oldest children were in school" learning about the modern world in unprecedented ways. Franz says that his son Jake, "very clever, still remembers a lot," has been able to apply some of his learning to his life in Mexico. Marie Hamm of Riva Palacios in Bolivia has her own nostalgia for life in Canada. She says that when she lived in Ontario she missed the slow melodies of the traditional *Lange Wiese* hymns sung in Bolivia. But then "here in Bolivia some Mennonites ... came from Mexico ... [singing] like they sing in Canada," and then she longed for the faster gospel songs of the north. Just because someone goes to Canada, says Marie, doesn't mean that he or she can cut ties to the Old Colony permanently.

Others who have gone north speak of the difficulty of reintegrating upon their return to the south. Elisabeth Harder of Sabinal was eighteen when her parents moved from Vanderhoof, British Columbia, back to their old home in La Batea, Zacatecas, in central Mexico. But they stayed in Mexico only for a short time because her parents "never felt accepted on La Batea." Everything seemed fine at first, with Katherina finding work as a maid at the nearby La Honda Colony. For her parents, though, the problem began when they showed up at La Batea in a "little van … carry[ing] all their belongings, and … Father was made to sell it because they weren't supposed to have a vehicle." Although he accepted this edict, he and his wife exacerbated the situation by exhibiting a Canadian-spawned desire for privacy. Thus, when they "built a fence around their yard, [they] offended people because they were used to walking across the yard." To make matters worse, "the La Batea people said the family was too 'educated.'" A sense of alienation quickly set in, and they packed up again and returned to Canada. Elisabeth remained behind in Mexico only because she was already dating Frank, her future husband.

Still, other returnees say that they gladly left the riches of the north for the simple ways of the south. Daniel Neudorf of Colonia California in Bolivia says that his "brothers in Canada want to return to Bolivia; they like the life in Canada but miss the people in Bolivia." Some Canadian sojourners readily list their preferences for the south. Christina Friesen, a young mother from Manitoba Colony, Bolivia, lived in Canada with her family for a year to meet Canadian citizenship requirements and has fond memories of Canada: "The youngest was born there, Jacob [my husband] worked in a factory, I stayed at home." After a time, she "started getting used to the stuff in Canada; life was easier." But to her mind, Bolivia has the advantages. Life is closer to nature since her "son can play outside year-round in Bolivia." Then, too, labour is cheap and housing affordable, so the family has "hired four Bolivians to make the verandah and the barn." But she says that mostly they "came back to Bolivia because of family," a small price to pay for the "songs sung in church [that] are too slow" and the constricted travel by horse and buggy. Life within the extended family trumps any promise of upward mobility in the north.

Other Old Colonists feel that, when they reconnect with loved ones, they also embrace a better lifestyle. Martin Martens of Progreso, who has spent time in Canada, prefers life in Mexico: "I can make a cheaper livelihood. I don't like Canada in some ways. I went to school a bit, and I wanted my kids to grow up here and not there…. It's easier to make a living here. Canada has a long, hard winter, and one has to work to keep warm. Here it's always been better for living, but it's not always the same for all." But others speak of dreams in the south that middle-class life in the north could never offer. Young Jacob Friesen of Manitoba Colony, for example, speaks of having succeeded in Canada but without lasting satisfaction. He says that in Canada he learned English, attending biweekly classes, and, unlike his brother, who was too late to obtain Canadian citizenship, he did, at age twenty-seven, "just before they changed the laws to stop people from ... retaining Canadian citizenship." But ultimately he didn't enjoy life in Ontario because it meant working year-round. In Bolivia a hiatus between the seasons lets people relax, and then, too, in Bolivia, he might just fulfill his dream of owning his "own land and working outside."

When Maria Froese and her daughter Anna of Colonia Trinidad compare Mexico and the United States, they think of both the simpler technology of the south and a strong sense of home. Anna reflects on the life of her sister in the United States and then on her own when she returned south: "Horse and buggies, that we knew very well from already before. It was just a bit unfamiliar when we moved back. We lived for so long in the States.... [But] it seems to be more pleasant, with the *Jemeent* and among all the *Dietsche*, it is pleasant like this." Maria agrees with her daughter but acknowledges the economic cost of returning home:

> It is more comfortable to be here among the people to whom
> one belongs.... One feels better, more at home, when one can
> [live] like this. When one lives among such folk, such folk of
> which one is not a part, or the English or Mexicans, we don't
> belong with them. And it always never feels at home there....
> We are very, very emotionally well here [even though] ... it is
> harder than it was in the States to make a living, but I say as
> long as we have enough to live on, as we have had until now,
> then we can be satisfied.... We always have enough food here.

She recalls very difficult times in Mexico, especially when they still lived in northern Chihuahua, but reasserts that life in the tropics of the south provides a steady subsistence income.

This conversation about life in Canada and the United States for Old Colonists recounts a dramatic difference between two worlds. On the one hand has been life in the individualistic and economically developed world of the north, and on the other has been life close to nature and community in the south. Their conversations seem to crystallize this difference based on ideas fundamental to horse-and-buggy societies. In telling their stories, they have reaffirmed particular realities.

Conclusion

Old Colony communities have not consisted of only the cultural artifacts and social networks on the inside or even of social boundaries keeping non-Mennonites at bay. These communities have also been defined by a particular cosmology, one that has pitted a simple life in Latin America against the consumption-based, capitalist societies of Canada and the United States. One world has been marked by simplicity, obedience, and community, the other by the lure of consumer goods and individual achievement. The conversations in this chapter have highlighted the ways in which Old Colonists see the wider world.

When Old Colonists in Latin America in particular were asked in different circumstances about their thoughts on Canada or the United States, they often spoke a common narrative. The Global North had a stronger economy, even a social safety net, that was attractive. In fact, many Old Colonists said that they had travelled to Canada and the United States, often as sojourners to pay off debts, buy goods that could be sold in the south for a profit, obtain their citizenship papers or green cards, or simply follow relatives and reconnect with them. Many Old Colonist families had a sibling or child who had gone north and not come back, but some also had one who had returned and in so doing reaffirmed old values, a life lived outdoors and anchored within community, separated from urban bustle.

The conversations reported in this chapter clearly envisage two places, each with its particular code of ethics, one open to folks acclaiming individual pursuits and rights, the other governing a people called to humility and community. By envisaging not only the ideal in the south but also the "other" society in the north, they reinforced the reality of the former.

Horse-and-Buggy Genius

In July 2009, I sat down with my host Jacob in an Old Colony community in the southern regions of Bolivia to ask him about his life. It was a mild winter day, and we were sitting on plastic chairs under a cascade of bright red flowers planted by his wife, Maria, the Andes Mountains visible on the western horizon. Taking the tack that oral historians do not press their subjects into corners or common templates, I simply asked Jacob to tell me his life story. He agreed, and I took out my pen and yellow sheets of paper. He told me in the simplest terms that he had been born in Mexico, married, and moved to Bolivia, where he bought this farm. When I prodded him with follow-up questions about a favourite teacher, his day of baptism, his feelings on having purchased the farm, his responses came in single sentences. The interview lasted no more than ten minutes.

Seemingly pleased that I finally put down my pen, that the unpleasant part of the afternoon was over, Jacob suggested that we go and plant potatoes. No sooner had we begun than he began an hour-long narration of when he, as a *Waisenamt*-appointed widow's *Gootmaun,* her official guardian, stood up for her in her unsuccessful bid to purchase some farmland, also eyed by a wealthy colonist, who bought it from under her with the support of a corrupt minister. After an incensed Jacob approached his Ältester in front of the colony store, the cleric used his ecclesial power to try to discredit Jacob by "officially" admonishing him with a "three-preacher" visit for consorting with evangelical Holdeman Mennonites. Jacob could only complain that a basic historical principle of Old Colony Mennonites had been violated: a widow's place in the community had not been protected.

Talking about his personal life in answer to my questions seemed to be of little interest to Jacob. The teleology of a life of steady personal improvement is not central to the imagined lifeworld of communitarian horse-and-buggy Mennonites. The struggle for fairness in the community and for purity from modernity is of interest to them. Ask these Mennonites about the past, and you quickly end up in the present. What does history mean in a society that values changelessness? What does it mean to remember old ways when the very present is supposed to encapsulate the ways of tradition? How do you remember something that you have chosen to live?

Throughout the research and writing of this oral history, a simple, central question ordered the interviews: What has changed? And changes were certainly identified. Houses of red clay brick have given way to houses of sturdy concrete; cotton dresses have succumbed to those of polyester; an organic fuel, wood, has disappeared with the coming of propane; open wagons have been outpaced by top buggies; herbs have been edged out by pills; occasional flatbed trucks have been overtaken by regular bus service; often household manufacturing and shop work have replaced farming; in some of the communities rubber-tired tractors have replaced those with steel wheels. Yet most horse-and-buggy people suggest that these changes have hardly been significant, for most can be accepted without violating the principles of simplicity, the slow, the humble.

In a similar fashion, the various migrations—regional or international—have not changed old ways, indeed they have served to resist change. Old Orders in Ontario who have moved within the southern region of the province have done so to seek inexpensive lands well away from the immediate hinterlands of bustling cities or more acculturated Mennonites. Old Colonists have built a life of migration, one based on the collective memory of their grandparents' great emigration from Canada in 1922. They have readily undertaken their own transborder moves, increasingly southward into Central and South America, to the "ends of the earth," where they have adapted to semi-tropical climates. But again, in every respect, these changes have not encouraged progress and efficiency and modernity; rather, they have enhanced the very aim of anti-modernity—the close-knit, self-sufficient agrarian community.

If conflict is a measure of historical change, then horse-and-buggy Mennonites have a claim to being agents of history. Yet the conflict that these people see is not that of a people who bend to modernity and lose their cultural distinctions to the homogenizing forces of glo-balizing culture. The well-to-do in the horse-and-buggy community certainly don't mind their status and power, but they have no interest in producing a permanent working class; rather, deeply engrained cultural habits of community building compel them to use their wealth to help secure new sources of land for their colonies, including the poor. Conflict is also ultimately squelched by the habit of stalwart members who have stayed the course, neither caring to denounce the more modern Mennonites nor seeking to convert them to accept tra-ditional values. Usually, those who have broken their vows to uphold the *Ordnung* and left the community—voluntarily or through excom-munication—are the most vocal critics of horse-and-buggy culture. Conflicts within communities are usually resolved locally, the most serious dealt with at an *Umfrage* or *Donnadach* or *Nokjoakj*, in conversa-tions not usually on the public record.

Still, horse-and-buggy people are rather open about talking of the struggle to keep old ways alive in the modern world. They seem sur-prisingly transparent about the details of their peculiar ways, about their faults and weaknesses. They speak readily about pressures on them to change their old ways. They highlight the difficulties of seek-ing anti-modern pathways in a global economy that has relentlessly as-saulted small farmers, mostly by lowering commodity prices through increased scales of economy and raising land prices with profits from large holdings. They highlight times when intrusive governments sought to integrate them into national or regional programs that they found threatening. They talk about crime—abusive neighbours, armed robberies, corrupt lawyers, and incompetent bureaucrats.

What they don't talk about is how their communitarian, simple ways are better than the life choices of other people. Horse-and-buggy people are not good at debating. They know that often they are not appreciated: missionaries cite them for being joyless, entrepreneurs for being inefficient, and journalists for lacking a sense of the primacy of individual rights. How do you defend yourself when you are intention-al about the very things for which others fault you? Horse-and-buggy Mennonites don't want a bold and certain faith that undermines the primary value of humility; they don't want to acquire large profits just to engage in the inefficiency of conspicuous consumption; they don't believe that the individual is best served by asserting "rights" when goodness comes from "belonging." But they don't seem to care to make their case in any other way than living it.

The various chapters of this book tell the stories of two sets of Mennonites who seem to be secure in their particular webs of life, their complex constellations of cultural symbols, their multifaceted social organisms, their imagined heaven-bound destinies. They are committed to migration for cultural ends. They have their institutions meant to provide for every social and spiritual need, from cradle to grave. They live within their households and clans, knowing that they have attained belonging simply through birth in a particular place. They have learned that success always depends on cooperation and consultation rather than on competition and unchecked growth. Status comes not so much in crossing boundaries to worlds built on upward mobility as in acquiring more fully the resources needed to keep the lure of the city at bay. They expend as much effort in remaining outside the wider world as the vast majority of modern humanity expends attempting to achieve full social and cultural citizenship in it. And in all of this their dialects of Low German or Pennsylvania Dutch not only ward off easy assimilation to the outside but also enhance their cultures with maxims that contain ancient wisdom and turns of phrase that accept the ironic, shame the brazen, praise the humble, reward the faithful.

What does a people who do not value progress, greater knowledge, and the latest labour-saving technologies, leisure, and entertainment talk about with ease? They keep certain stories to themselves; like all subjects of oral history, they do not want to share their most abject failures or shortcomings, though they seem to be much more open to doing so than many modern Mennonites whom I have interviewed. They are deeply ashamed of cases of sexual assault in their midst, of charges of incest, and they seek to address these atrocities in the imperfect ways that they have been taught: confrontation, censure, and forgiveness. But they do acknowledge their own incoherencies. They engage in self-deprecating humour, lampoon their own foibles, and laugh easily. They insist that they are not perfect, that things could be done better, that they need to figure out ways of confronting depression and other mental health issues. They speak about the stress of trying to locate their many children on lands of their own. They complain about one another, rich neighbours, lazy villagers, power-hungry ministers, weak bishops, abusive fathers, out-of-control youth, unkempt mothers, or ex-members who return as "sheep stealers." They might murmur in public, but they are curious and love conversation; they are welcoming of visitors who they sense are friends.

This book has set out to share the voices of some 250 horse-and-buggy people from thirty-five communities as they spoke to eight university-trained observers of culture and society, in both the past and the present. And as they did so, the common culture of two starkly different groups of Mennonites—Old Order Mennonites in Canada and Old Colony Mennonites in Latin America—became apparent. The Mennonite world generally reveals itself in a number of rather incredible sociological coalescences, as "neo-Anabaptist" critics of social injustice or as urban evangelicals emphasizing a personal faith, but both groups are increasingly likely to be middle-class residents of large towns and small cities anywhere in the world. But an untold story is the coincidental growth of two completely unrelated streams of Mennonites—the Swiss and the Dutch, the Old Colonists and the Old Orders—in an unanticipated historical outworking of teachings on submission, humility, and simplicity in the face of modernity with its clarion embrace of ease and individualism.

Certainly, pronounced differences have divided the worlds of the two peoples examined in this book. They come down to a fundamental approach to contesting modernity. Where Old Orders speak of finding theirs in the shadow of North America's largest cities, Old Colonists speak of finding theirs within privation at the ends of the earth. These disparate strategies have had their consequences: Old Orders have accommodated themselves to elements of modern North America, teaching children English, emphasizing personal morality, or answering to the judiciary of a modern welfare state; Old Colonists have maintained local life solely in Low and High German, worked at complete institutional self-sufficiency, and honed the idea of community transplantation. But a closer look reveals many more commonalities, for both Old Orders in Canada and Old Colonists in Latin America have struggled to contest modernity: they have had to decide which technologies, fashions, or state programs to adopt or reject;

they have maintained ancient dialects, distinctive peasant garb, and primitive transportation technologies; their men and women have worked hard to keep life simple in self-sufficient, production-oriented farm households.

Horse-and-buggy Mennonites have no great presumptions that their witness to simplicity and community-mindedness will be accepted by the wider world. They know that often the media turn them into people of failure, crime, or dysfunction. Certainly, the people who spoke to us knew these stories. But they were bewildered at how a world in which the death toll from car accidents and violent crimes is high, divorce is prevalent, the elderly are institutionalized, factory farms dominate agriculture, and lives are lived in asphalt jungles can be considered superior to theirs. Aware of this disjuncture, they continue to resist ingratiating themselves with consumer goods. They stay on the land as global society races toward reconstituting itself as a constellation of megalopolises. They emphasize life in community and proximity to nature, even as educational systems emphasize personal achievement and social decoupling.

The history of the last century is one of modernization. In rural districts throughout the world, technology has displaced the small farmer, governments have encouraged greater efficiencies, and mass media have commodified a common culture. It is a story of old ways left behind. The story in this book has been that of a people making changes required to keep history from unfolding as it has almost everywhere else. It is an account of keeping old ways alive in modern times. Indeed, it is a narrative of a people who believe that past ways might just be those necessary to negotiate the future. It behooves us all to listen to these voices in a world rapidly losing its tie to an agrarian past and its tolerance for cultural diversity.

Acknowledgements

My first thanks are to the 250 horse-and-buggy Mennonites who opened their homes and hearts to us the interviewers. They are the 30 or so Old Order Mennonites from southern Ontario and the 220 Old Colony Mennonites in Mexico, Belize, Paraguay, and Bolivia. They followed their teaching to welcome the stranger and they trusted us with their stories, not stories of their accomplishments but of their struggle to keep the ways of humility and simplicity that they had been taught. Almost always they offered us food and drink, and in multiple cases a place to sleep; in their friendly, warm farewells they invariably insisted that we visit again, soon. I especially want to thank Noah and Martha Weber, and the families of Paul Martin, and Amsey Martin, of southern Ontario for their hospitality, and Jacob and Maria Neudorf and Benjamin and Anna Guenther of Bolivia for theirs. On behalf of our team listed below, I also want to thank the dozens of families in Canada and Latin America who offered them such tremendous hospitality, and gifts of sustenance and shelter.

The second set of people to thank are my co-workers in the writing of this book. Kerry Fast, Tina Fehr Kehler, Jakob Huttner, Anne Kok, Andy Martin, and Karen Warkentin did the vast majority of the interviewing, while Anna Sofia Hedberg also assisted in conceptualizing the academic project and interview process. They were a well-trained, tenacious and curious, group, knowledgeable in ethnographic scholarship, willing to enter into strange communities and ask about the history of the horse-and-buggy way of life. Kerry Fast from Toronto visited Sabinal in Mexico and then the original colonies close to Santa Cruz, listening especially to stories by women about keeping faith with their calling to build their households. Tina Fehr Kehler entered the 10,000-strong newly established communities in Campeche in southern Mexico and used her personal skills to convince the interviewees to be tape-recorded, producing a rare and highly valuable archival source. Jakob Huttner travelled to both East Paraguay and Bolivia, speaking in Spanish and High German, building on his experience as a doctoral student here just a few years before. Anne Kok who lived in Belize after defending her MA in her native Amsterdam, employed her friendly nature to have the men at Shipyard Colony, using their Belizean market English, to talk about their challenges of life in a rapidly modernizing world. Karen Warkentin worked hard to learn the Low German needed to take her to the Old Colony frontier, east of the mighty Rio Grande in Bolivia. Andy Martin returned to the communities of his grandparents, Old Order people in both Waterloo and Huron Counties, finding his innate interest in theology as a pathway into the lives of a people he feels close to. Family matters kept Anna Sofia Hedberg from returning to Bolivia where she had undertaken her doctoral research, but before the birth of her first child, she was able to help shape the project at the initial workshop at St. Jacobs, Ontario.

Along the way numerous people have assisted. Dick and Kathy Braun, Alfred Koop, Ramont and Elizabeth Harder Schrock, Wilmer and Hannah Harder, Canadian service workers at Centro Menno in Bolivia, provided an entry way for many of us. Kennert Giesbrecht, editor of the *Mennonitische Post* in Steinbach, provided numerous other links and constant support. Kerry Fast, Mary Ann Loewen, and Hans Werner read the entire manuscript with utmost care and offered invaluable conceptual and editorial advice; Andy Martin and Sam Steiner gave their approval for the chapters pertaining to southern Ontario. Andrea Dyck and Susie Fisher offered their adroit assistance as research assistants. Conversations with Gerald Friesen, Joe Friesen, Howard White, Paula Peña, Alexander Freund, Ralph Friesen, Marlene Epp, James Schellenberg, Janis Thiessen helped hone the methodological approach. Papers arising from this research were first presented at the Mennonites and Anti-Modern Pathways conference held at the University of Winnipeg in October 2011, and several published in the *Journal of Mennonite Studies*. Parts of the book were presented at Clare Hall at Cambridge University in November 2013, at the Social Sciences and History Association in Toronto in

December 2014, at the University of Winnipeg in January 2015, and at Canadian Mennonite University in November 2015.

I want to thank the wonderful staff at the University of Manitoba Press—David Carr, Glenn Bergen, David Larsen, Jill McConkey, and Ariel Gordon—for shepherding this book to production. I thank Dallas Harrison for his careful copyediting and David Drummond for his genius in producing the cover.

I am grateful to the Social Sciences and Humanities Research Council of Canada for a major research grant, the University of Winnipeg for support in many ways including a research leave, the D.F. Plett Research Foundation for travel funds. The Shantz family of St. Jacobs, Ontario, offered their historic schoolhouse for our initial meetings. The first draft of the book was written in the winter of 2012 while resident in Santa Cruz, Bolivia, while the second draft was completed in the fall of 2013 as a visiting fellow at Clare Hall, Cambridge University, an exquisitely welcoming institution that provided office space and support staff.

As always I offer my utmost gratitude to my immediate family—my wife and children—for allowing me to tell too many stories of adventures among a fascinating people.

Notes

PREFACE

1   The following essays published in the *Journal of Mennonite Studies* 31 (2013) are by team members, based on their own fieldwork: Anna Sofia Hedberg, "Speaking of 'Peter Money' and Poor Abraham: Wealth, Poverty, and Consumption among Old Colony Mennonites in Bolivia," 87–104; Andrew C. Martin, "Echoes of Ancient Wisdom: Old Order Mennonite Spirituality in Monastic Perspective," 105–27; Karen Warkentin, "'*Emma jedohne*': Memories and Old Colony Mennonite Identity," 129–49; Kerry L. Fast, "Why Milking Machines? Cohesion and Contestation of Old Colony Mennonite Tradition," 151–66; and Anne Kok and Carel Roessingh, "Where 'God Sleeps at Night': Integration, Differentiation, and Fragmentation in a Mennonite Colony," 167–82.

INTRODUCTION

1   The original handwritten manuscript is in my possession. For a published version, see Levi Fry, "An Ontario Old Order's Reflections on Being Pilgrims and Strangers in a Demanding World," *Journal of Mennonite Studies* 31 (2013): 183–91.

2   In preparing to write this book, I benefited especially from works that have offered such critiques, including Charles Taylor, *Dilemmas and Connections: Selected Essays* (Cambridge, MA: Harvard University Press, 2011); Gregory Baum, *Karl Polanyi: On Ethics and Economics* (Montreal: McGill-Queen's University Press, 1996); and Ian McKay, "The Liberal Order Framework: A Prospectus for a Reconnaissance of Canadian History," *Canadian Historical Review* 81 (2000): 617–645, critiqued in Jean-François Contant and Michel Ducharme, *Liberalism and Hegemony: Debating the Canadian Liberal Revolution* (Toronto: University of Toronto Press, 2009).

3   Similarly, works that envisage a return to old values that predate technologized societies and attending philosophies, and that influenced this work, include Terry Eagleton, *After Theory* (London: Penguin, 2003); Wade Davis, *The Wayfinders: Why Ancient Wisdom Matters in the Modern World* (Toronto: Anansi, 2009); Jeff Rubin, *The End of Growth* (Toronto: Vintage, 2013).

4   For one recent example, see Donald B. Kraybill, Karen M. Johnson-Weiner, and Steven M. Nolt, *The Amish* (Baltimore: Johns Hopkins University Press, 2013). Its bibliography lists hundreds of academic works on the Amish in the United States.

5   All interviews reported on below are part of a Social Sciences and Humanities Research Council–funded project, "Canadian and Canadian-Descendant 'Horse and Buggy' Mennonites of the Americas: A Study in Anti-Modernity," and were conducted between 2009 and 2012 by me and a team of research associates, including Kerry Fast (Toronto), Tina Fehr Kehler (Winkler, MB), Anne Kok (Amsterdam), Andrew Martin (Elmira, ON), Anna Sofia Hedberg (Uppsala, Sweden), Jakob Huttner (Berlin), and Karen Warkentin

(Winnipeg). The interview instrument and approach were vetted by the University of Winnipeg Ethics Committee. Transcripts of the interviews are currently in the possession of the author and team members.

6   Matthew 5:15 and I Peter 3:15.

7   Works that have informed the oral history approach employed in this book include Alessandro Portelli, *The Death of Luigi Trastuli and Other Stories: Form and Meaning in Oral History* (Albany: SUNY Press, 1991); *They Say in Harlan County: An Oral History* (New York: Oxford University Press, 2011); Amy Starecheski, "Squatting History: The Power of Oral History as a History-Making Practice," *Oral History Review* 41, 2 (2014): 187–216; Troy Reeves and Caitlin Tyler-Richards, "Confessing Animals, Redux: A Conversation between Alexander Freund and Erin Jessee," *Oral History Review* 41, 2 (2014): 314–24; Warren and Steven High, "Memory of a Bygone Era: Oral History in Quebec, 1979–1986," *Canadian Historical Review* 95, 3 (2014): 433–56; and Linda Shopes, "'Insights and Oversights': Reflections on the Documentary Tradition and the Theoretical Turn in Oral History," *Oral History Review* 41, 2 (2014): 257–68. I wish to acknowledge Janis Thiessen for directing me to these insightful pieces.

8   See http://www.ego4u.com/en/cram-up/grammar/tense.

9   Jan Assmann and John Czaplicka, "Collective Memory and Cultural Identity," *New German Critique* 65 (1995): 127; Starecheski, "Squatting History."

10   For published histories of the Ontario Old Order community, see Winfield Fretz, *The Waterloo Mennonites: A Community in Paradox* (Waterloo: Wilfrid University Press, 1989; Isaac Horst, *A Separate People: An Insider's View of Old Order Mennonite Customs and Traditions* (Kitchener, ON: Herald Press, 2000); Donald B. Kraybill and Carl F. Bowman, *On the Backroad to Heaven: Old Order Hutterites, Mennonites, Amish, and Brethren* (Baltimore: Johns Hopkins University Press, 2001); Donald Martin, *Old Order Mennonites of Ontario: Gelassenheit, Discipleship, and Brotherhood* (Kitchener, ON: Pandora, 2003); Sam Steiner, *In Search of Promised Lands: A Religious History of Mennonites in Ontario* (Scottdale, PA: Herald Press, 2015).

11   For works that analyze Old Colony people from different perspectives and in specific locations, see William Janzen, *Limits on Liberty: The Experience of Mennonite, Hutterite, and Doukhobor Communities in Canada* (Toronto: University of Toronto Press, 1990); H. Leonard Sawatzky, *They Sought a Country: Mennonite Colonization in Mexico* (Berkeley: University of California Press, 1971); Calvin Wall Redekop, *The Old Colony Mennonites in Mexico: Dilemmas of Ethnic Minority Life* (Baltimore: Johns Hopkins University Press, 1969); J. Winfield Fretz, *Pilgrims in Paraguay: The Story of Mennonite Colonization in South America* (Scottdale, PA: Herald Press, 1953); Ben Nobbs-Thiessen, "Mennonites in Unexpected Places: Sociologists and Settlers in Latin America," *Journal of Mennonite Studies* 28 (2010): 203–24; Anna Sofia Hedberg, *Outside the World: Cohesion and Deviation among Old Colony Mennonites in Bolivia* (Uppsala: ACTA Universitatis Upsaliensis, 2007); Lorenzo Cañas Bottos, *Old Colony Mennonites in Argentina and Bolivia: Nation Making, Religious Conflict, and Imagination of the Future* (Leiden: Brill, 2008); Carel Roessingh and Tanja Plasil, eds., *Between Horse and Buggy and Four-Wheel Drive: Change and Diversity among Mennonite Settlements in Belize, Central America* (Amsterdam: VU University Press, 2009); David Quiring, *The Mennonite Old Colony Vision: Under Siege in Mexico and the Canadian Connection* (Steinbach, MB: Crossway Publications, 2003); and Larry Towell, *The Mennonites: A Biographical Sketch* (London: Phaidon Press, 2000).

12   See James C. Scott, *Domination and the Arts of Resistance: Hidden Transcripts* (New Haven: Yale University Press, 1990). For leading Canadian examples, see Beatrice Craig, *Backwoods Consumers and Homespun Capitalists: The Rise of a Market Culture in Eastern Canada* (Toronto: University of Toronto Press, 2009); Katherine A. Wilson, *Tenants in Time: Family Strategies, Land, and Liberalism in Upper Canada, 1799–1871* (Montreal: McGill-Queen's University

Press, 2009); Ruth W. Sandwell, *Contesting Rural Space: Land Policies and Practices of Resettlement on Saltspring Island, 1859–1891* (Montreal: McGill-Queen's University Press, 2005); and Kenneth M. Sylvester, *The Limits of Rural Capitalism: Family, Culture, and Markets in Montcalm, Manitoba, 1870–1940* (Toronto: University of Toronto Press, 2001).

13 For one example, see T.J. Jackson Lears, *No Place of Grace: Antimodernism and the Transformation of American Culture, 1880–1920* (New York: Pantheon Books, 1981).

CHAPTER ONE: CHANGELESSNESS IN CANADA'S HEARTLAND

1 All names related to the interviewees in this chapter are pseudonyms, recognizing a tradition in Old Order society not to have names published in public forums. The names are common Old Order names and were chosen by Andy Martin. The names of Old Order Mennonites mentioned along the way (unless they are close kin) are real, as is the name Noah Weber, the very helpful man whom I met at the Linwood church.

2 A pseudonym.

3 A pseudonym for Amsey Bearinger to honour the Old Order belief that he has been forgiven, but he is named here out of respect for his victims, who insist that there are wrong ways to forgive.

4 *Guelph Mercury,* 7 June 2006, https://secure.pqarchiver.com/therecord/access/1050804331.html?FMT=FT&FMTS=ABS:FT&type=current&date=Jun+8%2C+2006&author=&pub=The+Record&edition=&startpage=B.6&desc=Farmer+pleads+guilty+to+assaulting+16+children.

CHAPTER TWO: A NEW ORTHODOXY IN BACKWOODS ONTARIO

1 All names related to the interviewees in this chapter are pseudonyms, recognizing a tradition in Old Order society not to have names published in public forums. The names of bishops John Sherk and Paul Martin, whose farms I have visited in southern Ontario, and who have been most friendly and helpful, are not pseudonyms, nor are historical names such as Elam Martin.

CHAPTER THREE: VOWS OF SIMPLICITY IN THE SOUTH

1 A pseudonym for Mrs. John Hiebert.

2 A pseudonym for Mrs. Franz Ginter.

3 A pseudonym for Mrs. Wilhelm Penner.

4 A pseudonym.

5 A pseudonym.

6 A pseudonym.

7 A pseudonym.

8 *Time: World,* 17 August 2011, http://content.time.com/time/world/article/0,8599,2087711,00.html.

9 Personal interview with Johan Neudorf, Manitoba Colony, Santa Cruz, Bolivia, February 2012, fieldnotes.

10 A pseudonym for Mrs. Isaac Rempel.

CHAPTER FOUR: THE GENIUS OF COMMUNITY SURVIVAL

1   A pseudonym for Mrs. Jacob Wall.

2   A pseudonym for Mrs. Isaac Klassen.

3   A pseudonym for Mrs. David Fehr.

4   Pseudonyms, as children were minors at the time of the interview.

5   A pseudonym because of a request for anonymity.

6   A pseudonym for Mrs. Isaac Klassen.

CHAPTER FIVE: NURTURING FAMILY THE OLD COLONY WAY

1   The names in this paragraph are all pseudonyms.

2   Pseudonyms.

3   A pseudonym.

4   Pseudonyms.

5   A pseudonym.

6   A pseudonym.

7   Bernard Peters, *Eine Lehrreiche Ermahnung* (Santa Cruz, Bolivia: Johann F. Hamm, 2002), 22.

8   Ibid., 40.

9   Isaac and Johan are pseudonyms.

10   A pseudonym.

11   A pseudonym.

12   A pseudonym.

13   A pseudonym.

14   A pseudonym.

15   A pseudonym.

16   Anonymous interview; interviewer, Jakob Huttner.

17   A pseudonym.

18   Anonymous interview; interviewer, author.

19   Anonymous interview; interviewer, author.

20   Anonymous interview; interviewer, Kerry Fast.

21   A pseudonym.

22   A pseudonym.

23   A pseudonym for Mrs. Peter Friesen.

24   A pseudonym for Mrs. Abram Klassen.

25   A pseudonym for Mrs. Isaac Rempel.

26   A pseudonym.

27   A pseudonym.

28   A pseudonym for the sake of anonymity.

29   A pseudonym.

CHAPTER SIX: BOUNDARIES, RACE, AND THE MORAL ECONOMY

1   A pseudonym.

2   A pseudonym.

3   A pseudonym.

4   A pseudonym.

5   Pseudonyms.

6   Pseudonyms.

CHAPTER SEVEN: THE "OTHERING" OF ENGLISH NORTH AMERICA

1   A pseudonym for Mrs. Franz Bergen.

2   A pseudonym for Mrs. John Hiebert.

3   A pseudonym for the sake of anonymity.

4   A pseudonym for the sake of anonymity.

5   A pseudonym for the sake of anonymity.

6   A pseudonym for the sake of anonymity.

7   A pseudonym for Mrs. Isaac Rempel.

8   A pseudonym for the sake of anonymity.

9   A pseudonym for the sake of anonymity.

10 A pseudonym for Mrs. Franz Wiebe.

11 A pseudonym for the sake of anonymity.

Annotated Bibliography

The horse-and-buggy Anabaptists located in the Western hemisphere have generated a fair bit of interest over the generations. It ranges from mid-twentieth-century sociological and geographical works by North American Mennonites to late-twentieth-century works by non-Mennonite academics working in anthropology, economics, and history. Along the way, horse-and-buggy Mennonites themselves have offered testimonials on their lifeworlds. Each of these various genres has influenced this work.

Writings by these Mennonites themselves usually include works of apologetics, historical sermons, and testimonials of various kinds. For Old Colony Mennonites, such works appear in the German language. The most prominent are Isaak M. Dyck, *Die Auswanderung der Reinlaender Mennoniten Gemeinde von Kanada nach Mexiko 1970* (Cuauhtémoc, Mexico: Imprenta Colonial, 1993), a historical narrative of the migration of the 1920s written in the 1920s; and Bernard F. Peters, *Eine Lehrreiche Ermahnung* (Santa Cruz, Bolivia: Johann F. Hamm, 2003), an account similar in nature to Dyck's except that it focuses on the historic migration from Mexico to Bolivia in 1967. For other biographical writings, see also Jacob Harms, *Das Hinterlassene Heft vom Verstorbenen Jacob Harms, 1914–1993* (Strassbourgo, Chihuahua: Strassbourg Platz, 2001); and Abram G. Janzen, Aeltester *Johan M. Loeppky, 1882–1950 as I Remember Him* (Hague, SK: self-published, 2003).

For Old Order Mennonites, three recent works in English are noteworthy. They are Isaac Horst, *A Separate People: An Insider's View of Old Order Mennonite Customs and Traditions* (Kitchener, ON: Herald Press, 2000); Levi Frey, "An Ontario Old Order's Reflections on Being Pilgrims and Strangers in a Demanding World," *Journal of Mennonite Studies* 31 (2013): 183–191; and Andrew Martin, "Echoes of Ancient Wisdom: Old Order Mennonite Spirituality in Monastic Perspective," *Journal of Mennonite Studies* 31 (2013): 105–27. The first two works serve as apologias of the Old Order way, written by practising Old Order persons. The third work is part of a doctoral dissertation on the theology of Old Orders written by one of their descendants.

Mid-century surveys that are geographical and sociological in nature have analyzed the Old Colony groups in Mexico. They include Henry Leonard Sawatzky, *They Sought a Country: Mennonite Colonization in Mexico* (Berkeley: University of California Press, 1971), a work in historical geography; and Calvin Redekop, *The Old Colony Mennonites in Mexico: Dilemmas of Ethnic Minority Life* (Baltimore: Johns Hopkins University Press, 1969), a study in sociology. For other sociological works, see J. Winfield Fretz, *Mennonite Colonization in Mexico* (Akron, OH: Mennonite Central Committee, 1945); and J. Winfield Fretz, *Pilgrims in Paraguay: The Story of Mennonite Colonization in South America* (Scottdale, PA: Herald Press, 1953). For an insightful survey of these various works and the ambivalent way that northern academics at the time looked on the traditionalist Mennonites of the south, see Ben Nobbs Thiessen, "Mennonites in Unexpected Places: Sociologist and Settler in Latin America," *Journal of Mennonite Studies* 28 (2010): 203–24.

More recently, a number of European and American non-Mennonite scholars, especially in the field of anthropology, have undertaken cultural analyses, usually microanalytical in nature and usually rather positive in orientation. They include Anna Sofia Hedberg, *Outside the World: Cohesion and Deviation among Old Colony Mennonites in Bolivia* (Uppsala: ACTA Universitatis Upsaliensis, 2007), a study of Nuevo Durango in Bolivia; and Lorenzo Cañas Bottos, *Old Colony Mennonites in Argentina and Bolivia: Nation Making, Religious Conflict, and Imagination of the Future* (Leiden: Brill, 2008). For other graduate works by non-Mennonite scholars—Canadians and Americans—on Old Colony Mennonites in the Americas, see A.D. Bushong, "Agricultural Settlement in British Honduras: A Geographical Interpretation" (PhD diss., University of Florida, 1961); Kelly Hedges, "'Plautdietsch' and 'Huuchdietsch' in Chihuahua: Language, Literacy, and Identity among the Old Colony Mennonites in Northern Mexico" (PhD diss., Yale University, 1996); James W. Lanning, "The Old Colony Mennonites of Bolivia: A Case Study" (MSc thesis, Texas A&M University, 1971); Ronald Palmer, "Politics and Modernization: The Case of Santa Cruz, Bolivia" (PhD diss., University of California, Los Angeles, 1960); Edward Van Dyck, "Blumenort: A Study of Persistence in a Sect" (PhD diss., University of Alberta, 1972); Kelso Lee Wessel, "An Economic Assessment of Pioneer Settlement in the Bolivian Highlands" (PhD diss., Cornell University, 1968); and Martina Will, "The Old Colony Mennonite

Colonization of Chihuahua and the Obregón Administration's Vision for the Nation" (MA thesis, University of California at San Diego, 1993).

In 2013 the *Journal of Mennonite Studies* published a special issue (31) on horse-and-buggy Mennonites of Canada and Latin America. See, in this issue, Christopher Cox, "The Resilient Word: Linguistic Preservation and Innovation among Old Colony Mennonites in Latin America"; Lorenzo Cañas Bottos, "Marrying the Brother's Wife's Sister: Marriage Patterns among Old Colony Mennonites in Argentina"; Anna Sofia Hedberg, "Speaking of 'Peter Money' and Poor Abraham: Wealth, Poverty, and Consumption among Old Colony Mennonites in Bolivia"; Karen Warkentin, "'Emma Jedohne': Memories that Formed the Old Colony Mennonite Identity"; Kerry L. Fast, "Why Milking Machines? Cohesion and Contestation of Old Colony Mennonite Tradition"; Anne Kok and Carel Roessingh, "Where 'God Sleeps at Night': Integration, Differentiation, and Fragmentation in a Mennonite Colony"; and Martha Hiebert, "Stories of Betrayal and Hope among 'Horse and Buggy' Mennonite Women in Bolivia."

Lay scholars, writing in German, have made valuable contributions to the study of Mennonite groups in Latin America and Belize, studies not focused particularly on horse-and-buggy Mennonites but including them. See Walter Schmiedehaus, *Die Altkolonier-Mennoniten in Mexiko* (Winnipeg: CMBC Publications, 1982); Sieghard Schartner and Sylvia Schartner, *Bolivien: Zufluchtsort der konservativen Mennoniten* (Santa Cruz, Bolivia: self-published, 2009); Abe Warkentin, *Gäste und Fremdlinge: Hebräer 11:13; Strangers and Pilgrims: Hebrews 11:13* (Steinbach, MB: Mennonitische Post, 1987); Hans Theodore Regier, "Die Altkolonier in Paraguay," *Jahrbuch fuer Geschichte und Kultur der Mennoniten in Paraguay* 1 (2000): 39–60; Adina Reger and Delbert Plett, *Diese Steine: Die Russlandmennoniten* (Steinbach, MB: Crossway Publications, 2001); and Gerhard Rempel and Franz Rempel, eds., *75 Jahre Mennoniten in Mexiko* (Cuauhtémoc: Comité Pro Archivo Histórica y Museo Menonita, 1998).

For a selection of works by Latin American scholars, see Genaro Romero, *Colonización Menonita* (Asunción: Imprenta Nacional, 1933); Carlos Barney Almeida, "La colonización menonita en Chihuahua," *Estudios Americanos (Sevilla, Spain)* 5 (1953): 581–88; Maria Bjerg, *Historias de la inmigración en la Argentina* (Buenos Aires: Edhasa, 2009); Carlos J. Carafa, "Distribución especial e inmigración extranjera," in *La población* (La Paz, Bolivia: Instituto Latinamericano de Investigaciones Sociales, 1988), 67–73; Ivonne Flores, "Llegaron Para quedarse: La colonización menonita en Chihuahua," *Cuadernos del norte* 11 (1990): 4–7; Lyra Pidoux de Drachenberg, "Inmigración y colonización en el Paraguay, 1870–1970," *Revista Paraguaya de sociologia* 34 (1975): 65–123; and Gerhard Ratzlaff, *Entre dos fuegos: Los menonitas en el conflicto limitrofe entre Paraguay y Bolivia, 1932–1935* (Asunción: self-published, 1993).

For a variety of other works dealing with Mennonites in Latin America, see David Quiring, *The Mennonite Old Colony Vision: Under Siege in Mexico and the Canadian Connection* (Steinbach, MB: Crossway Publications, 2003); Jack Thiessen, *Mennonite Low German/Mennonitisch-Plauttdeutsches Wörterbuch* (Madison: University of Wisconsin at Madison Max Kade Institute for German-American Studies, 2003); and Delbert F. Plett, ed., *Old Colony Mennonites in Canada 1875 to 2000* (Steinbach, MB: Crossway Publications, 2001).

For some recent works on the Amish in the United States, see Donald B. Kraybill, Karen M. Johnson-Weiner, and Steven M. Nolt, *The Amish* (Baltimore: Johns Hopkins University Press, 2013); Donald B. Kraybill, *The Amish and the State* (Baltimore: Johns Hopkins University Press, 2003); Donald B. Kraybill, *The Riddle of Amish Culture* (Baltimore: Johns Hopkins University Press, 2001); Donald B. Kraybill and Carl F. Bowman, *On the Backroad to Heaven: Old Order, Hutterites, Mennonites, Amish, and Brethren* (Baltimore: Johns Hopkins University Press, 2001); Donald B. Kraybill and Steven M. Nolt, *Amish Enterprise: From Plows to Profits* (Baltimore: Johns Hopkins University Press, 2004); Donald B. Kraybill, Steven M. Nolt, and David Weaver-Zercher, *Amish Grace: How Forgiveness Transcended Human Tragedy* (San Francisco: Jossey-Bass, 2007); Steven M. Nolt and Thomas J. Meyers, *Plain Diversity: Amish Cultures and Identities* (Baltimore: Johns Hopkins University Press, 2007); and Charles E. Hurst and David L. McConnell, *An Amish Paradox: Diversity and Change in the World's Largest Amish Community* (Baltimore: Johns Hopkins University Press, 2010).

For a general history that encompasses these two groups, see Frank H. Epp, *Mennonites in Canada, 1786–1920: The History of a Separate People* (Toronto: Macmillan, 1974); and T.D. Regehr, *Mennonites in Canada, 1939–1970: A People Transformed* (Toronto: University of Toronto Press, 1996). For recent regional histories that encompass Old Colonists in Manitoba and Old Orders in Ontario, see John J. Friesen, *Building Community: The Changing Face of Manitoba Mennonites* (Winnipeg: CMU Press, 2007); and Sam Steiner, *In Search of Promised Lands: A Religious History of Mennonites in Ontario* (Scottdale, PA: Herald Press, 2015). See also general works on Mennonites in Belize by Carel Roessingh and Tanja Plasil, eds., *Between Horse and Buggy and Four-Wheel Drive: Change and Diversity among Mennonite Settlements in Belize, Central America* (Amsterdam: VU University Press, 2009); and on Paraguay by Edgar Stoesz, *Like a Mustard Seed: Mennonites in Paraguay* (Scottdale, PA: Herald Press, 2008). For general histories of Mennonites in the Western hemisphere, see Royden Loewen and Steven M. Nolt, *Seeking Places of Peace: North America: A Global Mennonite History* (Intercourse, PA: Good Books, 2012); and Jaime Prieto Valladares, *Mission and Migration: Global Mennonite History Series, Latin America* (Intercourse, PA: Good Books, 2010).

For some of my previous works that have shaped my approach to and interpretation of this book, see "Competing Cosmologies: Reading Migration in an Ethno-Religious Newspaper," *Histoire sociale/Social History* 47 (2015): 87–105; *Village among Nations: "Canadian" Mennonite Migrants across the Americas, 1916–2006* (Toronto: University of Toronto Press, 2013); "To the Ends of the Earth: Low German Mennonites and Old Order Ways in the Americas," *Mennonite Quarterly Review* (2008), 427–48; *Diaspora in the Countryside: Two Mennonite Communities in Mid-20th Century North America* (Urbana: University of Illinois Press; Toronto: University of Toronto Press, 2006); *The Making of Ethnic Farm Culture in Western Canada*, Canada's Ethnic Group Series (Ottawa: Canadian Historical Association, 2002); *Hidden Worlds: Revisiting the Mennonite Migrants of the 1870s* (Winnipeg: University of Manitoba Press; Newton, KS: Bethel College, 2001); "'Mennonite' Repertoires of Contention: Church Life in Steinbach, Manitoba, and Cuauhtémoc, Chihuahua, 1945–1970," *Mennonite Quarterly Review* 72 (1998): 301–19; and *Family, Church, and Market: A Mennonite Community in the Old and the New Worlds, 1850–1930* (Urbana: University of Illinois Press; Toronto: University of Toronto Press, 1993).

For some of the theoretical foundations of this work, see the following. For comparative analyses, see Juergen Kocha, "Comparison and Beyond," *History and Theory* 42 (2003): 39–44. For basic approaches to oral history, see Alessandro Portelli, *The Death of Luigi Trastuli and Other Stories: Form and Meaning in Oral History* (Albany: SUNY Press, 1991); and Michael Jackson, "Introduction," *Politics of Storytelling: Violence, Transgression, and Intersubjectivity* (Copenhagen: Museum Tusculanum, 2002).

For works that speak specifically to aspects of anti-modern protests, including low- and high-brow cultural responses, see Jeremy Stolow, "Transnationalism and the New Religio-Politics: Reflections on a Jewish Orthodox Case," *Theory, Culture, and Society* 21, 2 (2004): 109–37; Frances

Swyripa, *Storied Landscapes: Ethno-Religious Identity and the Canadian Prairies* (Winnipeg: University of Manitoba Press, 2010); Bryan D. Palmer, *Canada's 1960s: The Ironies of Identity in a Rebellious Era* (Toronto: University of Toronto Press, 2009); T.J. Jackson Lears, *No Place of Grace: Antimodernism and the Transformation of American Culture, 1880–1920* (New York: Pantheon Books, 1981); Nicholas Daly, *Modernism, Romance, and the Fin de Siècle: Popular Fiction and British Culture, 1880–1914* (Cambridge, UK: Cambridge University Press, 1999); and Lynda Jessup, ed., *Antimodernism and Artistic Experience: Policing the Boundaries of Modernity* (Toronto: University of Toronto Press, 2001).

For theoretical works that document migration and cultural studies, see Arjun Appadurai, "Global Ethnospaces: Notes and Queries for a Transnational Anthropology," in *Recapturing Anthropology*, ed. R. Fox (Santa Fe: School of American Research Press, 1991), 191–210; Pierre Bourdieu, "Structures, *Habitus*, Practices," in *The Logic of Practice* (Stanford: Stanford University Press, 1990, 52–79; Robin Cohen, *Global Diasporas: An Introduction* (Seattle: University of Washington Press, 1997); and Robert A. Nisbet, "Community as Typology: Toennies and Weber," in *The Sociological Tradition* (New York: Basic Books, 1966), 71–83.

Of special importance in shaping the philosophical underpinnings of this book are two works, both given as CBC Massey Lectures. Charles Taylor's *The Malaise of Modernity* (Concord, ON: Anansi, 1991), like his more recent *Dilemmas and Connections: Selected Essays* (Cambridge, MA: Harvard University Press, 2011), outlines the assumptions undergirding the individuated, secular basis of meaning and social organization under modernity. Wade Davis, *The Wayfinders: Why Ancient Wisdom Matters in the Modern World* (Toronto: Anansi Press, 2009), speaks to the same issue of modernity's limitations, albeit from the opposite perspective of outlining the benefits to premodern cultural complexity. Both authors, of course, represent but a tiny portion of a vast literature on modernity. But both also provide articulate, popular accounts of the limits of modernity and the promises of a complex and culturally composite world.

Illustrations

Index

A NOTE ON THE COVER IMAGE

The image of the horse and buggy on the front cover represents a generic horse-drawn buggy similar in style to buggies used by the Old Order Mennonites from time to time and by Old Colony people in the past. However, both the Old Order and Old Colony people use a variety of buggies. The Old Order Mennonites in Ontario tend to use mostly open buggies (with no roof or sides) on high "Sarven" wheels made of wooden spokes and steel rims (see page 16), but in southern Ontario closed buggies of the kind depicted on the cover are often used by older people or families with young children. The Old Colony Mennonites in Latin America once used a very similar closed buggy on high wheels. However, a generation after moving south the Old Colonists adapted their buggies to the hot sun of the South and its more rugged roads (see page 102). The buggies thus were opened to the sides, covered with a flat roof, and fitted with small, air-filled rubber tires.

R.L.

A NOTE ON THE TYPE

The text of this book is set in Baskerville (11/14), designed by John Baskerville in 1757. The title text is set in ITC New Baskerville, designed by John Quaranda for the Mergenthaler Linotype Company in 1978.